Look well to ...day

Look well to this day

A year of daily reflections

Tom Gordon

wild goose
publications  www.**ionabooks**.com

Wild Goose Publications
4th Floor, Savoy House, 140 Sauchiehall Street, Glasgow G2 3DH, UK
www.ionabooks.com
Wild Goose Publications is the publishing division of the Iona Community.
Scottish Charity No. SC003794. Limited Company Reg. No. SC096243.

ISBN 978-1-84952-301-1

Cover photograph © Tom Gordon
Stained-glass window design © Fiona Foley, used with permission

The publishers gratefully acknowledge the support of the Drummond Trust,
3 Pitt Terrace, Stirling FK8 2EY in producing this book.

Overseas distribution:
Australia: Willow Connection Pty Ltd, Unit 4A, 3-9 Kenneth Road,
Manly Vale, NSW 2093
New Zealand: Pleroma, Higginson Street, Otane 4170, Central Hawkes Bay
Canada: Novalis/Bayard Publishing & Distribution, 10 Lower Spadina Ave.,
Suite 400, Toronto, Ontario M5V 2Z2

Printed by Bell & Bain, Thornliebank, Glasgow

Dedication

To Catherine Cameron Dorward,
my aunt Kit,
for much love shared
and many lessons learned.

Preface

The Lebanese poet and spiritual writer Khalil Gibran is best known for his collection of mystical and spiritual teachings under the title of *The Prophet*. There have been more glimpses of meaning for me through the years from this book than from any other. But this was by no means Gibran's only piece of inspiring writing.

Gibran Khalil Gibran was born in the town of Bsharri in the north of modern-day Lebanon and emigrated to the United States with his family when he was a young man. There he studied art and began his literary career. In *The Wanderer,* a collection of mystical tales, he tells this story, entitled *The Path.*

There lived among the hills a woman and her son, and he was her first-born and her only child. And the boy died of a fever whilst the physician stood by. The mother was distraught with sorrow, and she cried to the physician and besought him saying, 'Tell me, tell me, what was it that made quiet his striving and silent his song?' And the physician said, 'It was the fever.' And the mother said, 'What is the fever?'

And the physician answered, 'I cannot explain it. It is a thing infinitely small that visits the body, and we cannot see it with the human eye.'

Then the physician left her. And she kept repeating to herself, 'Something infinitely small. We cannot see it with our human eye.' And at evening the priest came to console her. And she wept and she cried out saying, 'Oh, why have I lost my son, my only son, my first-born?' And the priest answered, 'My child, it is the will of God.' And the woman said, 'What is God and where is God? I would see God that I may tear my bosom before Him, and pour the blood of my heart at His feet. Tell me where I shall find Him.' And the priest said, "God is infinitely vast. He is not to be seen with our human eye.'

Then the woman cried out, 'The infinitely small has slain my son through the will of the infinitely great! Then what are we? What are we?'

At that moment the woman's mother came into the room with the shroud for the dead boy, and she heard the words of the priest and also her daughter's cry. And she laid down the shroud, and took her daughter's hand in her own hand, and she said, 'My daughter, we ourselves are the infinitely small and the infinitely great; and we are the path between the two.'

I'll share two more tales from *The Wanderer* later in the book. But, for now, let me tell you why this particular story matters to me.

All of my life as I've travelled my own path I too have been caught between the infinitely small and the infinitely great. There have been many times when I have realised how little I know, and, thankfully, other times when I have been excited by how much there is to discover. I have walked on pathways between the weakness of faith and the aspiration of fullness. I have worked in a belief-system which sits between the smallness of my insights and the hugeness of the truth of it all. In my humanity I am part of the infinitely small, and in my belief in a higher power I acknowledge the infinitely great.

Sometimes I have been discouraged by the infinitely small, when I fail to see the sense of things and don't know how to go forward. But I have also had times when I have been transformed by the infinitely great, and a glimpse of the vastness has made enough sense for now.

I am no different from you. I walk the pilgrim path which you also walk. This book, therefore, from the musings of a pilgrim companion, recognises the infinitely small of who we are and what we know and how little we understand. But I hope it also offers glimpses of the infinitely great of what's out there and what it can mean and how it can give transform us with hope.

The title of this book comes from a poem, *Look to this day*, attributed both to the writings of Rabindranath Tagore, the Bengali poet who was in 1913 the first non-European to win the Nobel Prize for literature, and to Kalidasa, a renowned 5th-century classical Sanskrit writer.

Regardless of its source, it is a poem familiar as a contribution to funeral and memorial services, weddings and birth celebrations, as well as anthologies of spiritual and reflective material.

Look to this day
for it is life
the very life of life.
In its brief course lie all
the realities and truths of existence
the joy of growth
the splendour of action
the glory of power.
For yesterday is but a memory
And tomorrow is only a vision.
But today well lived
makes every yesterday a memory
of happiness
and every tomorrow a vision of hope.
Look well, therefore, to this day.

Through these daily reflections, then, I invite you to look to each day, and to give thought to the small things and great things on your journey. And it is my prayer that these modest offerings might help you to live the occasional day a little better, and, as a result, have a more hopeful vision for tomorrow. 'Look well, therefore, to this day.'

Acknowledgements

My thanks for their support in the preparation of this book go to my wife Mary, for her constant support and encouragement; my family, for their advice, guidance and warmth; the staff at Wild Goose Publications, particularly Sandra for her unfailing wisdom and insight, and Jane for her artistic knowledge; Iain MacDonald, minister of Westray parish church in Orkney, and Jo and the staff at the Kalisgarth Care Centre for their permission to use the photograph of their window; the staff of the Port Seton Library and Community Centre for their unfailing assistance in the final editing period for this book; and all those who have read and commented on my previous writings, who have responded positively to my readings and who have encouraged me to write more. To all of them, and to countless unnamed others for their love and friendship, I offer my thanks.

Cover design

The stained-glass window depicted on the cover comes from the Kalisgarth Care Centre, Westray, Orkney. It was designed and made by Westray's schoolchildren under the artistic guidance of Fiona Foley. The photograph is copyright to the author. The photograph is used with the permission of the designer and the management committee of the Kalisgarth Care Centre.

January 1 – Beginnings

'Begin, be bold, and venture to be wise.'
Horace, Roman lyric poet

Like most children, I learned nursery rhymes when I was little. Here's one I now recall in adult years with quiet amusement …

> *I know a man called Michael Finnegan.*
> *He grew whiskers on his chin-a-gin.*
> *The wind came out and blew them in again.*
> *Poor old Michael Finnegan! Begin again!*
> *I know a man called Michael Finnegan …*

Then the whole unfortunate tale would indeed 'begin again' and a silly nursery rhyme would be repeated *an infinitum* – to the distraction of an increasingly impatient mother and irritated older sister. I know now what I didn't know then, that the injunction to 'begin again' was not only for a small child to repeat a rhyme. It was aimed at the unfortunate Michael Finnegan. Poor man! There he was, his whiskers growing as whiskers do, only to be thwarted by a change in the wind, so that his whiskers simply disappeared, pushed back into his chin, no less. 'Begin again Michael Finnegan' was the mantra. Don't be defeated. Whatever way the wind blows, beginning again has got to be worth it.

Whatever way the wind blows as the days of the coming year unfold, there will be times when things don't grow, despite our best efforts, or turn out as we hope – like Michael Finnegan's whiskers. So, beginning again could also be our mantra at the start of the year – and not just for hopeful beard-growers either!

When beginnings are hard, can I be patient with myself?
When beginnings are necessary, can I remain hopeful?
When beginnings are now, can I be encouraged
by the possibilities?

January 2 – Resolutions

'The native hue of resolution.'
William Shakespeare, Hamlet

When I was young, the advent of the New Year always led to long lists of 'self-improvement' promises. Resolutions ... not to rush my food, trying to heed the constant admonitions of concerned parents; to get homework done on time, fearful of yet another punishment exercise; to pluck up the courage to ask my favourite girl on a date – if everyone else could have a girlfriend, why couldn't I? The lists were sometimes long and detailed. But I never achieved everything I resolved to do. Meals were still rushed because they got in the way of play; punishment exercises still had to be endured; and my favourite girl is still waiting on my call ... New Year was filled with the 'native hue of resolution'. January the second was the dawning of reality.

I still make resolutions. But now they're not stored up to be ticked off on a long list at the turn of a year or at any other time. Resolutions are always with me, to be tackled one at a time when they need to be.

When a skilled climber is moving up a tricky rock-face, the instruction is always to keep three points of contact on the rock at all times – two feet and a hand, or two hands and a foot – and only to move one point of contact at a time. It's safer that way. Progress will be slow, but it will always be steady, and there will be no danger of falling backwards because too much is attempted at once.

New Year resolutions? Too much to ask at the start of a year, I suspect. Maybe a 'new day resolution' might be better ...

Self-improvement is good.
But when resolutions are overwhelming,
separating one from the other and doing a little bit every day
could be much better.

January 3 – Renewed

'Redeem me, and be merciful unto me.'
Bible: Psalm 26:11

The artist and art critic John Ruskin once spoke with a woman at a dinner party and had to suffer her assertion that there were some things which were irredeemable. She quoted stories of people who, she said, were so evil that there was no hope of any betterment. She affirmed that there were some situations that were beyond rescue, no matter how hard people tried. Ruskin took the opposite view and sought to convince his antagonist that through forgiveness and understanding redemption was always possible. He concluded with his belief that the Grace of God always offered hope in the face of evil and destruction.

The woman was unconvinced. And in the heat of the confrontation, as her *coup de grâce,* she unearthed from her small handbag a delicate white silk handkerchief on which, she reported, she had spilled some indelible ink earlier in the day. 'There,' she announced, indicating the clearly visible stain. 'The handkerchief is ruined, is it not? Why, a lady could *never* be seen using such a thing. It would be shameful. And no amount of cleansing will ever restore this 'kerchief to its former delicacy and usefulness. It is, indeed, beyond rescue, past renewal.'

Ruskin smiled and requested that he might have the handkerchief till the following day. When he and the woman met again a day later, Ruskin held the silk, lace-trimmed square in the palm of his hand, and there, with the ink-stain still at its centre, Ruskin had drawn the most beautiful, colourful and intricate design. In the right hands, it appeared, renewal was always possible ...

I am accepted; I am redeemed;
I am forgiven; more than I dreamed.

January 4 – Mistakes

'Wink at sma' fauts, ye hae great anes yersel'.'
(Wink at little faults, as you yourself have great ones.)
Scots proverb

Round the gallery in the former Viewforth Church in the centre of Edinburgh there is a series of carvings. Between the regularly spaced, ornate false-pillars and scrollings there are a number of attractively carved flower-heads. The carved flowers are identical, each one having five petals of equal size and form, turning outwards from the centre of the bloom.

Apart, that is, from one blossom. This one has *four* petals and not the usual five; and in this case the petals turn inwards from the centre and not outwards. It just looks wrong!

Spoiling the symmetry? The handiwork of someone who didn't listen to instructions? The result of an over-eager professional not checking that everything was correct before the gallery was completed? A mistake by a ham-fisted apprentice? Any of these ... But I like to think that this flaw in the workmanship was included *on purpose*, so that worshippers and preachers from then on would be faced with this reality – that no human enterprise is perfect.

We all make mistakes. We're not perfect. But if we can forgive ourselves then we can move on with life. And if we can forgive one another, how much more positive our future together might be.

'To err is human; to forgive divine,' Shakespeare wrote. If we can forgive ourselves and learn to forgive others – to 'wink at sma' fauts' – we *will* have the glimpse of the divine we all need.

> *To err is human; to forgive, divine;*
> *Forgiveness, too, is also mine,*
> *To know myself; and to forgive,*
> *That we in harmony might live.*

January 5 – Useful

'As much use as a chocolate tea-pot.'
Anonymous

The owner of the second-hand bookshop was used to people browsing his shelves. Customers in all shapes and sizes came and went, and their eccentricities of behaviour and varied choice of books made his job very interesting indeed.

That's why the shop's proprietor wasn't too concerned by a customer who'd been coming in every day, always around the same time in the morning. 'Customer' was, however, a bit of a misnomer because this man never bought a thing. He would simply arrive, go straight to the hardback section in the corner and browse for a short while before exiting with a nod to the owner. He never opened any of the books he took down from the shelves. Instead he would occasionally lay a chosen book on a small table, study it intently and jot something down on a scrap of paper before returning the volume to its place on the shelf. The intrigued bookshop-owner determined one day that he was going to ask his strange customer what he was up to. He didn't need to, for the next time the visitor appeared, after only one ritual with a book, he boldly announced, 'At last! This is the one.'

'Interesting choice,' the storekeeper remarked. 'Youlan Feng's *History of Chinese Philosophy Volume I*. Would you like me to keep an eye out for Volume II, by any chance?'

'Goodness me, no!' replied the customer. 'I'm not going to *read* this. I just need a book that's *exactly* the right thickness to prop up the broken leg of my sideboard.'

What's not useful in one way could be useful in another.
Something considered useless
could have something new to offer.
Usefulness comes in unexpected ways
and in unexpected people.

January 6 – Epiphany

'While there's life, there's hope.'

Ancient Roman saying

January 6th is celebrated in the Christian tradition as *The Feast of the Epiphany*, commemorating the arrival of the Magi with their gifts for the infant Christ – the arrival, mark you ...

Matthew's Gospel tells us: *After Jesus was born in Bethlehem in Judea, during the time of King Herod, Magi from the east came to Jerusalem and asked, 'Where is the one who has been born king of the Jews? We saw his star when it rose and have come to worship him.'* So all we know is that the Magi came from the east, they got to Bethlehem via Jerusalem and they followed a star. Epiphany is about their arrival but it tells us nothing of the journey, the time it took, or how many of them there were. The poet TS Eliot, however, takes Matthew's outline and seeks to fill in the gaps. In *The Journey of the Magi* he tells us of the travelling, well before the glorious arrival.

A cold coming we had of it,
Just the worst time of the year
For a journey, and such a long journey:
The ways deep and the weather sharp,
The very dead of winter.
And the camels galled, sore-footed, refractory,
Lying down in the melting snow ...

The arrival of the Magi with their gifts is worth celebrating, because, like you and me, they are travellers on a journey, with all the travail and hopefulness the journey contains.

'To travel hopefully is better than to arrive.'
Robert Louis Stevenson, *Virginibus Puerisque*

January 7 – Gifts

'If you have much, give of your wealth;
If you have little, give of your heart.'
Arab proverb

A couple of years ago, around the season of Epiphany, I tried to find a hymn which would express our feelings at a time when we remembered the gifts of the Magi, and allow us to celebrate the themes that underpin our commitment to giving. I couldn't find one, so I wrote this. We sang it to the tune *Epiphany* by Joseph Francis Thrupp. But it works just as well as a poem about using our gifts as well as we can.

Here we have gathered on this day of giving,
Feeling at home, and surrounded by friends;
Here we reflect on the message before us,
Seeking a Truth which we know never ends.

Now we have come like the wise men before us,
Bearing the gifts which we know we should bring;
Here is the service that marks our commitment;
Here are our praises; rejoicing we sing.

Here is our caring, our faith and our prayerfulness;
Here are the talents, whatever we have;
Here are the skills and our tender devotion;
Here is our passion, our service and love.

Look we have come like the Magi before us;
Humbly we give all our offerings to you.
Bless all our giving; accept all our service;
Touch all your travellers with blessings anew.

January 8 – Names

'Call me by my old familiar name'
Henry Scott Holland,
from a sermon on the death of King Edward VII

When Prince Albert, husband of Queen Victoria for 22 years, died tragically young in 1862, the Queen was grief-stricken with a sorrow that lasted many years. She had been almost entirely dependent on her Prince Consort. In her mourning she wrote, 'I have no one to call me Victoria now.' In the midst of being addressed by the familiar *Your Majesty* and *Ma'am* there was a yearning to be called by the name that defined her as a person and not as a Queen.

Names are important. I was baptised Thomas John Gordon, after my two grandfathers. I was known as Tommy at home and university – to distinguish me from my grandfather who was 'Tam'. I was only called Thomas by my mother when she was angry with me. I've been Tom all my working life. So, if I'm now called 'Tam', 'Tommy' or 'Thomas' I think people are talking about someone else. 'Tom' is my name. My father was Jimmy. When he went into hospital, the staff didn't ask him what he liked to be called. So they called him by the name on his notes – 'James' – and that's what was on the card above his bed. But when they used that name in conversation with me, I felt they were talking about a complete stranger.

When someone gets your name right today, you'll feel good about that because you've been recognised as the individual that you are. And when you use someone else's name today, and get it right too, you'll be giving them the important gift of valuing them as an individual and accepting their uniqueness.

Today, I give thanks for my name.
Today, I value the individuality of the names of those I meet.

January 9 – Complaints

'I by the tide of Humber would complain.'
Andrew Marvell, To His Coy Mistress

In his poem 'The Gulistan of Sa'di' (The Rose Garden), the 13th-century Persian poet Sheikh Muslih-uddin Sa'di Shirazi wrote:

> *I never lamented about time's changes or complained of the turns of fortune except on the occasion when I was barefooted and unable to procure slippers. But when I entered the great mosque of Kufah with a sore heart and beheld a man without feet, I offered thanks to the bounty of God and consoled myself for my want of shoes.*

You might have heard this sentiment in a modern version: *I cried because I had no shoes, until I met a man who had no feet.*

I was working with a group of people who were bereaved. Among them was a young student, devastated by the loss of her mother and struggling to make sense of her feelings. Also in the group was an elderly widow, married for fifty-four years, who regularly cried herself to sleep because she missed her husband so much. These two people had much to complain about in their loss. Yet both saw in the other another pain, deeper, it seemed, than their own. The depth of understanding between these two women was the beginning of healing. In a sense, each of them in their loss cried because they had no shoes. And each of them found in the other someone with no feet. They found true solace together, and perhaps, even in their bereavement, instead of complaining, found a way of offering 'thanks to the bounty of God'.

I complain, though I have little to complain about;
I cry that I've got no shoes,
though there are many with no feet – and worse.

January 10 – When I was a child

'Children are the keys of Paradise.'
Richard Henry Stoddard, 'The Children's Prayer', Songs of Summer

In 1 Corinthians 13 (New RSV), St Paul writes: *When I became an adult I put an end to childish ways.'* This is what this means to me.

When I was a child, I played, and in my playing
found a world where I belonged.
Now that I'm grown, I need to find that 'belonging' once more,
so that, being finished with childish things,
I don't lose the child that's always in me.

When I was a child, I cried, and in my crying
found comfort in a warm breast and a full embrace.
Now that I'm grown, I need to be able to cry again,
and know that I am enfolded to the breast of a Love
that understands the child that's always in me.

When I was a child, I believed that everything was simple
and found a world that was easy to understand.
Now that I'm grown, I need to know that I live with uncertainties,
and find again the clarity and certainty
that reassures the child that's always in me.

When I was a child, I knew with absolute conviction
that love mattered above everything else.
Now that I'm grown, I need to know, more than ever before,
that I can love, even as much as I am loved,
and to know how that feels, for the child that's always in me.

Adapted from 'When I was a child', *first published in* A Need for Living,
by Tom Gordon, Wild Goose Publications, 2001

January 11 – Change

'Change doth unknit the tranquil strength of men.'
Matthew Arnold, A Question

I remember the first time I travelled on a diesel-powered train. I had been brought up close to the railway station of a Highland town, so long journeys were most often taken by train. Northwards, up the West Highland line, southwards towards Glasgow, train journeys were long and noisy but immensely exciting for a small boy. Because, of course, train journeys were always by steam train, and the hissing of the brakes, the straining of the engine, the smoke of the chimney, the steam of the boiler, the clickety-clack of the wheels over the rails and the clatter over the points were all part of the train-journey experience.

When I first travelled on a diesel-powered train I was, therefore, surprised and disappointed. In the station, it seemed no different, with all the clamour and movement of the crowds; when we boarded, the luggage, seats and carriage looked much the same; it felt the same while we waited to go … But then, when we started to move, there was next to no noise, and no smoky smell, and no jolt when we pulled away from the platform. It was too quiet and much too smooth to be a *proper* train journey. It had all changed – for the better, according to my parents; for the worse, according to me, for there was no excitement any more.

Change is not always easy to cope with. For some, it will bring better things. For others it will mean things will never be the same again. 'More's the pity,' they'll say.

I enjoy travelling on diesel – and electric – trains these days. I know now what my parents knew – that changes *can* bring improvement, even if it sometimes means letting go of the romantic days of a childhood past.

Change and decay … or might it be change and 'Hooray!'?

January 12 – Obvious

'They can discover everything except the obvious.'
Oscar Wilde, An Ideal Husband

Benji had been wearing glasses since he was six. 'It runs in the family,' he'd once heard his mother say, though he didn't know what that meant, and his head hurt when he tried to work out things like that. So he didn't bother too much. Benji's mother wore glasses, big, chunky red ones. His father did too, frameless ones you might hardly notice. And so did Benji's big sister. She was on her third kind of glasses, as far as Benji knew.

Benji remembered his first glasses. There had been a lot of fiddling about with things at the 'oktishuns', where a man with a white coat had put a kind of chunky frame over his eyes and asked him to look at coloured lights and big letters on the wall. Benji wasn't allowed to *choose* his glasses at the oktishuns. *He* wanted an almost-invisible pair like his dad's; his *mother* said he had to get an ordinary pair because he was only six. So Benji was grumpy when he got home. 'Nice glasses,' his father remarked. Benji chose not to agree. 'How did he get on?' his father asked his mum. His mum told the whole story, most of which Benji didn't understand.

Just then, Benji's know-all sister arrived home. 'New glasses?' she remarked. 'So, what've you got them for, long sight or short sight? Eh? Eh? Have you got glasses because you have myopia or hypermetropia? Eh? Eh?'

'Oh, for goodness' sake,' Benji blurted, stating the obvious. 'I just wear glasses so I can *see* better!'

When you can't see the wood for the trees,
look at the trees;
that might be enough for now;
you'll find the rest of the wood soon enough.

January 13 – People

'Good people all, of every sort ...'
Oliver Goldsmith, Elegy on the Death of a Mad Dog

Knowing that the author of the Harry Potter books, JK Rowling, began her writing in an Edinburgh café, I thought I'd try it out. So I found a quiet café, ordered a coffee and set about my task. I'd just begun when a woman sat at the next table. She laid her shopping bags down, ordered a pot of tea and a scone and set about reading a magazine. I was hooked! What had she been shopping for? Had she had a stressful morning? I glanced at my laptop. I'd written half a sentence and forgotten how I was going to finish it.

I'd just returned to my task when two business gents took the table in the corner. There was animated conversation. Bundles of papers were spread out. The delivery of an espresso and a fruit juice hardly interrupted their flow. How vital were their discussions? What project were they planning? Looking at my laptop again, I discovered that I'd deleted my half-a-sentence, and I couldn't remember what it was anyway.

I'd typed three more words when two policewomen arrived. Soon they were in deep conversation with the counter assistant who was pointing at the toilet door then gesticulating at the till. One constable scribbled in a notebook. Had the till been rifled? Were reinforcements on the way? I closed my laptop. A café was obviously no place to find inspiration for my writing. People-watching was *much* more interesting.

As I went to settle my bill, I wondered if JK Rowling ever felt the same. Maybe there were times when she couldn't think of anything to write either, until she looked up and saw Harry Potter coming into the café.

Bless 'em all ... the people that I see;
Bless my soul! But they look just like me!

January 14 – Password

'A password is like a toothbrush.
Don't let anyone else use it,
and it's best to change it every six months.'
Anonymous

The Bible's Book of Judges tells us of the people of Gilead defeating the tribe of Ephraim in battle. The surviving Ephraimites try to cross the Jordan back to their home territory, but the Gileadites have secured the river's fords. To identify infiltrators the Gileadites ask each man who approaches, 'Are you an Ephraimite?' Of course the reply will be, 'No!' But the Gileadites have an ace up their sleeve. 'Very well. So say "Shibboleth".' They know that the Ephraimites' dialect doesn't have a 'sh' sound, so they can't pronounce the word properly. If anyone says, 'Sibboleth' they are the enemy. A lot of enemies are captured and killed as a result.

During World War II, some United States soldiers in the Pacific used the word 'Lollapalooza' as a Shibboleth when unidentified people approached checkpoints. Working on the premise that if they were Japanese infiltrators they were likely to confuse the letter 'r' with 'l', non-Americans could be easily identified – and dealt with. And there are reports that during the Nairobi massacre in 2013 the terrorists sought to identify non-Muslims if they did not know that the name of the Prophet Mohammed's mother was Amina.

It's sad when a starting position is to be suspicious of people because they're different, or speak strangely, or don't know our customs. If reconciliation had been the approach of the Gileadites, the lives of many Ephraimites would have been spared, and two warring forces might have found ways to live in peace.

Beware of unknown passwords,
because they can shut you out of sharing.

January 15 – Adversity

'Adversity is the first path to truth.'
Lord Byron, Don Juan

When I first met George he had two legs, lived alone, was in failing health because of his diabetes and, as a result, was rapidly losing his sight. But as far as his legs were concerned, he had the requisite number. That was soon to change. The diabetes continued to do its worst. George's right leg was affected first. Before long he was told he would have to have an amputation above the knee. George was stoical. If he felt bad about it before the operation, he never told me – even though I was convinced it would have helped him to talk things through with me.

I visited George in hospital after the amputation. This would be the time, I hoped, when I could help him come to terms with things, if only he would talk. I found him sitting up in his bed, the covers showing the shape of only one leg down the left side. I sat on the chair beside him. 'How are you?' I enquired.

'Not too bad,' George replied. 'But it's good you've come. There's something I need help with.' *This is it*, I thought, *the moment of revelation*. I leaned forward to create a closeness.

'What is it?' I asked. 'What's troubling you?'

George looked me straight in the eye with the most serious expression on his face I'd ever seen and a deeply furrowed brow. He took a deep breath, and asked, 'D'you know anyone with size nine feet who'd like a free gift of fourteen right shoes?' And the whole hospital ward was filled with the loudest guffaw I had ever heard.

A one-legged man helped me to learn.
He said he would be hopping mad if he had to throw out
fourteen perfectly good right shoes.
He taught me that smiling in the face of adversity
could actually be possible.

January 16 – Integrity

'Integrity is the loincloth round his waist.'
Bible: Isaiah 11:5

The author of *The Water Babies*, Charles Kingsley, in his book *Twenty-five Village Sermons*, wrote:

> *One good man – who does not put on his religion once a week with his Sunday coat, but wears it for his working dress, and lets the image of God grow into him, and through him, till everything he says and does becomes religious – that man is worth a thousand sermons. He is a living Gospel – the image of God. And men see his good works, and admire them in spite of themselves, and see that they are Godlike and that God's grace is no dream … They get a glimpse of God again in His saints and heroes …*

General William Booth, the founder of the Salvation Army, was passionate that his faith should not be only for himself. It drove him to a life of service to others, especially those who were most in need. He wrote this about that life-long commitment:

> *While women weep as they do now, I'll fight; while children go hungry, I'll fight; while men go to prison, in and out, in and out, I'll fight; while there is a poor lost girl on the street, I'll fight; while there remains one dark soul without the light of God – I'll fight to the very end.*

Lives are changed because saints and heroes show what they believe by how they live. They are worth a thousand sermons.

Might someone have a glimpse of God today
because of my integrity?

January 17 – Example

'A candle loses nothing by lighting another candle.'
Anonymous

'Set a good example,' my mother used to say, 'so that people know what kind of home you come from.' She was right – if you show a good example, then people will know your good motives. They will, indeed, know where you come from!

In the days before the pocket-torch, a blind man was visiting his friends. He had arrived at their home in the daylight, but, as the conviviality of friendship continued into the evening, the darkness of night had descended by the time the man was to return home. So, before he stepped into the dark, his friends insisted he carry a lantern to light his way.

'Thank you. But I have no need of a lantern,' the blind man protested. 'Light or dark, day or night, it's all the same to me.'

'Yes indeed,' his friends replied, 'of this we are well aware. But you will do well to carry the lantern none the less, so that it might be a sign that you are on the road, for fear that others would bump into you and cause you harm.'

The blind man assented and went on his way. But he had not gone further than the end of the street when someone collided with him and knocked him off his feet. 'You clumsy oaf,' the stranger shouted. 'Why don't you look where you are going?'

'But surely,' the unfortunate man replied, 'I have a light. Did you not see my lantern?'

'Lantern?' came the mocking reply. 'What use is a lantern if the candle has gone out?'

> *Candle, candle, burning bright*
> *In the middle of the night …*
> *Could it be the good I do*
> *Lights a path for such as you?*

January 18 – Little by little

'A tower of nine storeys begins with a heap of earth;
the journey of a thousand li starts from where one stands.'

Lao Tzu, Tao-te Ching

The physicist William Thomson, who became Lord Kelvin, was professor of Natural Philosophy (physics, that is) in Glasgow University in the second half of the 19th century. During his lectures, to illustrate the effect of small forces on large masses, he would have a heavy lump of metal weighing a hundredweight or more suspended from the ceiling and beside him a basket of scrunched-up pieces of paper. To the delight of his class, Kelvin would begin to bombard the heavy iron mass with the little balls of paper. At first nothing happened. Then after a while the iron weight would begin to move a little, then some more, till it was swinging in an arc. The arc would become wider than the students could have imagined at the beginning of the experiment – all through repeated blows with scrunched-up pieces of paper.

A protest song from the 1960s reminds us:

> *One man's hands can't break a prison down.*
> *Two men's hands can't break a prison down.*
> *But if two and two and fifty make a million,*
> *We'll see that day come round;*
> *we'll see that day come round.*

Little things, which appear to have little or no effect on their own, can achieve big things if we keep on going. It's the little, constantly repeated efforts that count.

If something worthwhile is to be achieved,
I need to know where to start, and then to keep on going.

January 19 – Perseverance

'If you wish success in life,
make perseverance your bosom friend.'

Joseph Addison, The Spectator *– 1711*

In his *Child's History of England*, Charles Dickens tells the story of
the parents of Thomas Becket. Gilbert Becket, Thomas's father, on
a pilgrimage to the Holy Land was taken prisoner by a Saracen
who had a beautiful daughter. She fell in love with Gilbert and
pledged her life to him in marriage. She loved him so much she
was willing to become a Christian, if only they could escape
together to a Christian country. Gilbert pledged his love in return.

In time he escaped from captivity with his servant Richard.
Returning at last to England, he forgot the Saracen girl. But the
young woman had not forgotten Gilbert. She left her father's home
in disguise and made her way to the coast. She knew only two
words of English – 'Gilbert' and 'London'. So she went about the
ships in the harbours, saying 'London' over and over again. Her
perseverance never diminished.

Eventually sailors pointed out a ship bound for London, and,
securing a passage in exchange for some of her jewels, the girl
boarded the ship and, in time, arrived in London.

One day Gilbert Becket, now a thriving merchant, was sitting
in his office when a servant arrived breathlessly saying, 'Master!
A Saracen lady is here. As I live, she is going up and down the
street calling out, "Gilbert! Gilbert!".' The merchant hurried out
to find her. When she saw him, the Saracen maiden fainted in his
arms. Their pledge was renewed, and marriage soon followed.

Perseverance, so we're told,
is like a postage stamp.
Its usefulness consists in the ability
to stick firmly to one thing till it gets there.

January 20 – Recognition

'Buying a camera doesn't make you a photographer;
it makes you the owner of a camera.'
Anonymous

I was rummaging through a box of old photographs of my grand-mother's. The small, faded, black-and-white pictures were jumbled and needed organising. So one by one I went through them with a view to putting them in an album later. Some of the photos were of people I knew – my mother before she was married; myself and my sister on a holiday beach; my grandfather in his gardening clothes; my granny's two sisters; my father's first car. And there were pictures of people and places I didn't know. Some had a name scribbled on the back – cousin Bert; Phamie and Ida; Ayr Races; Saltcoats Prom. But some of them were of strangers; there was no hope now of ever knowing their names.

One of the photographs was of members of a pipe-band – six pipers, four side-drummers and a bass-drummer posing in full Highland regalia. I knew none of them, and looked for a message on the back. There was none. I was about to discard the picture to the 'unknown' pile when I looked again at the pipe-band. There was something familiar about the drummer on the bottom left. A face I knew? And then it came to me, a vague recollection from childhood of my grandmother saying that her younger brother had been a drummer ... That's it! A drummer – in the Shotts and Dykehead pipe-band. What was his name? Alec! That's it! Uncle Alec, whom I'd met once when I was very small.

An unknown and unnamed bandsman from a past generation was now a living person, and a part of me. A stranger no longer, but a welcome family member come back with his pipe-band.

Sometimes we need the insight to see behind what's black and white,
to find all the colour and life that's waiting to be revealed.

January 21 – Prayer

'Pray without ceasing.'
Bible: I Thessalonians 5:17

The small band of young people had persuaded the skipper to take them out into the open sea. It was a calm day. The sky was blue. The sun was warm. And the spirits of the young people were high. They even sang hymns and songs as the boat chugged along. The skipper smiled and kept his eyes on the waters ahead.

The boat took them along the Sound and round the headland, with the promise of a couple of hours on an uninhabited island with time to explore the rolling dunes and beaches of golden sand. Spirits were high. All was right with the world … until a sudden squall blew up and the little boat began to be buffeted by the winds and the waves.

None of the young people had any protective wet-weather clothing. So, quickly soaked by the rain and the spray, they huddled together under a tarpaulin at the back of the boat and in the wheelhouse around the skipper. Soon some of them were crying. There was the occasional yelp of fear as the boat was raised high by another wave. One young man started to pray and soon many of the group were praying out loud with him. The skipper made no attempt to join them. Until, spurred by a mixture of fear and faith, one of the young people cried out, 'Skipper! Are you not going to pray along with us?'

The old sailor never took his hands from the wheel or his eyes from the bow. Instead he responded in a voice almost drowned by the wind. 'Young man, I prays when it is calm. But when it is stormy, I attend to my boat.'

> *When I pray with my hands as well as my mouth,*
> *my prayers are more real than ever,*
> *and God's response is already there.*

January 22 – Damaged

'An Archangel a little damaged.'
Charles Lamb, A letter to Wordsworth

One of the most striking pieces of modern art in Chichester Cathedral is the painting by the artist Graham Sutherland, *Noli me tangere* (Touch me not), the words of Jesus to Mary when she recognises him in the garden after the Resurrection, as recorded in John's Gospel. The immediacy and directness of Sutherland's depiction of this Resurrection scene in such a dramatic modern idiom was too much for some of the more traditional-thinking worshippers who considered such art to be too controversial for their ancient cathedral. One lady, we are told, was so outraged by what she considered offensive that she attacked the painting with her umbrella, tearing a hole in the canvas.

Some people said this act of vandalism confirmed that the painting was too radical and should be withdrawn from the cathedral. However, those who believed the painting said something important in a new and vibrant way prevailed. The tear was carefully repaired from the back of the canvas, so that, as the painting hangs in the cathedral today, it's hard to see the tear if it isn't pointed out. But the damage remains, as a sign of disagreement, distress and anger. The painting still holds its life and colour around the tear and goes on offering challenge to those who stand before it seeking to absorb its message.

Damage in life doesn't go away. It stays, surrounded by the bigger picture, still there to inform and to challenge, while life has a habit of growing around it.

When the damage does its worst,
and what's precious seems to be ruined,
let me learn patience to wait for the healing that will come,
so I can appreciate the bigger picture – damage and all.

January 23 – Generosity

'One who gives only when asked has waited too long.'
Anonymous

An Indian fable tells of a poor beggar who learned that the Maharaja was to come past the spot where he begged. His hopes were raised. 'The Maharaja will surely place some grains of rice or a small coin in the bowl of a poor beggar,' he thought. So the next day he waited by the side of the road for the Maharaja to pass by. He waited and waited, still at the roadside in the early evening. Then, when the procession eventually appeared, the beggar stepped in front of the Maharaja's chariot and asked for alms. But instead of giving him anything the Maharaja extended his hands and asked the beggar to give *him* something.

Disappointed that a wealthy ruler would be begging from a poor wretch, the beggar reluctantly counted out five grains of rice from the collection in his bowl and placed them angrily in the Maharaja's hands. With a cursory 'Thank you' the Maharaja went on his way.

With a heavy heart, the beggar returned to his home and with his winnowing-fan began to clean the rice that remained in his begging-bowl for his meal. As he did so, a small, glittering object attracted his attention. Picking it up, he saw that it was a grain of gold. Then he found another, then a third, and a fourth, and a fifth. And that was all, for no matter how keenly he searched, there were no more golden grains to be found. Five grains of rice to the Maharaja had brought the beggar five grains of gold.

'What a fool I have been,' he exclaimed. 'If I'd known *that* I'd have given him it all!'

'*Teach us, good Lord, to serve you as you deserve,*
to give and not to count the cost … '
St Ignatius of Loyola

January 24 – Success and failure

'He that is down needs fear no fall
He that is low, no pride.'

John Bunyan, The Pilgrim's Progress

The poem 'If' by Rudyard Kipling has been an inspiration over several generations. But there is one line that has always puzzled me. The stanza in question runs like this:

If you can dream – and not make dreams your master;
If you can think – and not make thoughts your aim;
If you can meet with Triumph and Disaster
And treat those two impostors just the same;
If you can bear to hear the truth you've spoken
Twisted by knaves to make a trap for fools,
Or watch the things you gave your life to, broken,
And stoop and build 'em up with worn-out tools:

'Triumph' and 'Disaster', both impostors? I can understand what Kipling means to this extent – if triumph and disaster come our way then they have to be treated equally. We have to face them as inevitable events on our journey of life. But impostors? That makes me think that they are 'pretend' things, to be suspicious of and treated with scepticism. But I don't believe that is what Kipling meant. Triumph and disaster, success and failure, devastation and elation all have much to teach us. And in *that* sense they are equals. They have to be faced up to, not run away from; seen as real, and not as unnatural impostors. Triumph and disaster *will* come our way. Let's learn equally from both.

Every disaster can become an opportunity.
Every opportunity can be a creativity.

January 25 – Try again

'Perseverance is not a long race;
it is many short races one after another.'
Walter Elliott,
The Spiritual Life: Doctrine and Practice of Christian Perfection

The church I attend sits in the middle of a fishing village on the East Lothian coast. Although fishing in the Firth of Forth and in the North Sea is well past its heyday, the village harbour, where pleasure boats mix with shellfishing boats and the occasional visiting trawler, is still a working environment.

The interior of my church, built in an Arts-and-Crafts style in the early years of the 20th century, is filled with sailing and fishing motifs. Stencils of fish cover the roof beams. A model of a trawler, with sails unfurled, sits above the chancel. A vibrant painting by the renowned artist John Bellany of a fishing boat at sea dominates the transept. And the roof-beams and spars are constructed to resemble the inside of an upturned trawler's hull. Come to church, and you know you're in a fishing village.

The most significant fishing symbol for me is contained in a small stained-glass window depicting Jesus' fishermen disciples throwing nets over the side of a boat. It comes from the Gospel story (John 21) when the disciples complain to Jesus that they have fished all night and have caught nothing. 'Cast your nets on the other side,' Jesus tells them. When they do, their nets are full.

There are many interpretations of this allegorical tale. But it speaks to me of trying again. When nothing's working, try again. When you're inclined to give up, try again. Of course it's hard if you cast your nets over a side of your boat you've never used before. But who knows what kind of catch you might achieve?

We could be distressed when we don't achieve,
but we should be when we don't try.

January 26 – Brothers

'Then let us pray that come it may,
(As come it will for a' that,)
That Sense and Worth, o'er a' the earth,
Shall bear the gree, an' a' that.
For a' that, an' a' that,
It's coming yet for a' that,
That Man to Man, the world o'er,
Shall brothers be for a' that.'

Robert Burns, For a' That

The concept of brotherly love epitomises an ideal, a 'sense and worth o'er a' the earth', where harmony and peaceful coexistence define the norm of a society. There is no more powerful exemplar of this than the relationship between David and Jonathan as recounted in the Bible in the First Book of Samuel. The bond between David, the shepherd and slayer of Goliath, and Jonathan, the son of King Saul, is brotherly love at its very best. The New International Version of the Bible puts it this way:

> *After David had finished talking with Saul, Jonathan became one in spirit with David, and he loved him as himself. From that day Saul kept David with him and did not let him return to his family. Jonathan made a covenant with David because he loved him as himself. Jonathan took off the robe he was wearing and gave it to David, along with his tunic, and even his sword, his bow and his belt.*

The King James Version puts it: *The soul of Jonathan was knit with the soul of David.* If more 'souls were knit with souls' what a peaceful and harmonious world would be the result.

*Where are the signs that the world of true brotherhood,
which Robert Burns believed in, is 'coming yet'?*

January 27 – The Holocaust

'We have to remember, always, but it's never easy.'
A survivor of Auschwitz

Holocaust Memorial Day provides an opportunity to remember the millions killed in the Holocaust and subsequent genocides in Cambodia, Rwanda, Bosnia and Darfur, and to challenge hatred and persecution wherever it is found. The Holocaust Memorial Day Trust works to raise awareness of Holocaust Memorial Day. This was their declaration of purpose:

We recognise that the Holocaust shook the foundations of modern civilisation. Its unprecedented character and horror will always hold universal meaning ... We believe the Holocaust must have a permanent place in our nation's collective memory. We honour the survivors still with us, and reaffirm our shared goals of mutual understanding and justice ... We must make sure that future generations understand the causes of the Holocaust and reflect upon its consequences. We vow to remember the victims of Nazi persecution and of all genocides ... We value the sacrifices of those who have risked their lives to protect or rescue victims, as a touchstone of the human capacity for good in the face of evil ... We recognise that humanity is still scarred by the belief that race, religion, disability or sexuality make some people's lives worth less than others'. Genocide, anti-Semitism, racism, xenophobia, we have a shared responsibility to fight these evils ...We will do our utmost to make sure that the lessons of such events are fully learnt ... We will continue to encourage Holocaust remembrance by holding an annual UK Holocaust Memorial Day. We condemn the evils of prejudice, discrimination and racism. We value a free, respectful, and democratic society.

January 28 – Discrimination

'All human beings are born free and equal
in dignity and rights.
They are endowed with reason and conscience
and should act towards one another
in a spirit of brotherhood.'
United Nations Declaration of Human Rights

We are invited to celebrate 27th January as Holocaust Memorial Day and to speak against hatred and discrimination. But one day is not enough. On 28th January there should be just as much concern about discrimination. The Office of the UN's High Commissioner for Human Rights offers us this current example:

> *Joseph Kanani and his family live as squatters in extremely poor conditions in Musigati, north of Burundi's capital, Bujumbura. 'We have no representation in government and anyone could build in the middle of our land. The public treat us like dogs that cannot bite,' Kanani says. The Batwa, a pygmy people, indigenous to the tiny Central African nation of Burundi, are marginalized. They want their rights and are demanding equal access to land, education and health services. The Batwa, 1% of the population, traditionally served as servants. The perception of them in servitude still dominates. Births are unrecorded. With no legal status they have no rights to public amenities such as health services.*

If we know people shouldn't be discriminated against because of their height or colour or place of origin, why should they suffer discrimination because of long-standing perceptions?

Is there discrimination in me I need to be aware of today?
And what might I need to do about it?

January 29 – Mourning

'Death leaves a heartache no one can heal;
love leaves a memory no one can steal.'

From an Irish gravestone

I once supported a gay man through the loss of his partner. His devastation was total and his mourning deep and lasting. But he could not grieve openly because his partner had not 'come out' to his family. So a grieving man, bereft of the light of his life, had to sit at the back of the crematorium for the funeral.

I tell the story in my book *New Journeys Now Begin*. But I mention it here because, while not everyone will understand the nature of a gay relationship, we *can* understand grief, and, therefore, glimpse the strength of the relationship from the depth of the mourning. We grieve because the bond of love is broken. When we recognise the depth of mourning, how can we not know the strength of love behind it?

Earlier I explored the love of David and Jonathan. Jonathan is killed in battle. Saul dies afterwards. This is how David mourns:

Then David chanted this lament: 'Saul and Jonathan, beloved and pleasant in their life, and in their death they were not parted. How have the mighty fallen in the midst of the battle! Jonathan is slain on your high places. I am distressed for you, my brother Jonathan; you have been very pleasant to me. Your love to me was more wonderful than the love of women. How have the mighty fallen and the weapons of war perished!'

'Your love was more wonderful ...' What depth of love! And what pain of sorrow in parting!

From brotherly love in life comes heart-rending mourning in death. How could it ever be anything else?

January 30 – Appointments

'Man is so made that he can only find relaxation
from one kind of labour by taking up another.'
Anatole France, The Crime of Sylvestre Bonnard

It began when I was in the waiting room at the doctor's surgery.
My appointment was for 10.50am. It was already five past eleven,
and there were at least two people to be seen before me. I had to
be on my way *very* soon or else I was going to be late for another
appointment later in the morning. The more I waited, the more
stressed I became; as my stress increased, the more angry I got;
the more angry I got, the more I doubted the point of making any
definite appointments at all!

I don't like it when all my day is governed by appointments,
with no room for contingencies. Something goes wrong early in
the day – like an appointment with a doctor taking longer than
expected, creating a domino effect of lateness for everything else
that's to follow – and the rest of the day is spent catching up, and
being very stressed. So I *try* to leave spaces to allow for the unexpected. It doesn't always work out. But I try – because appointments are important.

Appointments are promises made between people. They *are*
important. In some cultures, life isn't governed by appointments,
and things are handled in a much more *laissez-faire* fashion. I once
heard a tourist on a Scottish island ask a local what time a bus was
due to depart. The local looked languidly at his watch, stared for
a time at the bus, turned back to the tourist and replied, 'Sometime
today.'

So today I'll try to be more 'languid' and not be overstressed
about a missed appointment – or about when the next bus leaves.

Sorry, I have to stop now, I have an appointment ...

January 31 – Talk

'Don't let your tongue cut off your head.'
Persian proverb

Aesop, the philosopher and author of the *Fables* from 5th-century BC ancient Greece, was once asked what he considered the most useful thing in the world. He pondered the question for a while. 'The tongue,' he replied. And then he was asked what he believed to be the most *harmful* thing in the world. The response came without a moment's thought. 'The tongue,' he replied.

One of Aesop's fables tells of three bulls feeding together in a field in absolute peace and safety as the best of friends. Day after day a lion watched them in the hope of having something tasty for dinner, but as long as the bulls stayed together there was little chance to make them his prey. So the cunning lion devised a plan and began secretly to spread evil and slanderous gossip about one bull against the other. The vile rumours got back to the bulls, creating much mistrust and fearfulness, till there was a boiling up of jealousy and hatred among the three of them.

Not surprisingly, the bulls, each one now harbouring deep suspicion of the others, began to avoid each other and took to finding space to feed alone, as far apart as the boundaries of their field would allow them. Now the lion had the easy opportunity he had long hoped for. He fell on each one singly, for they no longer had the protection of being together, and made easy prey of them all.

'Careless talk costs lives,'
we were reminded during the war.
Actually, there might be more cost to careless talk
than we could ever imagine.

February 1 – Mornings

'Sweet is the breath of morn, her rising sweet,
With charm of earliest birds.'

John Milton, Paradise Lost

The poems of Robert Burns were inspired by what was around him – in nature, *Tae a Mouse*; in society, *The Cotter's Saturday Night*; in religion, *Holy Willie's Prayer*. So we can surmise that *Up In the Morning Early* was inspired by his own experiences as a ploughman or as an excise-man on a dawn raid.

Cauld blaws the wind frae east to west,
The drift is driving sairly;
Sae loud and shrill I hear the blast,
I'm sure it's winter fairly.

The birds sit chittering [shivering] in the thorn,
A' day they fare but sparely;
An' lang's the night frae e'en to morn,
I'm sure it's winter fairly.

Up in the morning's no' for me,
Up in the morning early;
When a' the hills are covered wi' snaw,
I'm sure it's winter fairly.

I'm with Burns on this one! I can't relate to Milton's 'sweet is the breath of morn'. The morning is simply a gateway to what's to follow. And if that's a reasonable day, that's enough for me.

When people complain that they're 'allergic to mornings',
like Charlie Brown in the 'Peanuts' cartoons of Charles Schulz,
I hope that doesn't put them out of sorts for the whole day.

February 2 – Passion

'Football isn't a matter of life and death.
It's more important than that.'
Bill Shankley, while he was manager of Liverpool FC

One of the greatest-ever football matches of my generation took place in Glasgow at Hampden Park on May 18th 1960. It was the final of what was then known as the 'European Cup' between Eintracht Frankfurt and Real Madrid, at that time the greatest club team in the world. The final score was 7-3 to Real Madrid, and the crowd of 127,621 – and the many others like me who watched the game as a black-and-white movie some years later – were treated to the kind of classy football which had never been seen before.

One of the Real Madrid stars was a Hungarian, Ferenc Puskás. Among a team of stars, it was Puskás who was the architect of the victory and the scorer of four second-half goals. The morning after the great game Puskás was being interviewed for the newspapers, and, of course, was very willing to talk. He told the reporters of his passion for the game he loved. 'When I don't play football, I talk football. And when I don't talk football, I think football.'

For Puskás, football was the passion of his life. And, building on his innate skill, it was his passion for the game that made him the master football-player he was.

A passion for something can become an obsession. If it's all anyone can talk about, then a life can become one-dimensional and that person ends up being a crushing bore to other people. But, on the other hand, none of us will become really good at anything unless we have a passion for it.

If I were to ask you to complete this sentence:
'For me, to live is ... ...',
what would you say is your passion in life?

February 3 – Selflessness

'When a man is wrapped up in himself,
he makes a very small package.'
Attributed to both Benjamin Franklin and John Ruskin

My granny was one of the most generous people I have known. 'She'd give you the sugar out of her tea,' someone remarked of her. My father had proposed marriage to my mother before he went on war service. He sent money back from overseas so she could buy an engagement ring. There wasn't enough money to pay for the ring my mother wanted. So my granny put the extra money to it – and it remained a secret from my dad for years.

I remember Christmas parcels arriving from my granny when I was a small boy. They weren't much, but when you don't have much, they were very special. In later years I learned of her generosity to the folk in her stair. A pot of soup would be made, far too much for one elderly lady, because the rest was for 'Auld Wullie, who disnae look after himself.' (*Old* Willie being twenty years younger than his neighbourly benefactor.)

But what I didn't know then, I certainly know now, and that is that my granny had never been a wealthy person. She never had much of her own. But she knew what it was like to have nothing. She knew about poverty. So what she had, she shared. What was hers was never hers alone, it was always for sharing with someone else, even if she went without.

My granny never gave *me* the sugar out of her tea. What was the point of that, when she was willing to give me the whole cup for myself, sugar and all?

Jesus said, 'Love the Lord your God with all your heart,
and soul and mind, and love your neighbour as yourself.'
Love yourself ... not selfishly, but so that you know
what is needed in your love for someone else.

February 4 – Partly

'What's done we partly may compute,
But know not what's resisted.'
Robert Burns, Address to the Unco Guid

Buddha had to deal with a theological conflict between two groups of monks. Some believed one thing and some another. Each group believed it alone was right. Neither group was prepared to give ground. So Buddha told them a story.

There was once a Rajah who summoned his servant and bade him gather at the palace all the men in the town who had been born blind. Then he commanded that an elephant be brought in. The Rajah had the blind men stand around the elephant with the instruction to explore what was in front of them. 'Each of you,' said the Rajah, 'is touching my elephant.' When they had all completed their exploration, the Rajah said to them, 'Now that you have all studied the elephant, tell me, what is your conclusion?'

The man who'd explored the head said, 'It is like a pot.' The one who'd touched the ear said, 'It is like a fan.' And for the others, the trunk was a plough; a tusk, a ploughshare; a foot, a pillar; the back, a granary; the tail, a pestle; the tail's tuft, a broom. Each blind man thought he knew the whole elephant because of the part he'd touched. So they began to squabble saying, 'An elephant is like this …' 'No, it is like this …' 'I tell you it is not …' 'You are quite wrong, an elephant is this way …' and so on, until, in the end, the blind men came to blows.

That, said Buddha to the feuding monks, is what you are like with the truth.

The world would be a more gracious place,
and religions would be more helpful to all of humanity,
if people didn't insist that they were always right.

February 5 – In a different light

'Whoso would be a man must be a nonconformist.'
Ralph Waldo Emerson, Self-Reliance and Other Essays

My friend is an Anglican priest and he's quite straight-laced. He's good company but he's always of a serious disposition. Trivial conversation will morph into heavy theology as he throws in a quote from something erudite he's just read; and exploration of current affairs will move seamlessly into an examination of recent developments in Christian ethics. Too much for me sometimes …

All that changed in the planning for the farewell social for a senior vicar in the town. A few of us were involved and there were the usual decisions about an appropriate venue, opening a subscription to a farewell gift, catering arrangements, speeches and, of course, entertainment. The cathedral choir was a must, as were the hand-bell ringers from the next town. But 'couldn't we do something different?' someone suggested. 'I can write parodies of familiar hymns,' an organist offered. 'What about some *Gilbert & Sullivan?*' was my contribution. My friend hadn't said much. 'Any thoughts?' I asked. 'I can do a tap-dance,' he replied. There was a stunned silence. 'A *what?*' I asked after a while. 'I can do a tap-dance. I was the all-England tap-dancing champion for my age before I went to Seminary. Just play the right music, and I'm away.'

The straight-laced vicar was the star turn at the farewell social. The crowd cheered to the echo when his tap-dancing was done. So now I see my friend in a very different light. When his serious disposition is too much for me, I just think of him tap-dancing as if his life depended on it, and I can't help but smile.

If you think you know all about someone,
try to see them differently.
If you do, you might find something new about yourself,
and then we can all celebrate our diversity.

February 6 – Always

'Let your love be like the misty rains,
coming softly, but flooding the river.'
Malagasy proverb

The language of Thomas Hood's poem is from the 19th century, but the sentiment is timeless.

I love thee – I love thee! 'Tis all that I can say;
It is my vision in the night, my dreaming in the day;
The very echo of my heart, the blessing when I pray.
I love thee – I love thee, is all that I can say.

I love thee – I love thee! Is ever on my tongue;
In all my proudest poesy that chorus still is sung;
It is the verdict of my eyes, amidst the gay and young:
I love thee – I love thee, a thousand maids among.

I love thee – I love thee! Thy bright and hazel glance,
The mellow lute upon those lips, whose tender tones entrance;
But most, dear heart of hearts, thy proofs
that still these words enhance.
I love thee – I love thee; whatever be thy chance.

Over many years of working in the healing of relationships, and, in particular, helping people come to terms with the loss of someone they have deeply loved, I have heard people say things like: 'But she knew I loved her, so I didn't need to say so.' 'We've always been in love. It didn't need to be put into words.' Thomas Hood's poem offers a different view – love is greatly enhanced when we say what we mean.

Is there someone you need to say 'I love you' to today?

February 7 – Sharing

'There is no delight in owning anything unshared.'
Seneca, Roman Stoic philosopher

On the west side of the island of Iona, facing the rigours of the Atlantic winds, is the Machair. A *machair*, common on many of the outer islands and the north-west coastlines of Scotland, usually stretches between outcrops of hill and rock. It is, the geologists tell us, a raised beach, left higher than an adjacent shore following a drop in sea levels millions of years ago. With its high shell content it is a fertile area amidst the barrenness of its surroundings, offering good grazing and often housing carpets of rare wild flowers.

The Machair on Iona, like such areas in other parts, is the common-grazing land for the island crofters. Given the dearth of good grazing on the islands, a *machair* is precious for ecology, agriculture and survival. So it is not apportioned to individuals nor controlled by a landowner. It is what it is – common ground for everyone's benefit. It is for sharing, for the good of all. Local knowledge of the Machair on Iona also reveals another common provision. For hidden in the dunes, often overgrown and changed by the ravages of the wind and rain, there is an eighteen-hole golf course, the home each year of the Iona Golf Championship.

The Machair, a place of sharing: common enjoyment of the wildness and the beauty of the island of Iona; common grazing for crofters' welfare; common sport for everyone's enjoyment. How good it is to share, and how important to know that everyone can benefit from a common purpose.

Thousands of candles can be lit from a single candle,
and the life of the candle will not be shortened.
Happiness never decreases by being shared.
Buddha

February 8 – Chains

'Man was born free, but everywhere he is in chains.'
　　　Jean-Jacques Rousseau, The Social Contract

In 1989, on study-leave in the USA, I took a personal pilgrimage to the tomb of Martin Luther King in Atlanta, Georgia. I arrived early in the morning in the Peachtree area of the city where King had grown up. The streets were deserted and I had time and peace to reflect on the all-too-short life of this remarkable man. I'd walked up to the memorial area from the Ebenezer Baptist Church where King had ministered and was overwhelmed by the simplicity and beauty of the memorial to his lasting legacy, a marble mausoleum set in the middle of flowing blue water.

With the morning sun catching the water's surface, the effect was truly moving. But this is no tomb at which to grieve for a fallen hero. For round the memorial is a living place – a centre for peace studies, a focus for the continuation of the civil rights movement, encouraging work for justice, equity and openness.

There are many symbols in the complex of what Martin Luther King and those who continue his work stand for. None is more graphic than a sculpture in glass, consisting of the arms of a black slave stretching upwards, with hands holding chains, and the chains are broken. 'Free at last, free at last ...'

Deeply moved by the whole place, I wanted to give thanks for it all and to offer quiet prayers for the continued work for justice and reconciliation. There was a multifaith chapel at the corner of the complex. I moved across to it to use it for a time of personal devotion. But the doors were shut. There was a big chain through the handles of the doors barring my way. A large sign in red letters announced, 'Chapel closed due to vandalism.'

In the midst of freedom some are in chains.
How can we set them free?

February 9 – Small things

'If you are faithful in little things,
you will be faithful in large ones'.
Bible: Luke 16:10

The great English architect Sir Giles Gilbert Scott designed both Liverpool's Anglican Cathedral *and* the red street telephone kiosk familiar since the 1920s. A grand public building and a humble, unadorned, simple utility came from the skill of the same man. I know little else about Sir Giles Gilbert Scott, so I'm happy to know that he gave his genius to a great modern cathedral, and was equally committed to the production of a telephone box.

It's easy enough to give your all to a great enterprise. It's what's expected, particularly when the effect of it is to produce something known and appreciated by many people. None of us is averse to a little bit of personal pride and the opportunity to earn praise! But true commitment and worth might be better measured by how committed and dedicated we are to the humblest of tasks. Real genius is being able to give our all to the grandest *and* simplest of enterprises.

No enterprise, no matter how humble, is unimportant. The dedicated carer, for example, who gives 100% to the most menial of tasks, so that a person in need is properly looked after, does small things well. They may not receive an accolade. But, 'faithful in little things', they are worthy of the highest praise. The street-sweeper looks after our communities so that our roads and pavements are free from litter. Taking pride in a basic task means that lots of other people benefit. In the service of others, there is no big and small, no important and unimportant. Telephone kiosk or great cathedral, everything matters.

Look at a stone wall. The big stones are no use on their own.
They need little stones in between them to make the wall strong.

February 10 – The Lord's Prayer

'Lord, teach is how to pray aright.'
James Montgomery, hymn-writer

The words of The Lord's Prayer have been familiar to generations of Christian worshippers.

Our Father, who art in heaven, hallowed be thy name; thy Kingdom come; thy will be done, on earth as it is in heaven. Give us this day our daily bread, and forgive us our debts as we forgive our debtors; and lead us not into temptation; but deliver us from evil. For thine is the Kingdom, the power and the glory, forever. Amen.

There are modern versions of the Lord's Prayer too, seeking to reinterpret some of the ideas to fit current thinking and language. But have you ever thought of writing your own version? It might make you think about familiar things in a different way and help you 'pray aright'.

Eternal God, giver of love, sustainer of life, healer of pain,
source of all that is and that will ever be,
let your holy name echo with our praises in all the world;
let your way of justice and peace be followed by every nation,
so that the wonders of heaven can be known, here and now.
Feed us with the food we need;
and when we have plenty, don't allow us to forget those who don't.
If others cause us harm, forgive them;
and forgive us too when we don't do much better.
When we are tested more than we can cope with, make us strong;
when we are hemmed in by evil thoughts and ways, set us free.
For your Way is right; your Truth is good; your Life is full.
So, to your glory we sing; forever we say, 'Amen!' So let it be!

February 11 – Shortcuts

'Shortcuts make for long delays.'
JRR Tolkien, The Hobbit

My friend makes her own bread. One day she decided to try a 'foolproof, no-kneading recipe' that she'd discovered in a magazine. The amount of liquid required *seemed* to be more than necessary for the amount of flour. But, encouraged by the reassurance that 'the dough should be slippery when wet', she set about her task. There was an unusual instruction that 'the dough should be mixed with one hand only', but, an experienced breadmaker, she didn't worry. The ingredients were placed in a large bowl and, having added the liquid, she plunged her right hand in. The result was an awful mess like thick, warm porridge. Getting nowhere with one hand, she used two, so that both hands were now engulfed in warm, wet stickiness. Then the phone rang!

Quickly scraping the mess from her hands under a running tap and seizing a towel, she answered the phone. A double-glazing salesman! Back in the kitchen she again attacked the mess of pottage, but all her mixing failed to produce anything like dough. It needed more flour. She'd already put the bag of flour back in the cupboard. So now, with cloggy hands, she had to open the cupboard door and retrieve it. Within moments she'd used *all* the flour and not much had changed! But having come so far she wasn't going to waste the result. So she slapped the mixture in two bread tins as best she could and rushed to the oven, the sticky mess dripping over the edges onto the floor.

My friend didn't divulge the outcome of her breadmaking. But she *did* say that with sticky dough all over the kitchen, she would never, ever again try taking shortcuts when making bread.

More hurry, less speed.
More cut corners, less chance of a predictable outcome.

February 12 – Hospitality

'In the cherry blossom's shade
there's no such thing
as a stranger.'

Kobayashi Issa, Japanese poet and lay Buddhist priest

Algernon Charles Swinburne was one of the most able lyric poets of the Victorian era and many consider him to be a key person in the criticism of the conservative values of his time. Much has been made, however, of Swinburne's physical appearance and strange personality. He was small and frail, and throughout the 1860s and 1870s he drank excessively and had numerous damaging accidents. Until his forties, he often had to return to his parents' home to recover from his illnesses and disasters.

We're told that in 1879 Swinburne visited his friend and literary agent Theodore Watts-Dunton and asked if he could stay with him. Watts-Dunton agreed, and Swinburne stayed for thirty years! While it sounds as though Swinburne overstayed his welcome, the truth is quite different. Watts-Dunton actually offered support during a time when Swinburne was dangerously ill. He ensconced Swinburne in a house in Putney and gradually weaned him from alcohol and from many of his destructive habits. Swinburne did indeed live for thirty years with his friend. Some say that Watts-Dunton cut Swinburne off from his friends, controlled the poet's money, and restricted his activities. But the fact is that he stopped the erratic conduct which could have resulted in Swinburne's death.

Thirty years of hospitality is above and beyond the call. But Watts-Dunton saved his friend's life and encouraged him to continue writing into his old age. Swinburne died in 1909 at the age of seventy-two.

Might a stranger be a friend you just don't know yet?

February 13 – Loosen up!

'Tension is who you think you should be.
Relaxation is who you are.'
Chinese proverb

I was invited to speak to a group of ministers near the end of their training and soon to be launched into the world of parishes. But during the talk I became worried that they were too serious by far and needed to loosen up a bit. We concluded with a question and answer session. One question took me by surprise. 'What gifts do you believe God has given you through which you have exercised your ministry?' I *could* have expounded on preaching ability, pastoral skills, communication issues, or whatever. But I was beyond the stage of offering a serious or weighty response.

So instead I answered: 'God has blessed me with three gifts which I value above all else.' Pens were poised; notepads at the ready. 'Firstly, God has given me the best wife in the world, without whom I could not function.' Notes were hurriedly scribbled. (I wondered if anyone had actually written *'Get wife!'*) 'Secondly,' I continued, warming to my task, 'God has given me … a telephone answering-machine, without which I wouldn't get my meals in peace.' More feverish note-taking … 'And finally, and arguably most importantly,' – edge-of-the-seat time for some, it appeared – 'God has given me … the gift of Laphroaig whisky, without which there's no point getting out of bed in the morning!'

Most of them had stopped writing things down. I suspect the majority had made a mental note to take me off their Christmas-card list or to pray for my eternal soul. But one or two folk laughed. At least a few trainee ministers loosened up a bit, and, who knows, maybe they're more relaxed than they might otherwise have been.

What gifts should I value? More relaxation would be a good start.

February 14 – What love means

'They do not love that do not show their love.'
William Shakespeare, The Two Gentlemen of Verona

Saint Valentine is a 3rd-century Roman saint commemorated on February 14th and associated, since the Middle Ages, with a tradition of courtly love. We don't know much about St Valentine except his name and that he died on February 14th on the *Via Flaminia* in the north of Rome.

St Valentine's Day, also known as the Feast of St Valentine, is an official feast day in the Anglican Communion, as well as in the Lutheran Church. The *Legenda Aurea* of Jacobus de Voragine, compiled about 1260 and one of the most-read books of the Middle Ages, tells of St Valentine refusing to deny Christ before the Emperor Claudius in the year 280. Before his head was cut off, Valentine restored sight and hearing to the daughter of his jailer.

This is far removed from the vast industry of cards and gifts that has built up around Valentine's Day, and the boxes of chocolates, bunches of flowers, romantic meals and other signs of affection which are integral to a day when expressions of love matter. But in the midst of all the sentimentality, give a thought to this: whoever St Valentine was and however little we know about him, we know he had faith, he offered compassion when it was needed and he had courage to stand up what for he believed.

If the love we show on Valentine's Day contains a fraction of the faith, compassion and courage of the Saint after whom today is named, we will have begun to move from our sentimental expressions of love to a Love that has all the depth and commitment that's needed. If we're to lose our head over love, let it be a love that is *really* like St Valentine's.

Love as if there is no tomorrow.
For there will be no real tomorrow without love.

February 15 – The Hub

'He that will not apply new remedies must expect new evils;
for time is the greatest innovator.'

Francis Bacon, Of Innovations

Visitors walking Edinburgh's Royal Mile towards the Castle cannot fail to be impressed by the imposing, gothic grandeur of what was formerly known as the Highland Tolbooth St John's Church. Indeed, as it is the highest point on Edinburgh's skyline, many will enquire as to the nature of this somewhat stark, steeple-topped building that merges with the twin towers of the General Assembly Hall of the Church of Scotland at the top of The Mound.

The recent name of Highland Tolbooth St John's Church is an indication that this gaunt building is the product of several changes and amalgamations in Church structures over the years. Originally known as the Victoria Hall it was built for the Church of Scotland both as a parish church and as a purpose-built General Assembly Hall. The General Assembly of the Church of Scotland last met here in 1929 when the Church of Scotland joined with the United Free Church of Scotland. But from 1979 when it closed, with the congregation uniting with the nearby Greyfriars Kirk, the building was left largely unused, a shell of its former grandeur. However, things change, and its current name and purpose have now anchored this building more effectively in contemporary Edinburgh. It is now known as 'The Hub', and it is the home of the Edinburgh International Festival, and a central source of information on all the Edinburgh Festivals.

A former church building as a *hub*; a church reinventing itself as a living, vibrant centre for the arts. A parable of what's possible when churches close down? I certainly hope so ...

A hub – a centre from which things radiate
so they can make a difference.

February 16 – Displacement

'When the music changes, so does the dance.'
African proverb

A man was sitting in his garden suffering from toothache. He was trying to decide whether he should visit the dentist or not. In the meantime, he thought he would make himself a cup of tea and accompany it with some bread and jam. So he got his tea and took a bite out of his bread and jam without noticing that a wasp had settled on it. No sooner had he bitten into the delicacy than the wasp stung him on the gum. It was extremely painful, and, rushing indoors, he saw in his mirror that the gum had quickly become swollen and inflamed. So he treated it as best he could, tenderly and carefully, and, in time, the pain began to subside. Soon enough, the pain disappeared, and when the pain from the bite had gone he realised that the pain from the toothache had gone too. I shared this story with a doctor friend. 'It's a common phenomenon in medicine,' she commented. 'Two pains can cancel each other out. It's strange, isn't it, that a way to get rid of one pain is to get a different one, and then they will eliminate each other.'

Of course it would never be right to advocate the *deliberate* creation of one pain to eliminate another. I'm told that this is why self-harm can come about, the creation of a physical pain to deflect from a mental anguish. But, instead, might it not be that the way to get rid of a bad thing in life is to replace it with a good thing? Displacement *could* work in our favour. When a gardener looks at a weed-infested piece of ground, he will, first of all, pull out the weeds. But he won't leave the ground empty. He will replace the weeds with something more useful or beautiful. Not emptiness, but displacement.

Thinking about our African proverb,
can we find a different dance when the music changes?

February 17 – God

'God moves in a mysterious way.'
William Cowper, Olney Hymns

'What is God like?' is a question I have been asked many times. Working on the assumption that the facile answer 'An old, grey-bearded man in the sky' isn't sufficient, explorations of a response are always revealing and challenging. As a parish minister, I would run regular classes for 'First Communicants', confirmation classes, where the basics of the Christian faith would be explored with a group of enquirers before they took their vows of commitment in a special worship service. The question 'What is God like?' would be part of that exploration. But rather than trying to give the definitive response – as if there was one – to satisfy everyone, I used the question as a way of getting the enquirers to think what God meant to them, and how they might express that.

Because I've always found it easier to explain things in pictures, I would ask the folk in the class what their picture was of God. Could they find a metaphor, an image that could communicate the nature of God in their own lives, even if they couldn't explain it in words? The pictures shared were enlightening, deep, expressive, emotional, challenging and much more besides. No one ever failed to come up with a picture. Everyone was right, and everyone learned from everyone else.

One young woman described God as a blanket of knitted squares which she could pull around her for warmth. It was brightly coloured and had no set pattern or form. But it was always there and always did its job. Sometimes when she pulled it too tightly the stitching came out somewhere. So she had to take it off and examine it carefully, and do a bit of mending before pulling it round her again.

So, what might your picture of God be now?

February 18 – Unexpected

'A Scout is never taken by surprise; he knows exactly
what to do when anything unexpected happens.'
Robert Baden-Powell, Scouting for Boys

When I was a minister in my first parish, our house was right next
to the church. Although it was set in the midst of a deprived
housing estate, its congregation was a beacon of goodness and
hopefulness. But while the church people didn't have to live next
door to the church, I did! As a consequence, my wife and I got
used to a procession of odd callers at all times of the day or night.
If there was a light on in the house, someone was at home; if
someone was at home, then someone was available. There were
many unexpected things to be dealt with in our front porch. In
addition, there was a secluded car park at the rear of the church
which backed onto our garden. We became security guards for
that too.

That's one of the reasons we got a dog, a small, black-and-white
Border collie. The dog was no more than a little pup when she
was first called into action. My wife saw something untoward
going on in the car park. So with a frisky collie pup on a lead, the
brave lady went out to investigate. The kids messing about were
highly amused. 'Haw missus,' chortled one, 'this your guard-dog,
eh? Magic! Man, ah'm scared, ha, ha … not!' With that, he bent
down to pick up the dog. And the wise beast proceeded to wee
down his front! 'Aye, good guard-dog, right enough,' my wife
reports that she concluded, 'and wets anyone who's up to no good
– on command! You should always be prepared for the unexpected, eh lads?'

Always expect the unexpected, we're told.
Even then, the unexpected sometimes takes us by surprise.
But when we're prepared for what might be different,
what a difference that might make!

February 19 – Imagination

'What is this life if, full of care,
We have no time to stand and stare.'
William Henry Davies, Leisure

When I was a small boy, my first primary school was only a stone's throw from the back of my house, so I walked to school. At the age of 10 I moved to a school that was about a mile away. But I still walked, because that's what everyone did. But when I began secondary school when I turned 11, that meant a three-mile journey. There were no school buses and my parents didn't have a car. So it was either an hour's walk – or get a bike.

A second-hand bike was procured and I cycled to school each day. My trusty steed did its job well. 'Trusty steed' was an apt description, for often I would be riding to school on a horse from a Wild West movie, roping steers on the way, or dealing with an Indian raiding party. On another day, I would be racing to school on a motorbike, doing Moto-Cross on the rutted paths across the moorland opposite our house. And on yet another, I would be a Maharaja mounted atop a huge elephant, slowly progressing on my regal way and waving to the crowds as I went. My bike was *seldom* merely a means of transport to get me to and from school. A vivid imagination made it *much* more than that.

Such an imagination dims quickly when adult years and responsibilities come along and our minds become filled with practicalities and the need to make decisions. Maybe it would be good to find a childhood imagination from time to time and be transported for a moment into the mystical, imaginary places of our hopes and dreams.

I was late for school one day.
I told my Latin teacher I'd got delayed on a cattle-drive.
He didn't believe me. Silly man! No imagination ...

February 20 – Suffering

'To each his suff'rings; all are men,
Condemn'd alike to groan;
The tender for another's pain,
Th' unfeeling for his own.'

Thomas Gray, Ode on a Distant Prospect of Eton College

A man was walking along the promenade of a seaside town with his grandson. During their leisurely stroll, they met a clergyman, an old, craggy soul, who was clearly not in the best of moods. To say he was disgruntled would be an understatement. Nothing in the world was right. Everyone and everything was wrong: from the state of the nation, to the morals of the young; from the cost of living, to the decline of the Church.

To make matters worse, the elderly clergyman complained that he was suffering from a slight touch of sunburn. 'This is all I need. *Sunburn*, indeed,' he muttered as he went disconsolately on his way.

The boy had been silent throughout the encounter – 'seen but not heard' – but had been listening intently. When he and his companion had walked on a short distance from the gloom-stricken old man the lad looked at his grandfather and announced, 'Grandad, I hope *you* never ever suffer from a sunset.'

He got the word wrong, right enough. But he got the idea right, don't you think? There *are* some people who suffer from a sunset. They live in a dark, dingy and disconsolate world. There are some people, as my granny often pointed out, 'who enjoy bad health' and are not hesitant in telling you about their woes.

Today, if I suffer from a sunset,
let me suffer in silence.
But if I get a glimpse of a sunrise,
let me share it with as many people as I can.

February 21 – Pathways

'Good company in a journey
makes the way to seem the shorter.'
Izaak Walton, The Compleat Angler

In a collection of short spiritual tales called *The Wanderer*, Khalil Gibran offers us this mystical idea:

> *In the valley of Kadisha where the mighty river flows, two little streams met and spoke to one another. One stream said, 'How came you, my friend, and how was your path?'*
>
> *And the other answered, 'My path was most encumbered. The wheel of the mill was broken, and the master farmer who used to conduct me from my channel to his plants, is dead. I struggled down oozing with the filth of laziness in the sun. But how was your path, my brother?'*
>
> *And the other stream answered and said, 'Mine was a different path. I came down the hills among fragrant flowers and shy willows; men and women drank of me with silvery cups, and little children paddled their rosy feet at my edges, and there was laughter all about me, and there were sweet songs. What a pity that your path was not so happy.'*
>
> *At that moment the river spoke with a loud voice and said, 'Come in, come in, we are going to the sea. Come in, come in, speak no more. Be with me now. We are going to the sea. Come in, come in, for in me you shall forget your wanderings, sad or gay. Come in, come in. And you and I will forget all our ways when we reach the heart of our mother the sea.'*

Truth, insight and purpose come not from everyone being on the same road, but from a deeper sharing when our paths intersect.

Mutual understanding leads to a greater goal.

February 22 – Growth

*'We are not yet what we shall be,
but we are growing toward it.'*
Martin Luther, In Defence of All the Articles

Peggy Kilgour was a Church of Scotland deaconess in the church in which I was brought up, and she had a singular effect on me. With her soft, greying hair and ready smile, she was a kindly 'auntie' figure for all the children. Miss Kilgour, as I knew her, had a passion for two things – the Bible and begonias. The Bible was fundamental to her life and she communicated that through 'The Good News Transport Fleet'. The chairs for each Sunday school class would be formed in a boat-shape, and every week the ship would sail with the great missionaries of the Church – Livingstone, Aylward and Grenfell – and heroes of the Bible – Joseph and Moses, Gideon and Ruth, Paul and Timothy. I don't know whether 'The Good News Transport Fleet' was Peggy Kilgour's invention or a tried-and-tested teaching method. It doesn't matter. Her commitment to the Bible's Good News was enough for me.

And the begonias? In every spare moment, Peggy Kilgour cultivated begonias. Every year, each child got a begonia to care for. Over the weeks, nurtured with care and attention, the begonias would flourish. The culmination was the annual Children's Begonia Show where a motley collection of plants would be displayed in the church hall, brought by a motley collection of children. There were no prizes, only the pleasure of a church hall filled with colour, life and growth.

I never was a great begonia-grower. But the growth of the Good News continues for me from those seedling days, planted by a church deaconess who loved making things grow.

*Today, with nurture and care,
I can grow a little more towards what I yet can be.*

February 23 – Sleep

'To sleep, perchance to dream.'
William Shakespeare, Hamlet

My father was a master of the catnap. He could sit in his chair by the fire, say he was going to sleep for ten minutes, be out-for-the-count for *exactly* the time stated – I know he was asleep, because I know a snore when I hear one – and waken up and be about his business on the dot. When he was on a shift as a bus-driver which allowed him to come home for lunch, he would have his meal, lie back for his catnap, rouse from his slumbers just when he needed to and be outside in time for the lunchtime bus that would take him back to the depot. Amazing! My mother said it was the sign of a peaceful mind. I reckoned he was just lucky. But, whatever it was, it never failed. My dad was never late going back to work.

Whether my father had dreams in his catnaps I just don't know – 'perchance to dream', possibly. To my shame I've got no real knowledge either of the meaning of the soliloquy from which Shakespeare's quote comes, nor am I familiar with the intricacies of the plot of *Hamlet*. But what I *do* know because of my mother's understanding of her husband is that a guilty conscience *can* deprive the body of the peaceful and restful sleep that leads 'perchance' to dreaming. If my father did have dreams before he went off to work, he did so because he had a clear conscience. And, with my mother's compliments on his catnaps, a peaceful mind seemed to be integral to my father's make-up.

I didn't inherit the 'catnap gene' from my father. But I do know that it's always best to lie down to sleep at any time with a clear conscience. That way, if dreams happen, they come from a place of peacefulness and rest.

Don't let the sun go down on your wrath – or your mistakes.
Give your dreams the best possible chance.

February 24 – Artistry

'There is musick, even in the beauty and silent note which
Cupid strikes, far sweeter than the sound of an instrument.'
Sir Thomas Browne, Religio Medici

Clara Schumann (*née* Wieck) was born in 1819. A German musician and composer, she was one of the most distinguished pianists of her day. She and her husband, the composer Robert Schumann, were early supporters of Brahms, Clara being the first pianist to give public performances of his works.

Clara Schumann was the breadwinner and main support for her family through a series of tragedies. Her first son, Emil, died aged one. Her husband had a breakdown, attempted suicide in 1854 and spent the last two years of his life in an insane asylum. In 1872 her daughter Julie died, leaving two small children, and a few years later her son Felix died aged 25. Her son Ludwig suffered from mental illness and, in Clara's words, had to be 'buried alive' in an institution. Her son Ferdinand died at 43 and she took responsibility for raising his children. She herself became deaf in later life and often needed a wheelchair.

A music critic said of Clara Wieck's Vienna recital in 1837: 'The appearance of this artist can be regarded as epoch-making ... In her creative hands, the most ordinary passage ... acquires a significant meaning, a colour, which only those with the most consummate artistry can give.' But should Clara Schumann not also be remembered as epoch-making for the people she loved? In such creative hands, the ordinary, and extraordinary, passages of family life were given new meaning and colour from the consummate artistry of someone whose love was, indeed, 'far sweeter than the sound of an instrument'.

What instrument of love might bring new meaning
to those we care for today?

February 25 – Humility

'I believe the first test of a truly great man
is his humility.'
John Ruskin, Modern Painters

A rabbi and a cantor and a humble synagogue cleaner were once preparing together for the Day of Atonement. It was a time of self-examination and repentance.

The rabbi beat his breast and said, 'I am nothing. I am nothing. I am nothing.' The cantor beat his breast and said, 'I am nothing. I am nothing. I am nothing.' The cleaner beat his breast and said, 'I am nothing. I am nothing. I am nothing.' Whereupon the rabbi turned to the cantor and whispered, 'Look who thinks he's nothing.'

True humility is, as John Ruskin affirms, the test of true greatness. True humility, given the human frailties known to us all, is hard to find. But when it is exhibited, true humility is like a light shining in a dark world of selfishness and arrogance.

Some tourists were visiting the home of the composer Ludwig van Beethoven. A young woman among them sat down at Beethoven's piano and began to play his 'Moonlight Sonata'. When she had finished she turned to the caretaker of the composer's home and said, 'I presume many musicians visit this place every year.' 'Yes, indeed,' was the reply, 'for the great Paderewski was here only last month.' 'Oh,' responded the visitor. 'And did he play on Beethoven's piano?' 'No, he did not,' the caretaker replied, 'for he did not think himself worthy.'

'He that is down needs fear no fall,
he that is low, no pride.
He that is humble ever shall
have God to be his guide.'
John Bunyan, *Shepherd Boy's Song*

February 26 – Irritations

'Nothing so needs reforming as other people's habits.'
Mark Twain, Pudd'nhead Wilson's Calendar for 1894

We all have things that irritate us. Top of my list of major irritations would be people who rustle sweet papers in theatres; drivers who don't indicate properly on motorways; and don't get me started on the misplaced apostrophe!

I have a friend whose major irritation is people who make lists of their major irritations. I'm surprised he's still my friend. In reality, irritations are just that – irritations, and minor ones too. In the great scheme of things 'nobody died', as the great tennis-player Boris Becker once remarked after losing a major match at Wimbledon. 'Nobody died!' So why does this Grumpy Old Man have such a long list of irritations?

What about the things that *really* matter? Should the oppression of the people of Palestine not be more important than people who rustle sweet papers? Isn't the spread of HIV across Africa more alarming than a misplaced apostrophe? And when a devastating earthquake leaves hundreds dead and thousands homeless, might my getting tetchy on a motorway not be seen for the minor irritation that it is?

When I think about it, my list of irritations is all about me. Carl Jung wrote: 'Everything that irritates us about others can lead to an understanding of ourselves.' So I need to look at the selfish me at the centre of the world which I want to be perfect for my own sake. Come on, Grumpy Old Man, you need to understand yourself better and have a more important list. Why not get really irritated about what *really* matters. The plight of those who are worse off than you are would be a good place to start.

So now it's irritating that I can't remember
what I do that's irritating to other people.

February 27 – Poverty

'Those who oppress the poor
show contempt for their Maker,
but whoever is kind of the needy honours God.'
Bible: Proverbs 14:31

The annual Christian Aid book sale in St Andrew's and St George's West Church in Edinburgh is a remarkable enterprise. Under the able and passionate guidance of Mary Davidson, and assisted by hundreds of volunteers, the book sale has raised more than £1.9m since its inception in 1974. With all the sanctuary utilised, the galleries filled with more books and boxes, the ancillary rooms housing the sale of art and ephemera, and with groaning tables spreading into the church's precincts, the church gives itself in its entirety to the sale for three weeks in May every year. Thousands of books are sorted over a two-week period. The week of the sale is a maelstrom of buyers and sellers, sorters and movers, browsers and visitors, all in support of Christian Aid's work in response to the world's poverty, suffering, disasters and strife.

'I can't believe that this year's sale took in £46,700 on the first day alone,' a volunteer said. 'And, once again, I bought more books than I donated! Where am I going to put them all?

Church folk give up their building for three weeks; volunteers give of their time; countless people have the pleasure of exploring and buying. As a result, Christian Aid's work benefits by over £100,000 each year.

One visitor said, 'I just *have* to buy a stack of books even if my bookshelves are near collapsing. Well, it's a worthy cause. When we are rich and others are so poor, it's the least I can do.'

*'For inasmuch as you do it for the least of these
my brothers and sisters, you do it for me.'*
Bible: Matthew 25:40

February 28 – Promises

'Promises are like babies –
easy to make but hard to deliver.'
Anonymous

In the hallway of our home hangs a collection of family photographs, from my wife's family and my own, recording as much of family history as we have photographs for, from recent grandchildren all the way back to sepia pictures of great, great grandparents from the end of the 19th century. Among the most precious for me are two postcard-sized, black-and-white pictures of my parents from 1940. My father cuts a dashing figure in the Air Force uniform of his war service, and my mother is a dark-haired beauty in her early twenties. These were the photographs these two young people had exchanged when they got engaged, my mother keeping her fiancé's photograph beside her when he was overseas, and my father carrying the picture of his girl through North Africa and into Italy as the war unfolded. There's a message written on each photograph for the other to remember. It's a promise of love, a commitment to build on the engagement when a new life could begin together. My parents were married in 1945 after the end of the war. The promise had been kept all the time they were apart.

These two black-and-white photographs remind me of my mother and father, long since gone from this world, and of a young couple who knew the importance of love. But they also symbolise promises made and kept. Without those promises I would not be here. I don't know whether their promises were easy to make or hard to deliver. But I do know that without promises like these the world would be a much poorer place.

A Hebrew proverb runs: 'Promise little and do much.'
It's keeping the promise that matters, not how much you promise.

February 29 – Proposals

'This is the day that the Lord has made;
We will rejoice and be glad in it.'
Bible: Psalm 118:24

A leap year (or 'intercalary year', to be accurate) contains one additional day in order to keep the calendar year synchronised with the astronomical. Because the earth doesn't orbit the sun in exactly 365 days, a calendar that had the same number of days in each year would drift over time. By occasionally inserting (or *intercalating*) an additional day into the year, the drift can be corrected. February 29th happens every four years and is called 'leap day'.

It's been a tradition over many years that women can propose marriage only in leap years. Some claim this was initiated by Saint Patrick or Brigid of Kildare in 5th-century Ireland. Others say it has its roots in a law of 1288 created by Queen Margaret of Scotland which required that fines be levied if a marriage proposal was refused by the man, compensation to be a pair of leather gloves, a single rose, £1 and a kiss. In some places the tradition was tightened to restricting female proposals to the modern leap day, February 29th. Whatever the origins of such traditions, it's clear that February 29th is special because it's not as frequent as other days. Spare a thought for those who are born on February 29th and only have a *real* birthday celebration every four years.

Whether February 29th is different because of female proposals of marriage, strange compensations for refusals, ancient laws or infrequent birthdays, it is no more or less than another day to be enjoyed and to be put to the best use possible. That's my proposal, and I'm not looking for any compensation either.

Look before you leap or even before you propose.

March 1 – Nationalism

'I am not an Athenian or a Greek, I am a citizen of the world.'
Attributed to both Diogenes and Socrates, Greek philosophers

Saint David (*Dewi Sant* in Welsh) was born towards the end of the 5th century. He was part of the royal house of Ceredigion and founded a Celtic monastic community at Glyn Rhosyn (The Vale of Roses) on the western headland of Pembrokeshire at the spot where St David's Cathedral stands today. Glyn Rhosyn became a renowned Christian shrine and the most important centre in Wales. When David was dying, it is reported that he said to his monks: 'Brothers be ye constant. The yoke which with single mind ye have taken, bear ye to the end; and whatsoever ye have seen with me and heard, keep and fulfil.'

St David was recognised as the patron saint of Wales at the height of Welsh resistance to the Normans. St David's Day was celebrated by the Welsh from the late Middle Ages. Indeed, the 17th-century diarist Samuel Pepys records how Welsh celebrations in London for St David's Day would spark wider counter-celebrations amongst their English neighbours: life-sized effigies of Welsh people were symbolically lynched, Pepys tells us, and by the 18th century the custom had arisen of confectioners producing 'taffies' on Saint David's Day – gingerbread figures baked in the shape of a Welshman riding a goat.

It's one thing having pride in your nation, its traditions, culture, history, music and all that binds people together in a national community. But when nation rises up against nation, even in the form of local prejudice and mockery, nobody benefits. We need more of the constancy of David and his brothers, so that hospitality and welcome outweigh discrimination and hatred.

'We're a' bairns o' Adam.'
Scots saying

March 2 – Disrespect

'Against the assault of laughter nothing can stand.'
Mark Twain, The Mysterious Stranger

When ministers and priests get together they will inevitably swap funeral stories. There is something about sharing the bizarre happenings at funerals that helps clergy cope with the sadness and pressure of difficult occasions. They can seldom share such things with others in case it might seem disrespectful. But when they get together, that's another story.

Early in my ministry, I told a story at a function of a funeral I had conducted. The coffin was in the house prior to the funeral and had to be taken downstairs to the hearse. The house was on the fourth floor of a tenement; the stairwell was narrow; the deceased weighed eighteen stones; and two of the funeral cars had been delayed getting to the house. So who had to manoeuvre the coffin downstairs to the waiting hearse? The hearse driver – who was seventy-six and had a heart condition; the undertaker, who was five-foot-five and only had one eye; and ... me! Space fortunately curtails my account of the long downwards transportation of the coffin. But I suspect you can imagine ...

Now, if I *had* told that story to ministers and priests, I'm sure the response would have been laughter. But, on this occasion, I'd forgotten my audience. There were no clergy present to empathise with my tale. Instead I was greeted with silence, furrowed brows and looks ranging from horror to displeasure. My story was clearly considered to be disrespectful.

I've now learned to be more aware of my audience and to remember that what is 'heard' by others might be different from what I wanted to say.

Being disrespectful is never a good idea!
You wouldn't like to be disrespected, would you?

March 3 – Disgrace

'Like a dull actor now
I have forgot my part and I am out,
Even to a full disgrace.'
William Shakespeare, Coriolanus

I was ten years old when I brought disgrace on my family. I was a member of the local Cub Scouts. Badges and campfires, knots and first aid, cook-outs and rambles, I couldn't get enough of it. And I'd risen 'up the ranks', from a 'tenderfoot' (a new boy) to a 'seconder' (second-in-charge of six boys). And then, the ultimate accolade, I was appointed a 'sixer', lead boy in the 'White' six. What a confidence boost! But I let the confidence go to my head ...

One night round a campfire I decided to add a few rude words to a Cub song – and a rude gesture as well! Akela, the pack leader, was furious. In front of the rest of the boys she tore the 'sixer' stripes from my arm and sent me home in disgrace. I was too ashamed to go home early. I hung about outside till it was the normal time for coming back. For three weeks I went out to Cubs, making sure my parents didn't see my sweater minus its sixer stripes. I told my folks I had a great time. But all I'd done was hang about in the cold till it was time to come home.

When the disgrace eventually came to light, I thought the world would end. It didn't! I learned from my mistake. My stripes were reinstated in time, but not before the effect of my disgrace was deeply enough imbedded in my psyche never to be forgotten.

The Scout movement tells us that Akela is 'a symbol of wisdom and authority'. I wish I'd realised that. Perhaps then I wouldn't have needed to experience such abject disgrace.

Thank God for forgiveness and redemption.
Disgrace need never be the end.

March 4 – Contrasts

'There are dark shadows on the earth,
But its lights are stronger in the contrast.'
Charles Dickens, The Pickwick Papers

Humans have always tried to predict the weather or explain meteor-ological patterns. All civilisations have their weather-related rhymes, anecdotes and 'old-wives' tales'. For the farmer planting crops, the merchant sending ships on trade, the family arranging a barbeque, the couple planning a wedding, advanced knowledge of tomorrow's circumstances might mean the difference between success and failure. *When windows won't open, and the salt clogs the shaker, the weather will favour the umbrella maker!* It isn't hard to figure, is it? *A cow with its tail to the West makes the weather best; a cow with its tail to the East makes the weather least.* I'm not so sure I would trust *that* one though. Would you? And at the end of this month there's *March comes in like a lion and goes out like a lamb* – from the storms of winter to the tranquillity of spring. Contrasts … the wild and the gentle; the difficult and the easy.

The writer of the book of Isaiah also says something about lions and lambs. But instead of contrasts, there's a promise of togetherness. Whatever the extremes, the outcome is peaceful. That's hopeful, and maybe even helps us take the bad weather with the good.

The wolf also shall dwell with the lamb,
The leopard shall lie down with the young goat,
The calf and the young lion and the fatling together;
And a little child shall lead them.
The cow and the bear shall graze;
Their young ones shall lie down together;
And the lion shall eat straw like the ox.
Bible: Isaiah 11:6-7

March 5 – Stuff

'The want of a thing is perplexing enough,
but the possession of it is intolerable.'
Sir John Vanburgh, The Confederacy

Some years ago when I was on holiday with my wife and children, we got word that there had been a burglary at our home while we were absent. As it turned out, the thieves had been disturbed so not much was stolen and there was minimal damage. But, not surprisingly, before that reassurance settled comfortably on me, I was anxious about what might have happened. Had my paperwork been disturbed? Was my computer intact? Had my desk been rifled? I was expressing these concerns to my wife when I was met by this thought-provoking rejoinder: 'What's back at home is only "stuff", not necessities. It can all be replaced. It's what we have here – the two of us and our children – that really matters.'

In *David Copperfield*, Charles Dickens has Mr Micawber utter this familiar sentiment:

Annual income twenty pounds, annual expenditure nineteen [pounds] nineteen [shillings] and six [pence], result happiness. Annual income twenty pounds, annual expenditure twenty pounds ought and six [pence], result misery.

For Micawber it was clear enough – live within your means and you will be happy. But for many of us it's not just being debt-free that brings happiness and contentment. It's being surrounded by our 'stuff', much of which we don't actually need. Maybe we shouldn't wait for burglars to make us think about what really matters, but give some thought to de-cluttering ourselves of 'stuff' and concentrating on the things that are *really* important.

What stuff do I have that I can do without today?

March 6 – Art

'Fine art is that in which the hand, the head
and the heart of a man go together.'
John Ruskin, Selections from the Writings of John Ruskin

What is art? That's a question that has exercised the minds of discerning people for centuries. Some will see art in the paintings of Renoir or Monet, while others will value the modernism of Hockney or Emin. Some will make disparaging comments about the graffiti art of Banksy or the surrealism of Dali, while others will criticise the predictability of Constable. Some will choose to browse the National Gallery and know their favourite rooms within it, while others will be regular visitors to the Tate Modern. If 'beauty is in the eye of the beholder' then the answer to 'What is art?' will be as varied as the person who is that art's beholder.

When I was a student for the ministry I attended a seminar with a well known art critic exploring the spiritual aspects of art. He was asked what he considered the most moving piece of art he'd ever seen. He replied without hesitation, 'The Burma Road near Mallaig.' The beauty of the road, he said, was not only in its construction by a local man, wonderful though this was, but in the fact that the road had been built single-handedly for the good of others. It was beautiful because it was an offering of service.

I thought at the time that an *avant-garde* arty type was playing to his audience. I was right. There *is* no Burma Road at Mallaig. The story comes from a novel, *The Edge of the Glen,* by Clifford Geddes. But the point the artist was making stayed with me. Isn't there beauty in every act of service and the wonder of art in every loving action? That makes each one of us an artist, and offers every beholder the beauty they seek.

Is there anything that is beautiful that is not art?

March 7 – Just as I am

'Trust in thine own untried capacity.'
Ella Wheeler Wilcox, Achievement

Charlotte Elliot was born in Clapham in London in 1789. For years she struggled with her faith and one evening while she was living in Brighton with her vicar brother, Henry Venn Elliot, who ran a girls' school, she was alone, downcast and full of doubts and fears. She then recalled a meeting, twelve years earlier, with a preacher, Dr Caesar Malan, a conversation that had never left her. A seed had been sown and in her darkest hour it took root. At that moment she felt compelled to write down how she felt. Trusting her 'own untried capacity', she found peace for her troubled soul.

Just as I am, without one plea,
But that Thy blood was shed for me,
And that Thou bidst me come to Thee,
O Lamb of God, I come, I come.

Just as I am, though tossed about
With many a conflict, many a doubt,
Fightings and fears within, without,
O Lamb of God, I come, I come.

Just as I am, Thou wilt receive,
Wilt welcome, pardon, cleanse, relieve;
Because Thy promise I believe,
O Lamb of God, I come, I come.

Just as I am, Thy love unknown
Hath broken every barrier down;
Now, to be Thine, yea, Thine alone,
O Lamb of God, I come, I come.

March 8 – Acceptance

'Acceptable unto God'
Bible, Romans 12:1

Charlotte Elliot's hymn has expressed for many people who struggle for meaning and purpose what it means to find peace through believing in yourself and being accepted as you are.

> *Just as I am, though tossed about*
> *with many a conflict, many a doubt,*
> *fightings and fears within, without,*
> *O Lamb of God, I come, I come.*

In her lifetime, Charlotte Elliot collected over a thousand letters from people telling her of the important spiritual help they had received through the words of her hymn. Indeed, her own brother, Henry Venn Elliot, testified to its usefulness in his ministry when he wrote, 'In the course of a long ministry, I hope I have been permitted to see some fruit of my labours; but I feel far more has been done by a simple hymn of my sister's.'

In St Oswald's churchyard at Grasmere is a row of tombstones of the Wordsworth family, including that of Dora, William Wordsworth's daughter. On it is a carving of a lamb with a cross behind it. Someone had sent a copy of Charlotte Elliot's hymn to Dora when she was very ill, and the words brought her comfort as she was dying. 'That is the very thing for me,' she said, and asked for the words to be read over and over again. At the foot of Dora's tombstone is a text from John 6:37: *Him that cometh to me, I will in no wise cast out* – the same text Charlotte Elliot had put at the top of the page when she'd first penned her hymn.

> *To be feel accepted you first have to accept yourself –*
> *just as you are.*

March 9 – Being me

'Encourage all your virtuous dispositions,
and exercise them whenever an opportunity arises.'
Thomas Jefferson, Letter to Peter Carr

In my book *A Blessing to Follow*, I wrote a story about a 'showman preacher', suggesting that whatever 'virtuous dispositions' the preacher had it was only for his own glory. Inspired by Charlotte Elliot's hymn, *Just As I Am*, I ended the story with this poem.

'Just as I am,' I hear you say,
I should come close to you today.
And yet, mistakes get in the way – just as I am.

'Just as I am,' I hear you call;
completely me, regrets and all,
knowing how often I can fall – just as I am.

'Just as I am,' I hear your plea,
knowing your voice calls out to me,
this showman, down on bended knee – just as I am.

'Just as I am,' I hear your word.
With me you will not be deterred
by what you've known and seen and heard – just as I am.

'Just as I am,' I hear your praise;
you will be with me all my days;
I'll know, through Grace, forgiving ways – just as I am.

'Just as I am,' I hear you shout!
Come with your faith and with your doubt.
This is what following is about – just as I am.

March 10 – Procrastination

'Procrastination is the thief of time.'
Edward Young, The Complaint: Night Thoughts

I have a friend whose motto is, 'Never put off till tomorrow what you can put off till the next day ... or even the day after that.' He's the most unstressed person I know. But the trouble is that important things often don't get done at all!

'Never put off till tomorrow ...' Which of us has not been guilty of putting things off, perhaps not so expertly or with such total commitment as my friend, but nonetheless ... ? Difficult things that we prefer to avoid because they're just too difficult; that tricky job that gets delayed because there are much more interesting things to give attention to; that promised task that *will* reach the top of our to-do list but just never does.

Maybe we're more like my friend – and more often – than we like to admit.

But what of the good things? Isn't it disappointing that these things often get put off too? The phone call to someone who's been in trouble that ... well ... you don't get around to; the card to send on the anniversary of a friend's bereavement that ... well ... you forgot to take a note of; that visit to make which you *promised* you would do ... well ... when you have time. Maybe, even with the *good* things we're more like my friend – and more often – than we are prepared to admit.

When you put things off, of course it's because some things aren't much fun. That's human nature, isn't it? But when the good things get postponed too ... well ... there are other people that miss out on a bit of loving and caring, don't you think?

'Forgive us for what we have done
and what we have left undone.'
General Confession, Book of Common Prayer

March 11 – Reasons

'Reason has always existed,
but not always in reasonable form.'
Karl Marx, The Manifesto of the Communist Party

On a recent visit to County Mayo in the west of Ireland, my wife
and I drove through the beautiful countryside of Connemara, on
a route known locally as 'Joyce's Country'. Among the memorable
locations of our day-tour was the village of Recess (*Sraith Sailsach*
in Irish, 'The Stream of the Willow Tree'). Recess sits on the edge
of the Glendalough Lake surrounded by the quartzite peaks of the
Twelve Bens, home of the Connemara green marble quarries. And
there we found Joyce's Craft Shop and Art Gallery, one of the best
of its kind we'd come across.

Parking our car, we couldn't fail to notice a massive concrete
statue dominating the car park. This crouching, fearsome figure
was none other than Connemara himself. But most enlightening
was the full inscription on the statue's plaque.

This is
CONNEMARA
(Conn, son of the sea)
BUILT IN 1999
by Joyce's Craft Shop
for no apparent reason

Irish humour at its best! 'For no apparent reason', indeed! For
why should everything have a reason, when, apparently, even a
massive statue at the side of a lake can make people smile?

'I think, therefore I am.' (Decartes)
'I do because I can.' (Joyce's Craft Shop)
'I smile – for no apparent reason.' (The author)

March 12 – Self-love

'Manifest plainness; embrace simplicity;
reduce selfishness; have few desires.'

Lao-tzu, Tao te Ching

'If she was chocolate, she would eat herself,' I heard a colleague say recently of someone she knew. A *very* disparaging comment, I thought, but it was clearly heartfelt. Someone was obviously so full of herself that it affected how she was viewed by others.

A Greek myth tells us of Narcissus, who was an absolute stunner with long, flowing blond hair, beautiful bright blue eyes and white, even teeth. Lots of young ladies fell in love with him, including the nymph Echo. Echo had upset Hera, the Queen of the Gods. As a punishment Hera made Echo unable to speak except to repeat the last three words of the person she was talking to.

Echo fell in love with Narcissus, but she could never tell him how she felt. Narcissus teased Echo and she ran away in tears. Aphrodite, the goddess of love, seeing what had happened, decided to punish Narcissus. As he came to a pool, Narcissus saw his face in the water and fell in love with the vision he saw ... his own reflection. If he was chocolate, he would eat himself! Narcissus was in love with himself, but every time he tried to touch the face of the vision he loved it broke up on the shimmering surface of the water.

Narcissus stopped eating, lost his beautiful looks, pined for his love and faded away and died. Aphrodite took pity on him and made a flower grow in his place on the bank of the lake.

So there! Be careful not to eat yourself if you're chocolate. Be careful you don't fall in love with your own image. Self-esteem is one thing. Self-love – a Narcissus kind of love – is quite another.

The truth is – if you are *chocolate and you* do *eat yourself
there will be no chocolate left to do any more good!*

March 13 – Memory

'Memory is the diary we all carry with us.'
Oscar Wilde, The Importance of Being Earnest

How's your memory? Read this piece carefully and then follow the guidance.

The Great Panjandrum

She went into the garden to cut a cabbage-leaf to make an apple-pie; and at the same time a great she-bear, coming up the street, pops its head into the shop. What! No soap? So he died, and she very imprudently married the barber: and there were present the Picninnies, and the Joblillies, and the Garyulies, and the great Panjandrum himself, with the little round button at top; and they all fell to playing the game of catch-as-catch-can, till the gunpowder ran out at the heels of their boots.

Now see if you can recite the passage without a mistake. OK? Either you haven't bothered or you've not got very far and needed to check out your mistake. Ah well, at least you tried.

This remarkable piece was written by Samuel Foote in the mid-18th century to test the much-renowned memory of the actor Charles Macklin. Macklin boasted that he could recite any paragraph given to him without mistakes, having read it through only once. History doesn't tell us whether Macklin succeeded or failed in this particular test. But we *are* told that Foote regularly shared the story and the passage in subsequent years.

Memory matters. When people lose their memory for whatever reason, they lose so much. Be patient with those whose memory is fading. After all, it might be yours one day.

Remember the important moments – and remember why.

March 14 – Right and wrong

'There is no right way to do wrong.'
The author's grandmother

I was on the top deck of a bus at a bus stop the other day when a shop sign in the window of a local hairdressing emporium caught my eye. I recognised the red-and-white-striped pole projecting over the pavement. But the sign in the window confirmed it was a:

GENTLEMEN'S BARBER

As I said earlier, the misplaced apostrophe is high up my list of irritations. I don't know why. It just riles me. But here, on a huge shop-sign, was the *correct* use of the apostrophe. Well done the shop owner and the signwriter! They'd got it *right* for once. But then as the bus drew away from the stop I looked further down the window. There it was … right turned to wrong!

MENS' HAIRCUT'S
NO APPOINTMENT'S NECESSARY.

Aaarrrggghhh! Was the misplaced apostrophe confirmed on my irritation list? Indeed it was – and now right at the top!

It's sometimes the way of things, though. Good one minute, when we get it right; bad the next, when we get it wrong. Right and wrong; success and failure. So maybe irritation is useful if it helps us notice our mistakes and concentrate on getting it right next time.

I know I'm not always right,
and I hope I do more right than wrong,
but I need to stay irritated with myself
so that I know the difference.

March 15 – Books

'I've never known any trouble
that an hour's reading didn't assuage.'
Charles de Secondat, Baron de la Brède et de Montesquieu,
Pensées Diverses

In introducing the hero of *Don Quixote*, Miguel Cervantes writes:

> *You must know ... that the above-named gentleman whenever*
> *he was at leisure (which was mostly all the year round) gave*
> *himself up to reading books of chivalry with such ardour and*
> *avidity that he almost entirely neglected the pursuit of his field-*
> *sports, and even the management of his property; and to such*
> *a pitch did his eagerness and infatuation go that he sold many*
> *an acre of tillageland to buy books of chivalry to read, and*
> *brought home as many of them as he could get.*

Hopefully, despite his neglect of his field-sports, property affairs and 'tillageland', some of Don Quixote's troubles were duly assuaged. However, his reading clearly became an obsession.

> *He became so absorbed in his books that he spent his nights*
> *from sunset to sunrise, and his days from dawn to dark, poring*
> *over them; and what with little sleep and much reading his*
> *brains got so dry that he lost his wits.*

My grandmother said some people were 'so heavenly minded that they are no earthly use'. Maybe if Don Quixote had not lost himself in his fantasy world of chivalry he might have kept his wits. Books matter, but only if they help us to be more earthly use.

A good book is a friend that turns its back on you
but still remains a friend.

March 16 – Superstitions

'These gloomy presages and terrors of mind.'
Joseph Addison, Household Superstitions

My grandmother refused to go out of the house on Friday the thirteenth. 'Best stay safe at home in case bad luck befalls,' she would say, and hope that she didn't have any *indoor* accidents!

Why are there superstitions associated with Friday the thirteenth? In some cultures thirteen is an unlucky number and in others Friday is an unlucky day. Put them together and you have my granny's 'unlucky Friday'. She also reckoned that since there were thirteen people sitting round the table at Jesus' last supper, it's bad to have thirteen of anything to work with. And what she would have to say about Stock Market crashes being associated with 'Black Friday', I cannot imagine.

And it wasn't just Friday the thirteenth that was a problem for my granny. There was no walking under a ladder propped against a wall; no opening an umbrella indoors; no putting new shoes on a table; she would throw a pinch of salt over her shoulder if salt had been spilled on the table; and as for superstitions associated with New Year, the list goes on and on.

My grandmother never analysed any of this. She was just responding to superstitions handed down through the years, 'old wives' tales'.

Oh, and it was OK for me to go to *visit* my grandmother on Friday the thirteenth. That way, she was safe at home, while I was the one who had to face any bad luck going around. I was never struck by some unfortunate happening – though I once came close to it when I suggested to my grandmother that she was an 'old wife' ...

'Lucky people make their own luck.'
The author's grandmother

March 17 – Fullness

'All that we behold is full of blessings.'
William Wordsworth,
Lines Composed a Few Miles Above Tintern Abbey

The music for the hymn *Be Thou My Vision* is 'Slane', a traditional Irish folk-tune. Slane is a village in County Meath in Ireland, set on a steep hillside close to the River Boyne. The village centre dates from the 18th century, but the surrounding area contains many historic sites dating back over five thousand years.

'Slane' – *Baile Shláine* in Irish Gaelic – means 'homestead of fullness'. Legend has it that in AD433 on Slane Hill St Patrick defied the pagan High King Lóegaire of Tara by lighting candles as a Paschal Fire on Easter Eve. The light couldn't be doused by anyone but Patrick, and it was also here that Patrick used the three-leaved shamrock to explain the doctrine of the Trinity.

There's another legend that is, perhaps, better known. It credits St Patrick with banishing all the snakes from Ireland, chasing them into the sea after they assailed him during a forty-day fast he was undertaking on top of a hill. Maybe this was on the Hill of Slane too. The trouble with *this* legend, though, is that all evidence suggests that post-glacial Ireland never had any snakes, so there was nothing for St Patrick to banish!

So we're left with lighting candles on the top of the hill in defiance of a pagan king. Maybe this legend isn't true either, but it leaves me with an admiration that Patrick had enough faith in his light – whatever it was – to know it could offer defiance, even to a king. Vision, defiance, fasting, preaching, symbolism ... Even if there were no snakes, there was still for Patrick a 'homestead of fullness', a light that shone, no matter what.

When the light goes out,
why should our thankfulness sleep?

March 18 – Recognised

'Don't worry when you are not recognised,
but strive to be worthy of recognition.'
Attributed to Abraham Lincoln

An American soldier, based in Sweden, was spending the day in Stockholm. Travelling across town on a bus he fell into conversation with the man sitting next to him. The man correctly identified him as an American and they got to talking about the soldier's home country. The soldier expounded his pride in his nation, especially the value of American citizenship. 'The United States of America,' he proclaimed, 'is the most democratic country in the world. Ordinary citizens may go to the White House to see the President and personally discuss things with him.'

The man listened intently, and when he had the opportunity to interject offered, 'Sir. I am delighted with that. But it is nothing to what we have here. For in Sweden, the King and the people travel on the same bus.'

With that, the man rose to leave the bus as it arrived at his stop. The soldier was left somewhat bemused, but everything was clarified when the man sitting behind him leaned forward and informed him that he had just been talking with King Gustav Adolf VI of Sweden.

You never know whom you might be sitting beside or whom you might be called upon to help. Perhaps we might begin by recognising our own humanity, and our own needs, in every stranger we meet.

'Passing stranger! you do not know how longingly I look upon you,
You must be he I was seeking, or she I was seeking,
(it comes to me as of a dream)
I have somewhere surely lived a life of joy with you.'
Walt Whitman, *'To a Stranger'* in *Leaves of Grass*

March 19 – Jumping to conclusions

'When you jump to conclusions
you often skip over the truth.'
Anonymous

Recorded in *Boswell's Life of Johnson*, the 18th-century Samuel Johnson offers this advice:

> *There is a wicked inclination in most people to suppose an old man decayed in his intellects. If a young or middle-aged man, when leaving a company, does not recollect where he has laid his hat, it is nothing; but if the same inattention is discovered in an old man, people will shrug their shoulders, and say, 'His memory is going.'*

We can reach the *wrong* conclusion all too readily. I was once telephoned by a man who was looking for my help. His speech was slurred and he struggled to make himself understood. Because I knew something of the family's circumstances I concluded that he was drunk and I was immensely irritated that he'd bothered me in such an incoherent state. I told him I'd see him when he was more able to have a conversation. When I called at his home, I was horrified to discover that he'd recently had a stroke which had left him with slurred speech – and he hadn't touched alcohol for months. I apologised as profusely as I could.

I'd like to report that my apology was accepted, but I can't. I wasn't able to help the man or his family again, because jumping to the wrong conclusion had ruined any relationship we had.

*Exercise is not ... jumping to conclusions,
running off your mouth, stretching the truth,
pushing your own views, bending over backwards or
side-stepping your responsibility.*

March 20 – Explorers

'I had determined never to stop
until I had reached the end and achieved my purpose.'
David Livingstone, missionary

The explorer had been gone for a long time. For months the people waited for his return, eager to know what lay beyond their settlement. The great river was the unknown. Where did it go? Could it lead them to new lands? The explorer would be their salvation, for when he came back they would know for certain whether the great river was their highway to freedom.

When the explorer returned, there was much rejoicing. The people eagerly awaited the news of the great river. But the explorer was perplexed. For so great had been his experiences during his months of travelling that he did not have the words to convey his feelings and emotions around all his discoveries. And he could not find the expressiveness to describe all the wonders he had seen. 'You must go and see for yourselves,' he said. And to guide them, he drew them a map on the animal skins provided for him. The map outlined the twists and turns of the great river; the rapids and the shallows; the sights and the discoveries; the wonders and the images.

When he was done, the people were ecstatic. *Now* they knew about the great river. They revered the map. They hoisted it on two poles in the centre of the settlement. They covered it with a great awning to keep it safe from the heat of the sun and the beating of the autumn rains. They made copies of the map. And all who had a copy, and all who studied the original map, considered themselves experts on the great river, every twist and turn, every wonderful sight. Yet not one of them ever experienced the delights and wonders of the great river for themselves.

There is a danger in drawing maps for armchair explorers.

March 21 – Criticism

'Never criticise a man
until you have walked a mile in his moccasins.'
Native American proverb

When I qualified as a minister, I worked in a housing estate in Glasgow among some very supportive and honest people. And it was their honesty that allowed me to really learn about ministry. One Sunday I had preached what I considered to be an *excellent* sermon, based on the words of Jesus from Mark 10:14: '*Suffer the little children to come to me, and forbid them not; for of such is the kingdom of God.*' It was in my opinion the definitive exposition of this familiar text. Consequently, as I shook hands with the worshippers at the end of the service, I was glowing with pride. There was the occasional 'thank you', 'nice service', and 'the weather's better'. Then Edna appeared.

Edna was the school-crossing-patrol lady, a regular at church and a supportive friend. And she was well known for 'telling it as it is'. Shaking my hand she asked, 'Can I have a word with you about your sermon?' I smiled, expecting this to be the pinnacle of the morning's accolades. 'Of course,' I announced. 'Well,' said Edna, 'all I can say is … it was rubbish!' My beaming grin vanished. I was crushed. This was criticism I hadn't expected. But Edna continued, 'So let me suggest how it might have been better …' and in two or three sentences a 'rubbish' sermon was greatly improved.

If Edna had stopped at the 'rubbish' part, my fledgling confidence might have been severely and permanently dented. But because she offered wise advice as well, it turned out to be the best lesson in sermon construction I've ever had.

I never realised someone could walk in my moccasins
without my even knowing it.

March 22 – Wonder

'If eyes were made for seeing,
Then beauty is its own excuse for Being.'
Ralph Waldo Emerson, The Rhodora

I was delighted to learn recently of the existence of The Cloud Appreciation Society. I was given a book for my birthday which the society had produced entitled *Clouds That Look Like Things*. The introduction to the book begins in this way:

Is it a bird? Is it a plane? No, it's a ghost carrying the shopping. Or a pink elephant. Or an enormous pair of Mick Jagger lips. At The Cloud Appreciation Society, we love finding shapes in the clouds. It's what lazy afternoons in the park were made for and we think everyone should do more of it.

The book is filled with remarkable photographs of what people have seen in the sky above them – from airborne animals to a body-builder flexing his muscles; from a witch on a broomstick to Santa having a bad-hair day; from Homer Simpson befriending a squirrel to a broken heart. They're all there, and people with an eye for such things have recorded some remarkable sights.

And that's the point, and that's why I'm delighted that The Cloud Appreciation Society exists. The world is an amazing, beautiful, quirky place. There are some things that will take us by surprise and fill us with wonder – if only we would be in the mood to notice. The delicate beauty of a flower; a spider's web covered in morning dew; a sunset, where oranges and purples blend like nowhere else; and, of course, Mick Jagger lips in the clouds.

Keep your eyes open. Be prepared to be amazed. You'll be surprised how much in our world can fill us with wonder.

And I think to myself, what a wonderful world.

March 23 – Potential

'Knowledge is limited,
whereas imagination embraces the entire world.'
Albert Einstein, Cosmic Religion: With Other Opinions and Aphorisms

I have a painting of a small croft house beside a track somewhere in the Highlands of Scotland. It's a colourful picture, vibrant and dramatic, and made all the more effective by the bright red of the croft's roof, framed against the yellow of the fields beyond, and in sharp contrast to the pristine white of the croft walls. The artist is famed for his use of bright colours and bold brush strokes. So the red roof of the little croft house is not at all surprising.

Some years after acquiring the painting, I learned from the artist that the croft's roof wasn't originally bright red. It had been a rather dull, unattractive rusty brown, the corrugated iron of the roof showing the effects of many years' exposure to the wilds of Highland weather. A vivid red, therefore, looked *much* better on the croft, showing the house in a much more attractive fashion.

When the owner of the croft discovered that his house had been painted with such a wonderful red roof, far from being offended or feeling criticised, he bought the requisite amount of paint and proceeded to paint his roof bright red to match the painting! When I went recently to visit the scene, I had no doubt which croft was the subject of my picture, for its vivid red roof could be seen for miles around.

A skilled painter saw the potential of a scene and what it could look like. With an artist's imagination the image was transformed on his canvas. A crofter saw through the artist's eye what could be, and made the change come about.

Might others see potential in us that
we've never thought about before?
Might we be able to change so our potential comes to life?

March 24 – Home

'A happy home is the single spot of rest which a man has upon
this earth for the cultivation of his noblest sensibilities.'
Frederick William Robertson,
Sermons preached at Trinity Chapel, Brighton

In the times I have been away from home over the years I can't
recall being particularly homesick. Perhaps if I'd lived abroad for
a while, I might have pined for my native Scotland. But I haven't,
so I've just had to appreciate what other people have told me about
homesickness and leave it at that. I did, however, have a personal
glimpse recently of what others have lived through ...

I was on a pilgrimage with my wife to the Holy Land and we
were to spend time on the Sea of Galilee on our final day. We
boarded the 'Jesus Boat' (as it's known locally) arranged for our
party, and while we moved off from the pier I was delighted when
a Scottish Saltire, our St Andrew's Cross, was raised to the top of
the mast. I was just about to comment on this when music began
to pour out from the PA system – the rousing strains of 'Scotland
the Brave', pipe-band and all. The group cheered and clapped.
Those who knew the words sang along. There were smiles all
round. But for *this* sentimental pilgrim there were tears in the eyes,
an overwhelming sense of pride in my country and a deep feeling
of homesickness.

What better place to be reminded of home than sailing on the
Sea of Galilee? What better time to value the security of home
than at the conclusion of a pilgrimage of life and faith?

'Home is the resort
Of love, of joy, of peace, and plenty; where
Supporting and supported, polished friends
And dear relations mingle into bliss.'
James Thomson, *The Seasons, Autumn*

March 25 – Interpretation

'Spring bursts today,
For Christ is risen and all the earth's at play.'
Christina G. Rossetti, Easter Carol

My older grandson will have every right to give me a hard time if he happens to read this in the future, but I can't resist telling you this story ...

When he was five and in Primary 1 he was involved with the Easter story in a school setting for the first time. The school, it appears, was careful in making sure that the Easter story was unfolded clearly and accurately – amidst all the excitement of the forthcoming holiday, Easter bunnies, chocolate eggs, and a host of other trappings of this season of the year.

Concerned that it had all made sense to the little lad, I decided to do a bit of 'quizzing' to make sure he'd understood it all. I got the story about Jesus being dead and being alive again – even if it was understood as Jesus 'getting to be dead and then getting to be alive every Easter', and, 'I want to be Jesus when I'm bigger 'cause you get not to be dead sometimes when you should be dead ...' But when I gave him his Easter egg I asked the obvious question, 'What have Easter eggs got to do with Easter?'

'It's about the stone rolling,' came the helpful and encouraging response.'

'Good,' I said. 'That's right. But do you know how the rolling of the stone fits into the Easter story?'

'Yes,' he replied. 'A big stone rolled down the hill and killed Jesus. And that's why we roll eggs down hills at Easter.'

I had nothing to say after that, other than to take a mental note to explore Easter and eggs and stones again in a year's time ...

'Wouldst thou learn thy Lord's meaning in this thing? Learn it well.'
Julian of Norwich, in *Revelations of Divine Love*

March 26 – Improvisation

'A wise man will make more opportunities
than he finds.'

Francis Bacon, Of Ceremonies and Respects

My father was one of eight children brought up in a tenement flat in Fort William in the 1920s. His father had died young and a single mother was left to look after a large family. The tiring effects of keeping a family together before the days of the Welfare State were all too apparent. So the family clubbed together to arrange a week's break for their mother, and after much persuasion she went off for a holiday. Looking after the family fell to my father's elder sister. The older ones were working and my father and the younger ones were still in school. So the first task was to make sure that everyone got up in time for work and school on the Monday morning.

A plan was hatched. The tenant of the next flat worked in the local baker's and had to be there at 4 in the morning to light the fires for the ovens. He was instructed to knock his neighbours' door when he came home for breakfast at 6.30. But no one stirred. The entire household was late for work and school. The plan had to be rethought. My father's sister decided that as she slept next to the window she would tie a long piece of string to her wrist, attach a small weight to the other end and have the string hanging out of the window while she was asleep. When the baker's man came home for breakfast, he was to pull the string. This would wake her and she would make sure everyone else was up in time. It worked a treat! No one was late for the rest of the week.

Improvisation is sometimes necessary. Finding ways round an apparently insurmountable problem may tax our ingenuity, but when it works, it's certainly well worth it!

The imagination to improvise! Where would we be without it?

March 27 – Lives

'Every man's death diminishes me,
because I am involved in mankind.'
John Donne, Meditation XVII

The Forth Bridge is a remarkable feat of Victorian engineering. Connecting Scotland's capital city, Edinburgh, with Fife and beyond, the iconic bridge was opened on March 4th 1890, and spans a total length of 2,528.7 metres (8,296 ft). Described in the *Collins Encyclopaedia of Scotland* as 'the one immediately and internationally recognised Scottish landmark', it's been nominated to be added to the UNESCO World Heritage Sites in Scotland.

'Painting the Forth Bridge' is a colloquial expression for a never-ending task, coined on the erroneous belief that at one time the repainting of the bridge always recommenced immediately after the previous repaint had been completed at the other end. No one is quite sure whether such a practice ever existed, but it makes for a good story. In any event, a recent repainting of the bridge completed in 2011 means that the current 'paint job' should last for 25 years or more. No more necessity for the continual round of painting and repainting.

More important, though, was the monumental nature of the bridge project, which, at the time, pushed engineering and construction techniques to their very limits. At its peak, approximately 4,600 workers were employed. Ninety-eight lives were lost. Hundreds of workers were left crippled by serious accidents, and one logbook of accidents and sickness had 26,000 entries.

It's worthwhile remembering that behind any enterprise are the lives of valuable people. Whether a project is continual or a one-off, monumental or a simple task, where people's lives are involved, that's worth more consideration that anything else.

Everyone matters. But do they matter to everyone?

March 28 – What's in a name?

'What's in a name? That which we call a rose
By any other name would smell as sweet.'
William Shakespeare, Romeo and Juliet

When my two daughters were young they were members of 'The Brownies', the junior section of the Girl Guide movement. The Brownies were first organised by Lord Baden-Powell in 1914 to complete the range of age groups for girls and boys in Scouting. For many years they were the youngest group in the Guide Association, though nowadays the youngest section is 'The Rainbows' for girls aged five to seven. My daughters got a great deal of pleasure from their time in the Brownies. Games and fun, badges and service, songs and trips combined to make being a Brownie a great experience. And, of course, there were good role-models provided by their Brownie leaders – Brown Owl and her helpers.

Brownies wasn't the original name, however. At first they were called Rosebuds, but the girls complained that they didn't like the name (girl-power, it seems, is not new) and Baden Powell had it changed. The revised name came from a story called 'The Brownies' by Juliana Horatia Ewing in which two children learn what helpfulness means. And with young girls in a youth organisation learning what it means to be helpful, the name seemed right.

And that's the point … The Brownie Guides have a law which runs, 'A Brownie Guide thinks of others before herself and does a good turn every day.' So it doesn't matter whether the name is Rosebud or Brownie. What matters are principles which guide a young life. And thinking of others before yourself and doing a good turn every day seems to me to be a pretty good place to start.

A name might change, as people do.
But serving others' needs remains the same.

March 29 – Winds

'There's the wind on the heath, brother;
if I could only feel that, I would gladly live forever.'
George Borrow, Lavengro

Ode to the West Wind was written by Percy Shelley in 1819. Perhaps more than anything, Shelley wanted his message of reform to take hold, so the wind becomes a metaphor for spreading the word of change. Shelley and his wife, Mary, had lost their son William earlier that year, and their son Charles was to die seven years later. The pain of loss was a profound influence.

> *O wild West Wind, thou breath of Autumn's being,*
> *Thou, from whose unseen presence the leaves dead*
> *Are driven, like ghosts from an enchanter fleeing, …*
> *Wild Spirit, which art moving everywhere;*
> *Destroyer and preserver; hear, oh hear!*

It's hard to get the flow of any poem from a few lines. But whatever Shelley knew of the physical effect of the 'wild West Wind', he also knew a 'Wild Spirit' was changing his life. For whatever the wind does, we are powerless to stop it. It will come, to destroy or preserve, and will go, leaving us to assess its effects.

The word for wind in Hebrew is *ruach*. It is the same as the word for spirit. The wind will bring change. And when that change is the reform or revolution which Shelley believed was necessary for the betterment of his world, then the 'Wild Spirit' of God – the *Ruach Yahweh* – is surely at work.

> *We may not know where the wind comes from,*
> *but we can see its effect.*
> *We may not understand where the Spirit comes from,*
> *but we can marvel at what it does.*

March 30 – Precious

'Every man knows well enough that he is a unique being,
only once on this earth; and by no extraordinary chance
will such a marvellously picturesque piece of diversity
in unity as he is, ever be put together a second time.'

Friedrich Nietzsche, Schopehhauer as Educator

A birthstone is a gemstone that symbolises the month of birth in the Gregorian calendar, introduced by Pope Gregory in 1582. The calendar has poems matching each month with its birthstone. The birthstone for January is the garnet; for February, the amethyst; March, the bloodstone; for April it's diamonds; May, emeralds; June gives us the agate; July is marked by the ruby; those born in August should wear the sardonyx; for September, it's sapphire; October is associated with opal; November with topaz; and December with turquoise.

The idea behind all of this goes back to the 1st-century Jewish historian Josephus, who believed there was a connection between the twelve stones in Aaron's breastplate *(Exodus 28:17-20)*, the twelve months of the year and the twelve signs of the zodiac. The precise list of birthstones can be found in St John the Divine's amazing vision of the 'end times' in the book of Revelation *(Revelation 21:19-20)* where the foundation stones of the new Jerusalem are listed, though the identification of some of the stones is a bit uncertain.

But do we *really* need to be connected to a precious stone to be precious ourselves? Are we not precious in our own right by virtue of our uniqueness and individuality? A person who wears diamonds isn't more precious than someone who doesn't. So let's celebrate uniqueness, and value the preciousness that makes us, and everyone else, special, regardless of any birthstone.

Be yourself. It was surely what you were meant to be.

March 31 – Delays

'Away with delay –
it always injures those who are prepared.'
Marcus Annaeus Lucanus, The Pharsalia

I was in a hurry. There was just enough time to get from the train station to my meeting close by. It *should* have been OK. The train was on time – a good start! It disgorged its passengers onto the platform, and the crowd of commuters, tourists and shoppers headed for the ticket-barriers – the new, efficient, slick ticket-barriers which had recently been installed as part of the station's modernisation. The crowd slowed. One by one the passengers made their way through the three, green-arrowed barriers. Tickets were placed in the 'in' slot at the front and retrieved when they popped out from the 'out' slot at the top. Efficient and slick, indeed ... And for each passenger, the barrier opened and another traveller was on their way. Until, that is, *I* arrived. My ticket went in the 'in' slot and duly came out of the 'out' slot, but the barrier didn't open. I tried again – in went the ticket, and out it came once more, but the barrier remained firmly closed.

The crowd was building up behind me, muttering with impatience. There was some pushing and jostling. The people at the back ducked into the line for another barrier. Eventually, when the crush eased, I was able to reverse out of my 'stall'. I found a 'barrier operative', a helpful station official, who listened to my problem and ushered me through an open gate without a word. People behind me were now using *my* barrier with apparent ease. Why didn't it happen for me?

I'd like to be a 'barrier operative' and un-stick tricky barriers or offer a way through when folk are stuck. Maybe then I would be more aware of the damage barriers do in the first place.

What doors do I need to open for people today?

April 1 – Fools

'April Fool, *n*. The March fool
with another month added to his folly.'
Ambrose Bierce, The Devil's Dictionary

April Fools' Day is celebrated in different countries around the world on April 1st every year. It's a day marked by good-humoured hoaxes and other practical jokes of varying sophistication against friends, family, teachers, work colleagues, and the like. In France and Italy children (and adults sometimes) traditionally tack paper fish on each other's backs as a trick and shout 'April fish' (*Poisson d'Avril!* and *Pesce d'Aprile* in French and Italian respectively). In Scotland, April Fools' Day was traditionally called 'Hunt-the-Gowk Day' (*Gowk* is Scots for a cuckoo or a foolish person). The traditional prank was to ask someone to deliver a sealed message requesting help of some sort. In fact, the message reads *Dinna laugh, dinna smile. Hunt the gowk another mile.* The recipient will explain he can't help but knows someone else who can, and sends the victim to another person with an identical message, with the same result. And so it goes on.

No one really knows when all of this began. Its origins might be in the Roman festival of 'Hilaria' on March 25th, or the Medieval 'Festival of Fools' on December 28th. In the Middle Ages, New Year's Day was celebrated on March 25th in most of Europe. In some areas of France New Year was a week-long holiday ending on April 1st. Maybe April Fools' Day began when those who celebrated on January 1st made fun of those who celebrated on other dates. Who knows? But what we *do* know is that an ability to laugh at ourselves is important. And a gentle ribbing might be just what we need to stop taking ourselves too seriously.

Fool me once, shame on you; fool me twice, shame on me.
Chinese proverb

April 2 – Uncomplaining

'When any fit of gloominess, or perversion of mind
lays hold upon you, make it a rule
not to publish it by complaints.'
Samuel Johnson,
as quoted in The Life of Samuel Johnson *by James Boswell*

My mother was an only child, born to parents who worked on 'Corporation Farms' on the outskirts of Paisley in Scotland. These were farms run by Paisley's Council for the benefit of the town, providing much-needed farm produce, grain, meat, milk and eggs. My grandfather was a cattleman, my grandmother a milkmaid. Both of them were employed on a 'piece-work' basis – they only got paid for what they did. The more work they completed, the more they earned. Life was hard. Money was scarce. Conditions – largely in 'tied' accommodation – were often primitive.

To compound it all, when my grandmother was pregnant with my mother there were complications around the time of the birth. The baby had to be delivered by caesarean section. This was by no means a straightforward procedure in those pre-NHS days. As a result, my grandmother couldn't have any more children. But more pressing was the fact that, if she didn't work, she earned no money. Consequently, unable to recuperate for as long as the doctors wanted, she went back to the milking, and took her little baby with her. So she would milk a cow by hand then nurse her baby; lay the child in the straw, and milk another cow; finish that, then suckle my mother; lay the baby down, and see to another cow. She did her job as a milkmaid, and brought a wage into the home. And she did her job as a mother, and brought up a wonderful daughter.

Complaining is part of our humanity.
But which complaints really *matter?*

April 3 – Oops!

'Alas! how easily things go wrong!
A sigh too deep, or a kiss too long,
And then comes a mist and a weeping rain,
And life is never the same again.'

George MacDonald, Phantastes, A Fairy Story

Tommy was having a clear-out. Christmas wasn't far away and he hadn't saved as much as he'd thought. A desperate situation needed a desperate solution. There were things he could get rid of – at a price! He decided to put an advert in the local paper.

FOR SALE: One sock, green with red dots, size for boy of 9
Will soot someone with simlar sock
Price negoashable – apply Tommy 27 Primrose Drive.

The man at the paper office said his advert wasn't suitable. And, anyway, it was going to *cost*. What was the point of *that* when you were supposed to be *making* money for Christmas presents and not spending the little you had? So Tommy arranged to have a sale in his back garden. He got his dad's pasting table from the shed, sorted out all his unwanted stuff, put sticky labels with prices on them, and put up handwritten notices all over the street.

The sale went well. He cleared the whole table and even got rid of one green sock with red dots, which Mandy from number 22 said she could use as a bed for her hamster. He'd made £7.69! He was just about to put his dad's pasting table back in the shed when he heard his mum shouting. 'Tommy. Tommy! Have you seen the pair of gloves auntie Kath bought me for my birthday? I'm *sure* I left them on the kitchen work top.' Oooppps!

'Never say, "Oops." Always say, "Ah, interesting." '
Anonymous

April 4 – Real

'An honest man's the noblest work of God.'
Alexander Pope, An Essay on Man

One of the hardest things to learn in life is to be true to ourselves.
I wrote this on Iona, working with a very varied group of people.
And I know it can apply to everyone. We all need to discover the
value of being true to what we are.

Be real, and not pretend; do right, and do not spend
your time being what you're not.
Be what you are, and know being real's the way to go –
in fact, it's all you've got.

Be true to what you are, ev'n if being true's by far
the hardest thing to do,
When others put you down, and there's no one around
who might believe in you.

Be true when you need most the confidence you've lost,
and tried so hard to save.
When faith in self has gone believe you've been loved from
the cradle to the grave.

Be true to what you know, ev'n when the 'me' you show's
not what you want to be.
So love yourself, and hear this whisper in your ear,
'You're loved by God and me.'

Adapted from 'Be Real' from
New Journeys Now Begin *by Tom Gordon,*
Wild Goose Publications, 2006

April 5 – Tragedy

'In the midst of life we are in death.'
Burial of the Dead, Book of Common Prayer

My cousin and I were at the Ibrox Disaster of 1971. A crush among the crowd at the Rangers v Celtic football match at Ibrox Park on January 2nd caused 66 deaths. Eighty thousand fans attended the game and, at the other end of the ground and before mobile phones, we knew nothing of the devastating events till we got home. One wag had wisecracked: 'With so many ambulances around, it looks like the only way we're getting home tonight is on a stretcher.' Little did we know … Several children died, including five schoolmates from Markinch in Fife. My parents were at their wits' end by the time I got back. With no news of where I was, they'd feared for my life.

The disaster was the beginning of much-needed improvements in stadium safety. But this was the *second* major disaster at Ibrox, the first interrupting a Scotland v England match on April 5th 1902. The game was only a few minutes old when the back of a wooden stand collapsed. Twenty-five people died and 517 were injured out of a crowd of over sixty-eight thousand. Naturally, play stopped when people realised what was happening, and the injured were attended to by stewards, police and even some of the players. But after a while the game resumed, and was played to a 1-1 draw, despite the frequent stoppages to allow injured spectators to be taken across the pitch.

I'm struck by the random injustice and arbitrariness of such tragedies. Why does a disaster affect some, while thousands walk away? But I'm also aware that life goes on, including a football match played to its conclusion. It doesn't diminish the injustice or the horror of the tragedies. But it is the truth – in the midst of life there is death; and in the face of death life is yet to be lived.

When tragedy strikes others, does it not affect us all?

April 6 – Words

'As long as words a different sense will bear,
And each may be his own interpreter,
Our airy faith will no foundation find;
The word's a weathercock for every wind.'

John Dryden, The Hind and the Panther

It's a well-known fact that church notices, bulletin-boards and newsletters are a rich source of amusement. Doesn't someone proof-read these items? Mind you, if they did, we wouldn't have such funny pieces, would we? Here are a few that tickled my fancy.

The fasting and prayer conference this coming Saturday will include a meal.

This morning's sermon: Jesus goes to the wilderness
This evening's sermon: Searching for Jesus.

Ladies, don't forget about the bring-and-buy sale. It's a chance to get rid of those things not worth keeping. Bring your husbands.

Don't let worry kill you, let the church help.

The sermon tonight, 'What is Hell?'
Come early and listen to the choir practice.

More of these later ... But as I read such amusing pieces I am reminded of this – how important it is that we say what we mean and we mean what we say. We pray: 'God be in my head and in my speaking.' Put another way, let's think before we speak.

'Oh, be careful little lips what you say ...'
Victorian Sunday School song

April 7 – On the shoulders of giants

'Glimpses that would make me less forlorn.'
William Wordsworth, from Poems in Two Volumes

John of Salisbury was a 12th-century English author, educationalist and diplomat who became Bishop of Chartres. However, in his earlier years he described himself as *Johannes Parvus* – John the Little – perhaps because of his humble background as a clerk before he rose to the great heights of education and learning in the University of Paris. Or he may simply have been a very small man!

In 1159 John of Salisbury wrote his most important works, including *Metalogicon*, invaluable as sources of information about the education of the age and remarkable for their cultivated and humanitarian style. The idea of contemporaries 'standing on the shoulders of giants' of antiquity – more commonly associated with Sir Isaac Newton – first appears this work.

> *We are like dwarfs on the shoulders of giants, so that we can see more than they, and things at a greater distance, not by virtue of any sharpness of sight on our part, or any physical distinction, but because we are carried high and raised up by their giant size.*

Whatever his elevated circumstances as a scholar, writer or churchman, John of Salisbury never forgot his humble beginnings. *Johannes Parvus* might have been a small man and may have started life as a humble clerk, but he knew he could rise to giant size because of the efforts of those who had gone before.

> *When I cannot see far enough, or know well enough,*
> *I can stand on the shoulders of giants,*
> *and try to make good use of my new elevation.*

April 8 – Retirement

'The company gave me an aptitude test and I found out the
work I was best suited for was retirement.'

Anonymous

My friend was about to retire. His job had been a rewarding one,
but the hours had been long and the pressure often very intense.
He was good at what he did, but he didn't have much else to
interest him. I was worried how he'd cope in retirement. So I
broached the subject.

'Any plans for your retirement?' I enquired, hesitantly. He
smiled, not at all disturbed by my question. 'Yes indeed,' he
replied. 'Oh,' I responded, 'and what do you have in mind?'
'Simple,' he continued. 'I intend to do two things … First, I'll write
with a fountain pen; and, second, I'll sit on the road with the pro-
testers when they blockade the missile convoys to the nuclear sub-
marine base at Faslane.'

Seeing the surprised look on my face, he went on to explain his
reasoning. The fountain pen was the symbol of a choice – to take
more time and care; to write to friends; to pen his memoirs. A
working life had all been about pressure and speed, and a regular
supply of ball-point pens were part of that consumer, disposable,
be-quick-with-everything environment. Using a fountain pen once
more had been something he'd looked forward to for a long time.

More importantly, he wanted to join his colleagues and friends
in expressing his opposition to nuclear weapons being sited on
Scottish soil. If he'd been arrested at a protest while he was
working, he would probably have lost his job. But free from work,
he would be his own man, able to follow his passion and protest
as he chose.

Retirement is a gift of itself, which needs to be well used.
Who needs a gold watch?

April 9 – Little friends

'Life has no blessing like a prudent friend.'
Euripides, Greek tragedian

I have a motto that I've returned to for guidance in all my years of ministry. 'It's the little people that make the world go round.' Pillars of the Kirk or of society are fine. No one denies them their importance or their place. But without the little people, well … Have you come across Aesop's fable of the lion and the mouse?

One day when a lion was asleep a little mouse began running up and down on him, this way and that, from head to toe. Not surprisingly, this soon wakened the lion, who was not best pleased. So he placed one of his huge paws on the mouse, and opened his big jaws to swallow him.

'Pardon, O great King,' cried the little mouse. 'Forgive me this one time, and I shall never forget it. For who knows but that I may be able to do you a good turn one of these days?'

The lion was so tickled at the idea of the mouse being able to help him that he lifted up his paw and let him go. Some time afterwards the lion was caught in a trap. The hunters were jubilant, and resolved to carry the lion alive back to their leader. So they tied their captive prey to a tree while they went in search of a wagon to carry him.

Just then the little mouse happened to pass by, and seeing the lion's sad plight, went up to him and soon gnawed away the ropes that bound the King of the Beasts. 'Was I not right?' said the little mouse. And he might have added, for the lion's benefit and for ours, 'Little friends may prove great friends one day – given the chance.'

Give thought today to your little friends.
Maybe they need you to say 'thank you' for their friendship.
And it might encourage them to say thank you to you, too.

April 10 – Connections

'Live in fragments no longer. Only connect!'
EM Forster, Howard's End

When I was a small boy and our family had holidays at my grandparents', there was always a sports programme on TV at lunchtime on a Saturday. At that time my own family didn't have a television, so I was enraptured by my grandmother's small TV – only a black-and-white one, of course. The Saturday sports programme on the commercial channel always included a boxing match, usually from the USA.

My grandfather was a boxing fanatic, so he looked forward to the televised boxing match even more than I did. He would settle down in his chair with his pipe and get so excited by the boxing that he would inevitably end up sitting close to the edge of his seat, almost on the floor. The trouble was, he had Parkinson's disease, and before the days when medication could control a Parkinsonian tremor, he often shook uncontrollably. The more animated he got in his excitement at the boxing match, the more violently he shook.

Sometimes he wasn't ready in time before the programme began and would still have a box of matches in his hand. So, the more excited he got, the more he shook, and the more he shook, the more he rattled his box of matches. My grandmother would often be heard shouting, 'For God's sake, man, will you give up on the maracas. I cannae hear myself think.'

To this day, more than fifty years later, I can't watch a boxing match, hold a box of matches or hear maracas in a band without thinking about my grandfather. 'For God's sake, man ...' Yes indeed! For God's sake, I'm so glad I have such connections.

Even if it's only a fragment of a memory,
it still makes for a strong connection.

April 11 – Persevere

'Persevere even though Hell and destruction
should yawn beneath your feet.'
Percy Bysshe Shelley, Letter to Edward Fergus Graham

The motto of the Port of Leith is 'Persevere'. Although Leith merged with the City of Edinburgh in 1920 and is no longer a separate municipal burgh, it has a long and distinguished history. The *Proclaimers'* hit 'Sunshine on Leith' defines what Leithers would say of their own home patch – 'You're now in sunny Leith.'

Why 'Persevere' as Leith's motto? Maybe it was because of the struggle to preserve their independence from 'big brother' over the boundary. But it might have been for another reason.

The earliest documented recording of golf refers to 'Leith Links', a green space at the heart of the town. In 1457 the Town Council, at the request of King James II, banned 'gouff' (golf) to 'discourage distractions from archery practice'. But did 'gouff' stay banned? Not a bit of it. It continued and flourished. And if the golfing Leithers hadn't persevered, we might not have had the Royal & Ancient and the Open Championship, or had the opportunity to enjoy the skill of Jack Nicklaus or Tiger Woods.

But more than that, 'persevere' could be a motto for *all* golfers. Keep going, even after playing a bad shot, for the next one might be the best ever. Persevere! There's a whole eighteen holes to finish. You can't give up now. After all, there's an amazing run of shots just waiting to happen – if you persevere.

I know several Leithers who've made up their own story about why 'Persevere' is their town motto. But wherever it came from, it's a good motto for all of us. Why should Leithers get to keep it for themselves?

Might you create a little corner of 'Sunny Leith'
for yourself and others around you
because you persevere today?

April 12 – Madness

'Your own self-love might impair your judgement.'
Seneca the Elder, Epistulae

'You're driving me mad' might be a comment familiar to us from a tense situation within a family or between good friends. 'You're doing my head in.' Something that someone has done or said, or an attitude they are portraying, destabilises you to the extent that you feel they're not the rational, controlled person you'd like them to be. But what is madness? Is not thinking straight or being uptight or being unstable madness? No, and many books and academic papers have been written to explain why not

A more important question would be 'What is mental illness?' We live in a world where it is easy to make assumptions about people simply by how they look. If someone's walking with crutches, you know they have a problem with their legs. If someone wears an eye-patch, you know there's something wrong with their sight. If someone has stitches in a wound, you know there's been some damage or another. But when someone is depressed, how do we know? Or psychotic? Or delusional? Or schizophrenic? Or paranoid? This is not about madness, it is about mental health. But it's unseen, the hidden illness, if you like.

There are wounds that people are living with that never show on the body, because they are hidden deep within their being. These wounds might be more painful than any obvious injury or visible weeping sore. Their healing might begin when we leave aside our judgement and show a willingness to reach into the depths of the suffering.

Be careful not to jump to conclusions.
Stop yourself making assumptions.
Reach beyond the 'hidden'
and try to understand the whole person.

April 13 – Accidents

'Accidents will occur in the best regulated families.'
Charles Dickens, David Copperfield

I was visiting a couple recently whom I'd only begun to get to know. Archie, the husband, was making a cup of tea with me in the kitchen, while Phyllis, his wife, was busy in the lounge. I was peering at some photographs on a noticeboard when I heard an almighty crash. I turned round to find that the cups, saucers and plates had slipped off the tray Archie was carrying and had smashed on the kitchen floor. 'Oh, well. Accidents will happen,' I was going to offer, but I wasn't quick enough. Instead, Archie said, 'Dear, dear, something else for Phyllis to clear up.' *Phyllis?* I thought. *How sexist is that? He expects his wife to clear up after his accident. What kind of marriage is this? What kind of husband?*

Just then Archie shouted, 'Phyllis! Phyllis! You need to come now.' And there was his wife bustling into the kitchen and surveying the detritus on the floor. 'Oh, Archie,' she scolded. 'Be more careful, won't you?' And, with that, she dived into the cupboard under the sink, unearthed a dustpan and brush and began to clear up the mess. *What?* I thought. *How subservient is that? Without complaint, she's expected to clear up after her husband. What kind of arrangement? What kind of wife?*

Archie must have seen the puzzled look on my face. 'Oh, sorry,' he said. 'I should explain. When we got married we made a pact – if either of us had an accident, the other one would clear it up. It works out about 50/50. *And* it helps us be more patient with each other. Because, as we all know, accidents *will* happen.'

In the random nature of our living,
random accidents will happen.
Can we ensure random acts of kindness
make a difference too?

April 14 – Letters

'Don't judge by appearances.
A rich heart may be hiding under a poor coat.'
Scottish proverb

I once worked with a man who was so devastated by his wife's death that he turned in on himself, declined offers of help and began to 'let himself go'. He said he had 'nothing to live for any more'. Concerned for him, I called at his home and was greeted on the doorstep by an unshaven, unkempt man, wearing a grubby shirt and no shoes, smelling of drink, with his hair uncombed and with shaky hands. He was in no fit state for a visit, so we arranged that I would call the following week. In case he forgot, I sent him a letter, handwritten on headed notepaper, to confirm the appointment. I reminded him I would call on the Monday at 3.30; I told him that he was a good man and that there were people around to help; I reassured him that he could be in touch any time.

On Monday at 3.30 I was greeted at the door by a transformed man, with combed hair and wearing a shirt and tie and polished black shoes. We shook hands and I was invited into the kitchen where he was making coffee. I saw my handwritten letter attached to the freezer with a fridge-magnet. Underlined in red was 'Monday 3.30'. *Sensible*, I thought. But double-underlined in red was the phrase 'You're a good man'. He saw the puzzled look on my face. 'Wondering why that's underlined?' he enquired. I nodded. 'Well,' he said, 'no one has ever said that to me in the whole of my life.'

An affirmation in a letter; a positive comment; a compliment; a good thing said. How rare, it seems. But how transforming!

If it matters a lot when someone says a good thing about you,
why not make a difference by saying a good thing to someone else?

April 15 – Fresh start

'Be willing to be a beginner every single morning.'
Meister Eckhart, Wisdom for the Soul

Fresh Start is an Edinburgh-based charity which offers support to homeless people in the city. In 1997 a small group of people, from a variety of backgrounds and some with their own experience of homelessness, were brought together by Edinburgh churches. They quickly realised that there were a number of areas in which church folk could provide immediate practical support to those who were trying to break the cycle of homelessness. In partnership with the City Council, businesses, schools, individuals, and community and faith groups, Fresh Start now offers a complete package of services. 'Starter packs' provide basic household utensils, bedding and crockery for people in a new tenancy. There's a 'recycling centre' in which people can learn new skills and from which furniture and equipment is made available for new homes. Fresh Start also tests and reuses small electrical appliances that are useful in everyday living.

But, for me, the most imaginative aspect is the 'Hit Squads'. This is a unique and successful approach to helping people who've been homeless establish and maintain their tenancy by providing assistance with painting and decorating. The 'Hit Squads' are teams of volunteers who work alongside new tenants in their home, typically decorating up to two rooms. The service is available to new tenants in the first eight weeks of their tenancy, with referrals coming via recognised support agencies. I have a friend who is 75 who is part of one of these 'Hit Squads'. He gives his time, up ladders and on his hands and knees, to paper and paint, so that people have a decent home to live in. A 75-year-old helping someone have a fresh start? I like that a lot ...

It's never too late to start afresh, or to help someone else to do so.

April 16 – Music

'Music religious heat inspires,
It wakes the soul, and lifts it high,
And wings it with sublime desires,
And fits it to bespeak the Deity.'

Joseph Addison, A Song for St Cecilia's Day

Among the repertoire of the Australia-based Scot Eric Bogle is a song he wrote after being deeply moved by a newspaper account of the death of a young black man during the apartheid regime in South Africa. The man had been sentenced to death. In prison, awaiting his fate, he was distraught. At the time of his execution he was so distressed and weak that his legs couldn't hold him up. So, half carried, half dragged, he was taken to his ultimate end. As they saw the young man go to his death, the other prisoners started to sing. One by one they joined in and, as the singing filled the prison with its intertwining African harmonies, a broken young man was strengthened on his final journey. Eric Bogle called his song 'Singing the Spirit Home', encapsulating the emotion of the event and the sustaining effectiveness of song.

Whatever the spirit is, that which is truly unique in us needs to be sustained on its journey. Many things can do that. But singing is surely one of the most important. There's a Gospel song which touches on the same issue. It reminds us that when we are too weak for the journey, like a young black prisoner in South Africa, singing can carry our spirit home too.

Over my head I hear music in the air;
Over my head I hear music in the air;
Over my head I hear music in the air;
I really do believe, I really do believe
There must be a Heaven somewhere.

Traditional Gospel song

April 17 – The truth

' "What is truth?" said jesting Pilate,
and would not stay for an answer.'

Francis Bacon, The Essays: Of Truth

When I was about eight years old my sister was knocked off her bike by a car taking a corner too fast. The driver didn't notice me and my sister coming along the road on our bikes (he said!) so he cut across us. I managed to take avoiding action but my sister wasn't so lucky. She went one way and her bike went the other. The bike got the worse of the car's impact. My sister wasn't injured, but was badly shaken by the accident. The driver was charged with dangerous driving and, of course, there had to be an investigation. The police came to the house to interview my sister. And, being the 'star witness', I was interviewed too. Two policemen took me and my mum into our kitchen for their questioning. And with notebooks out, they began their inquiries.

'We're going to ask you some simple questions and we're going to write your answers down,' they began. 'OK,' I replied. 'Now, what is your name?' the questioning started. 'Tommy,' I said. 'And where do you live?' 'Here,' was the obvious answer – though my mum felt she had to offer more details. 'And where were you born?' the inquiry continued. 'I was handed to my mum over the garden fence by the District Nurse,' I responded. The two policemen let out a huge guffaw. My mum was covered in confusion – and felt, once again, that she had to expand with more accurate information. But why the amusement of the policemen and the embarrassed look on my mother's face? I'd only told the truth. It's what my parents always insisted I do. And, after all, hadn't I told the policeman *exactly* what my mum had told me?

So what is truth?
And why should the truth be so difficult?

April 18 – Justice

'Justice is truth in action.'
Benjamin Disraeli, Speech, February 11th 1851

Albert Schweitzer was a theologian, organist, philosopher, physician and medical missionary. Born in Alsace-Lorraine, then part of the German Empire, he studied the music of JS Bach and influenced the organ reform movement. He qualified as a doctor, became a medical missionary and founded a hospital in Lambaréné, now in Gabon, west central Africa. He received the Nobel Peace Prize in 1952 for his philosophy of 'Reverence for Life'.

Schweitzer could have excelled in any of his chosen professions, but his passionate quest was to discover a universal ethical philosophy and make it available to all of humanity. In a sermon preached in 1905, before he had told anyone of his plans to dedicate his life to being a doctor in Africa, he said this:

> *I will not enumerate all the crimes that have been committed under the pretext of justice. [We] robbed native inhabitants of their land, made slaves of them, let loose the scum of mankind upon them. Think of the atrocities that were perpetrated on people made subservient to us, how ... we have ruined them with our alcoholic 'gifts', and everything else we have done. We decimate them, and then, by the stroke of a pen, we take their land so they have nothing left at all.*

Albert Schweitzer was not universally popular. But would anyone who has such a passion for justice be expected to court popularity?

> *Let judgement run down as waters,*
> *and righteousness as a mighty stream.*
> Bible: Amos 5:24

April 19 – Promise

'We promise according to our hopes,
and perform according to our fears.'
François de La Rochefoucauld, Maxims, No. 39

Who will do the remembering when we're dead and gone?

Will you promise to remember me when I am long since gone,
When you see me in the setting sun, or hear me in our song?
Will you promise me you'll think of me, and not forget too long?
Yes! I promise to remember when you're gone.

Will you promise to remember? Did you pick up all my cues –
How to work the tumble-dryer, and make casseroles and stews;
When the Council Tax needs paying; how to safely change a fuse?
Yes! I promise to remember when you're gone.

Will you promise to remember all the wonders of our days;
All the years we spent together – even shrouded in a haze;
All those special, precious moments; all my funny little ways?
Yes! I promise to remember when you're gone.

Will you promise to remember what we talked about back then,
Of your favourite piece of music to be listened to again;
And the hymns you have to organise for singing at the Crem?
Yes! I promise to remember when you're gone.

Will you promise to remember, even when you cry and fret?
Will you hold me in your memory for a little longer yet?
For I'll live in your remembering – and in times when you forget ...
Yes! I promise to remember when you're gone.

Adapted from 'Will you?' from New Journeys Now Begin,
Tom Gordon, Wild Goose Publications, 2006

April 20 – Bridges

'Everyone speaks well of the bridge which carries him over.'
Chinese proverb

Stretching across the river Liffey in the centre of Dublin is a pedestrian crossing known as 'The ha'penny bridge'. It got its name because a 'ha'penny' was the toll for a pedestrian to cross over the bridge, and the toll-keeper had the strict responsibility of ensuring that all the fees were appropriately collected.

One night, just after closing time in the local hostelries, two locals, clearly the worse for drink, appeared at one side of the bridge. 'A ha'penny each to cross,' insisted the toll-keeper. The two travellers were filled with consternation, for they only had *one* ha'penny between them. One of them could go over, but the other would have to stay behind. But they were not to be outdone. 'And what, my man,' asked one of the men, 'is the cost of baggage if we were to take it across your bridge?' 'Oh, there is no cost for baggage,' was the reply. And with that the man hauled his companion on to his back, paid his ha'penny, and proceeded on his way – carrying his 'baggage' across the bridge.

Whatever bridges we have to face in life, there will be those who find it hard – or downright impossible – to cross on their own. They will need the companionship of fellow travellers and the support of those who are prepared to negotiate the tricky parts of the journey with them. But there will also be times when they will have to be carried across, because they can't make it under their own steam. And the cost? More than a ha'penny or any monetary value. How can you put a price on friendship?

No friend's a friend till [they shall] prove a friend.
Beaumont and Fletcher (attrib), *The Faithful Friends*

April 21 – Traditions

'The less there is to justify a traditional custom,
the harder it is to get rid of it.'
Mark Twain, The Adventures of Tom Sawyer

Brother James had been the father figure for the religious community for as long as people could remember. A wise and much revered man, he was looked to for wise counsel, sound theology and tender pastoral care. But the passing of the years took its toll and Brother James became frail and unsteady. So he took to using a stick. A strong branch from a thorn tree was fashioned into a sturdy cane. Brother James would lean heavily on his walking stick when he came to worship in the community's chapel, especially to steady himself as he mounted the altar steps. But he was a proud man and was determined to stand behind the altar unaided. So he would lay his stick against the altar during worship. The thorn-tree stick became as familiar in the chapel as the lectern and the altar. Worship never happened without it.

When Brother James died, the community kept the stick where it had been for many years. From that time on there was no worship without the stick at the side of the altar. Years passed. The community grew. When a new chapel was planned, there *had* to be a walking stick at the side of the altar. 'Goes back centuries ...' 'Sound theological reasons ...' 'It's a rule,' they all agreed. So the new chapel was built with a gold walking stick attached to the end of the altar. A service of blessing was written, 'A Reverence for the Holy Stick.' A Brother was appointed 'Keeper of the Stick'. People came to believe that the holy cane had healing powers. 'Prayers to the holy healing stick' were offered. A new Brother asked, 'Why is there a gold cane attached to the side of the altar?' 'It's a tradition,' he was assured.

Something may be traditional, but is it always best?

April 22 – Cartoons

'A flattering painter, who made it his care
To draw men as they ought to be, not as they are.'
Oliver Goldsmith, Retaliation

The legendary *Tom and Jerry* cartoons created for MGM by William Hanna and Joseph Barbera were a *must* for any discerning student in the late 1960s. The TV room in my university Hall of Residence was packed every week as the never-ending rivalry between the cat, Tom, and the mouse, Jerry, was played out for everyone's enjoyment. The endless chases and battles and the extremes of comic violence were applauded, pored over and discussed with much enthusiasm. I've been a fan of cartoons ever since. But it wasn't till I was well beyond my student years that I discovered that a 'cartoon' wasn't originally a 'movie' at all.

Newspapers and magazines are full of cartoons, of course, which poke fun, create a caricature or make a telling point. But centuries ago cartoons were very different. In the Middle Ages they were preparatory drawings for a piece of art. The word cartoon comes from the Italian *cartone*, a term for heavy paper or pasteboard. A full-size sketch would be made on the *cartone*, so that the artist could work out what the final artwork might look like. Sometimes little pinpricks were made along the outlines of the cartoon. Soot would then be scattered over the cartoon, so that an outline of black dots provided a template for the artist on a wall, paper or cloth. Some of these cartoons – such as those of Leonardo da Vinci – are now much sought after in their own right.

The artists of the Middle Ages wouldn't have had *any* idea what the students of the 1960s would call a cartoon. But I wonder if these same students knew that their enjoyment of *Tom and Jerry* actually linked them to great artists of a bygone age.

When you think you see it all, try looking at the bigger picture.

April 23 – Courage

'Either life entails courage, or it ceases to be life.'
EM Forster, Pharos and Pharillon

St George, the patron saint of England and the paradigm of Englishness for many people, wasn't English at all. He was a 3rd-century Greek who became an officer in the Roman army. And far from being limited to one country's affection, St George, a Christian martyr, is one of the most venerated saints in the Catholic, Anglican, Eastern Orthodox and Oriental Orthodox churches.

A dragon has made its nest near a spring which provides water for the city of Silene. To get to the water, the people of Silene have to get the dragon off its nest long enough for them to fill their water jars. So each day they offer the dragon a sacrifice. A sheep is first. And if there's no sheep, a young girl will do. Really? Yes, that was their plan, and the unfortunate girl was chosen by the drawing of lots. One day, the random choice picks out a princess. The king begs for her life, but, rules being rules, his appeal fails. So the princess is offered up to the lip-smacking dragon. But all is not lost. Enter St George! He sees the distress of the townsfolk, hears the cries of the princess and comes to the rescue. Facing the dragon, he protects himself with the sign of the Cross. The dragon is killed. The princess is rescued. There is much rejoicing. The people of Silene convert to Christianity. And everyone – apart from the dragon – lives happily ever after.

We may not have mythical beasts to face, nor have a princess to rescue or a city to save. But we do have our own dragons to slay and our own dramas to engage with. And if that's the case, are we equipped, as St George was, with courage – human or divine – ready to be used?

Do we have what it takes to face our demons?
What tactics might we need,
and what might be our weapons of choice?

April 24 – Achievement

'Nothing will ever be attempted,
if all possible objections must be first overcome.'
Samuel Johnson, Rasselas

The film *Blindsight* is a 2006 documentary directed by Lucy Walker. Set against the remarkable backdrop of the Himalayas, *Blindsight* follows six Tibetan teenagers on their journey to climb the 23,000-foot Lhakpa Ri mountain, close to Mount Everest. The almost impossible, and extremely dangerous, journey is all the more remarkable because the teenagers are blind.

Many Tibetans believed that you were blind because you were possessed by demons. Not surprisingly, therefore, the blind children had been rejected by both family and community. But hope was at hand in the person of Sabriye Tenberken, a blind German social worker who had established the first school for blind people in Lhasa. With her encouragement, the students invited the famous blind mountaineer Erik Weihenmayer to visit their school. Weihenmayer had conquered Everest and had written about his climb in *Touch the Top of the World*. When Tenberken had read passages from the book to her students they found inspiration in Weihenmayer's success. 'If he can do it, then we can too,' they said. So Weihenmayer arrives in Lhasa and helps the students and their educators climb higher – physically, mentally and emotionally – than they have ever been before.

When one person achieves the seemingly impossible, is it any wonder others are inspired? When one person rises above what anyone expected, should we be surprised that others seek to reach higher than they have before? When one person succeeds, many others can reach for the sky.

*What we achieve, we achieve not for ourselves alone,
but so that others might know what is possible.*

April 25 – Showers

'Whenever April showers come along.'
BG De Sylva, April Showers

There is no doubt that the arrival of 'April showers' is a well known weather phenomenon. Spring rains are familiar in April, as the jet stream moves northwards allowing large depressions to bring winds and rain in from the Atlantic. In one day the weather can change from springtime sunshine to winter rain – and even sleet and snow. *April showers bring May flowers,* we are told. But the flowers of May are no more than a distant dream when you're being continually soaked by April rains!

There's a song called *April Showers* too. The De Sylva and Silvers song first appeared in 1921 sung by Al Jolson in a Broadway musical, *Bombo. April Showers* became a Jolson standard and he recorded it several times – as have many others. Clearly, every generation knows what April showers are about!

Morecambe and Wise did a wonderful skit based on the song. When straight-man Ernie Wise sang, he had to endure only a light sprinkling of water. But when it was the hapless Eric Morecambe's turn, he had to endure buckets of water soaking him from head to toe. April 'showers', indeed ...

However *April Showers* is understood, the opening words of the song hold an important and universal truth:

Life is not a highway strewn with flowers ...

Life isn't all sunshine. So what might our hopefulness be when we have a bucket of water falling on us when we thought a little drizzle was as much as we can manage? Maybe it's ...

*'Keep on looking for the bluebird
and listening for his song,
whenever April showers some along.'*

April 26 – Support

''Tis not enough to help the feeble up,
but to support them after.'
William Shakespeare, Timon of Athens

I have never been tall. The 5ft 6in of adult life was matched proportionally when I was growing up. I was always small for my age. I was bullied because of my lack of height. But smallness has its uses, and that's what I now recall with pleasure.

As I said earlier, I was 'drummed out' of the Cub Scouts for being rude to Akela. My confidence was so low and the shame so deep I abandoned scouting altogether and, instead, joined the Boys Brigade. I was back at the bottom of the pile once more: too new to be given responsibility; too apprehensive to excel at the rough-and-tumble of games; too small, I suspected, to have any meaningful part in the annual Boys Brigade Display Night.

The Display Night was the highlight of the BB year. Skills in marching, PE, team-games and overall discipline were offered to adoring parents and church folk. The best part was the Company Pyramid. This consisted of *all* the boys being formed into a human pyramid, the strong ones on their hands and knees at the bottom, two rows of other boys kneeling on their backs, two smaller boys on top of that, and, right at the apex, the smallest boy in the company – and that was me! Carefully I would climb up the backs, position myself right at the summit, and smile on cue … and the applause was loud and long.

Small boys on the top of human pyramids enjoy an accolade for sure. But small boys on the top of pyramids can't do it alone. They have to be supported by lots more underneath.

When I'm on top, I say a quiet 'thank you'
for all the people underneath who helped make it happen –
and hope they don't collapse under me!

April 27 – War

'There never was a good war, or a bad peace.'
Benjamin Franklin, Poor Richard's Almanac

I'm not old enough to remember World War II. My father was in the RAF during the war and he came back safely, as did all those he knew. Many didn't, and countless families received the dreaded telegram with the news that a loved one was 'missing in action' or 'presumed dead'. For those of us who have no experience of that, it is almost impossible to conceptualise what it was like.

Two recent experiences, however, have opened windows onto the reality of those who have lost folk in wars. The first relates to a friend whose son was seriously injured in a bombing in Afghanistan. The young man lost two comrades in the same explosion and he wasn't expected to survive. But through the highest-quality medical care, the support of the military and the love and commitment of family and friends, he has survived. Life is very different for him now, but he's going forward with a strength of character that can only be admired.

The second experience was told to me by another friend about the death of his grandfather in the First World War. The family originated from the Outer Hebrides and his grandmother received the news of her husband's death at her island croft. Having read the telegram, she went outside to face the ferocious Hebridean winds and shouted a prayer she'd learned in childhood from Job 1:4-5 – *Yea though he slay me, yet will I trust him.*

I have no direct experience of war. But I'm glad I now have glimpses through these windows of character, support, commitment and faith in the face of suffering, fear, waste, destruction and death.

What goodness can I trust in
even when I am being slain?

April 28 – Lasting effects

'Success, like happiness, cannot be pursued; it must ensue.'
Viktor Frankl, Man's Search for Meaning

The village of Bunessan sits on 'The Ross of Mull', the southern peninsula of the island of Mull, a few miles from the ferry terminal for the island of Iona. It was originally a small community of crofters, with a mill, weavers and a small fishing fleet until the 1900s. Today around three hundred people live in a village which has one hotel, a primary school, a village hall, a church, two grocery shops, a craft shop, a car-park, and a scattering of homes.

Perhaps the most recognised thing about Bunessan is that it gives its name to the tune of the familiar Christmas carol 'Child in the Manger'. A century and a half ago, Mary Macdonald lived close to Bunessan. A native Gaelic speaker, she wrote a hymn, *Leanabh an Aigh* (Blessed is the Infant), to a traditional tune. The hymn was later translated into English by Lachlan Macbean, giving us the beautiful words we sing today, and he named the melody after the village. Fittingly, there's a monument to Mary Macdonald, just off the road across Mull as it drops down into Bunessan village.

In the 1920s Eleanor Farjeon, commissioned by the editors of the hymnbook *Songs of Praise*, wrote new words to the tune. So the 'Morning Has Broken' and 'Bunessan' marriage became familiar in the second half of the 20th century. It even entered the 'hit parade' in the early 1970s, the singer Cat Stevens doing much to anchor words and melody in popular culture.

Mary Macdonald never pursued success. It ensued for her. But could an ordinary woman from a crofting village on Mull ever have thought that the traditional melody for *Leanabh an Aigh* would take the name of her village into the whole world?

*Who knows the lasting effects of what we might offer
in sincerity and truth?*

April 29 – Combinations

'Eagles fly alone, but sheep flock together.'
Polish proverb

When my grandfather was a farm labourer, part of his working-man's clothing was his 'combinations'. Combinations, or 'coms' as they were commonly known, had been introduced in Victorian times, mainly for young men, and consisted of an all-in-one shirt-and-leggings garment, made of stout cotton or flannel. They were healthy, robust, warm and practical, and had been described as a 'complete and most sanitary costume'. Well, that's as maybe, but when I saw my grandfather's 'coms' many years later, I thought they were hilarious.

Of course, the term 'combinations' can also mean something different – things or people coming together into one entity, unable any longer to have an independent existence. I *suppose* that's what a combination of the top and bottom of a male under-garment was about. But that's funny underwear, isn't it? I was more familiar with Morecambe and Wise, The Lone Ranger and Tonto, Laurel and Hardy ... or fish and chips, bangers and mash, bacon and egg. Combinations ... when things or people combine to make something that's bigger and better.

In 1 Corinthians 13 St Paul talks about 'faith, hope and love'. Each one matters on its own. But what a combination! And what about justice and peace; hope and joy; loving God and your neighbour and yourself? Each part has its own wonder and importance. But as a combination?

So, what about me and you; give and take; honour and truth; to love and to cherish; now and for ever? Where are the combinations that really matter?

Where do you fit in, so that what you are part of
is greater and better than what you are on your own?

April 30 – Retribution

'Every transgression or disobedience
received a just retribution.'
Bible: Hebrews 2:3

It's been said that one advantage of being bald is that you can hear a snowflake. But I know lots of *disadvantages* to being bald – feeling the cold in the winter, or a bald pate shining in bright lights, or being the butt of jokes about 'slapheads'. But despite all of that, I've never really been too bothered about being short of hair. It's just one of those things. What I *do* know for certain, however, is that I've never sought to inflict punishment on anyone who might make fun of my baldness. Unlike the prophet Elisha! The KJV Bible records this story in 2 Kings 2:23-25:

> *Then [the prophet Elisha] went up from there to Bethel; and as he was going up the road, some youths came from the city and mocked him, and said to him, 'Go up, you baldhead! Go up, you baldhead! So he turned around and looked at them, and pronounced a curse on them in the name of the Lord. And two female bears came out of the woods and mauled forty-two of the youths. Then he went from there to Mount Carmel, and from there he returned to Samaria.*

'Baldy! Baldy!' is the cry. So Elisha summons up two bears from the woods and forty-two cheeky kids are mauled in front of his eyes. And off he goes, without a by-your-leave.

I was taught as a child that 'Sticks and stones might break my bones, but names will never harm me.' A good lesson to live by! So it looks like Elisha had a lot to learn. Did forty-two youths have to suffer his retribution just because they called him names?

Reputation matters; name-calling will pass.

May 1 – Mayday

'Every day is the best day in the year.'
Ralph Waldo Emerson, Collected Poems

May Day, the first day of the month of May, is an ancient spring festival in the northern hemisphere and a traditional public holiday. It's related to the Celtic celebration of *Beltane* and the Germanic festival of *Walpurgis Night*. In farming communities it marks the end of the winter half of the year when farming is difficult and it has traditionally been an occasion for popular and often raucous celebrations.

In many countries May Day is also a time to celebrate the value of 'the working classes'. And in a society where class divides are thankfully less pronounced, it's still important to value the contribution we all make to a wholesome togetherness – labour and intellect, the work of brawn and brain. So May Day can also bring to mind various struggles for rights and better conditions for working men and women – International Workers' Day or Labour Day.

May Day when I was a student was very different. I recall getting up at dawn and going up a hill to wash my face in the May Day dew. It was supposed to make people more beautiful. (It didn't work for me!)

Perhaps the most intriguing association with this day, however, isn't actually anything to do with the first of May at all! *Mayday* is an emergency word used internationally as a distress signal in radio communications.

All of this associated with this one May Day – a promise of a good harvest; a holiday for the Spring; a celebration of working folk; the promise of beauty; a cry for rescue from danger. So much for the one day; such a lot to give thanks for as another day dawns.

What help might I offer someone on any important day?

May 2 – Martyrs

'The tyrant dies and his rule is over;
the martyr dies and his rule begins.'
Søren Kierkegaard, Papers and Journals

Haymarket for me has always been associated with Haymarket Station in Edinburgh. The area got its name from the times, long ago, when there was a market in the vicinity for the selling and buying of hay. There's a Haymarket in London too, probably for the same reason.

The name Haymarket, however, has taken on a different meaning for me since I read about 'The Haymarket Affair'. In the early days of May 1886 the city of Chicago in the USA was in the grip of a three-day general strike, during which the police had shot and killed four strikers. The following day, labourers and immigrants, artisans and merchants gathered at Haymarket Square to show solidarity with those who had died and with all working people who were oppressed and mistreated. Towards the end of the rally the police moved in to disperse the event and opened fire on the unarmed crowd. A riot ensued, and, when the dust settled, a dozen people lay dead, including one policeman.

Later, a dramatic show-trial took place. Eight defendants were openly tried for their political beliefs, leading to the public hanging of four alleged anarchists. They became known as the 'Haymarket martyrs', and they are still commemorated through various May Day workplace events and parades.

Throughout history, many have struggled for better conditions for working people. On this day after May Day we should remember that there are many who have given their all for what is right and fair and good.

Today, we remember many martyrs.
They are always worth remembering.

May 3 – Preparations

'Why not seize the pleasure at once? How often is happiness
destroyed by preparation, foolish preparation.'

Jane Austen, Emma

During my hospice chaplaincy I sat on an interview panel for an
important job. Each of the shortlisted candidates had been asked
to prepare a ten-minute presentation on a specific question. The
appropriate technology was available. The first candidate used
PowerPoint – and it was awful! Every word she spoke was also
written on a slide on the screen. There was nothing *whatsoever* to
make the presentation interesting. When she had finished reading
the paragraph on one slide, she moved to the next one and read
every single word from that one too. So it continued, for ten,
excruciating minutes. She finished on time – I'll give her that! But,
if there's such a thing as boredom by PowerPoint, that was it.

The second candidate had a better PowerPoint presentation –
clear, uncluttered and succinct. He spoke to it well. But he interrupted himself several times by going to the side of the room
where he'd placed an ice-cream tub, taking from it a wet sponge,
wringing it out with both hands and replacing it in the tub before
returning to the presentation. He never explained why. There was
no *dénouement* to his performance. We never asked ...

The third had asked for an overhead projector. When she sat
down and opened the folder containing her acetate sheets they all
fell on the floor, skidded across the carpet and ended up at our
feet. She sighed. 'I told my husband before I left the house that
this wouldn't work,' she said, clearing up the mess. 'I'll just do
without them.' She spoke for *exactly* ten minutes. The presentation was superb. There was more visual material in her words than
we could have expected. She got the job!

Be prepared to adjust your preparations when you need to.

May 4 – Hugs

'You can't wrap love in a box,
but you can wrap a person in a hug.'
Anonymous

A hug is a great way to reveal our feelings for someone else. Whether you throw your arms around their neck or slap them heartily on the back; whether the hug is 'barely touching' or a bear-like one; whether it's begun with a handshake or accompanied by a kiss ... a hug is a wonderful way of expressing physical intimacy. It can show familiarity or friendship; it can be an indication of comfort or support; it can be a sign of affection or happiness; it can be part of a romantic exchange. And if it's a 'group hug', lots of people benefit. Of course we know that an unexpected or over-demonstrative hug can be an invasion of someone's personal space. We know how rigid some people get when a hug is *not* welcome. But we also know that when a hug is reciprocated it can be very special indeed.

Research into hugs has thrown up some interesting facts. For instance, the optimum length of a hug is said to be three seconds. It seems to be in the human make-up that three seconds of this kind of physical contact is deemed sufficient for the hug to do its job. And think on this – hugging has been proven to have health benefits. One study has shown that hugs increase levels of *oxytocin* – a beneficial hormone – and lower the blood pressure.

Three seconds of that kind of benefit in the midst of a stressful day or a difficult time has to be worth it, hasn't it? And maybe the optimum of three seconds of physical contact might be an indication of more friendship, comfort and affection that's available – and for much longer than three seconds too!

A sign in the hallway of a home:
'Hug Department: Always Open'

May 5 – Comfort

'He that conceals his grief finds no remedy for it.'
Turkish proverb

Rabbi Harold Kushner tells the story of a small boy being sent to the corner shop for some groceries for his mother. He's late coming home, not by too much, but enough for his mother to be worried. When he does return, unaware of his mother's anxiety, he is surprised that she gives him a scolding. But it is the way of things, and she needs to remind him of how worried she has been. She tries to get to the bottom of the delay. 'What kept you? Why were you so long?' she asks.

'Sorry, mum,' the child replies, 'but on my way home I met my pal and his bicycle was broken, so I stopped to help him.'

'But, child,' the exasperated mother continues, 'you are far too small for such things, and you know nothing about mending bicycles.'

'I know that. I know. So I sat down on the ground beside him, and I helped him cry.'

***

A missionary translator, struggling with the language of a tribe in the mountains of Mexico, found it hard to get the right word for 'comfort'. Then one of his helpers asked for a week's leave, explaining that his uncle had died and he wanted some days off to visit his grieving aunt 'to help her heart around the corner'.

'To help a heart around the corner.' This was exactly the expression for comfort the translator needed.

'Comfort' is not a wishy-washy extra when all else has failed.
It is a stronger offering of help than we might think,
and is filled with purpose, resolution and commitment.

May 6 – Influence

'In my father's house are many mansions.'
Bible: John 14:2

We carry the influence of people with us as our life goes on.

The people I've met with; the folk that I've fought;
The ones that I've cared for; and those that I've not;
The people who matter; the ones I'd disown;
Pray tell me – but where have they gone?
They come along with you in memory's store,
They're part of your life since they've come through your door;
Their influence stays with you, never to go;
They'll always be with you, you know.

What, even the bad ones I'm happy to shun;
And those that I've damaged, who hate what I've done?
I want them to leave me, to let me alone.
Please tell me that they have all gone.
I'm sorry to tell you, but that's not the case;
The worst of encounters has not gone to waste.
You're moulded and shaped by experience; so
They'll always come with you, you know.

The people I've failed with; the folk who've done wrong;
The ones who've rejected me, laughed at my song?
You tell me they matter, whatever their tone?
You mean that they'll never be gone?
It's not just your saints who will shape you and mould
Your character, purpose and future; so hold
To the truth of the matter, and watch how you go –
You are what they've made you, you know.

From With an Open Eye, *Tom Gordon, Wild Goose Publications, 2011*

May 7 – Paradox

'The paradox is the source of the thinker's passion.'
Søren Kierkegaard, Philosophical Fragments

The Gilbert and Sullivan opera *The Pirates of Penzance* is one of my personal favourites. I sang the lead tenor role of Frederick at the age of seventeen in my school production. Like all G&S operas, the plot has many twists and turns. Frederick is indentured to a pirate king till he's twenty-one. It should have been a *pilot* but Ruth, his nursery maid, misheard. Now his time is up! Freedom awaits! But at the eleventh hour Ruth remembers that Frederick was born on the twenty-ninth of February in a Leap Year, so, as far as *birthdays* go, he'll not reach his twenty-first birthday for a *long* time. And as he'd been indentured till his twenty-first *birthday,* he's stuck as a pirate! It is, Ruth sings, *A paradox, a paradox, a most peculiar paradox.* It works out OK in the end, of course, but not before the paradox has caused confusion and consternation.

A paradox is a kind of circular reasoning, a logical statement that leads to a contradiction or a situation which defies logic or reason. Simply put, it's a real puzzle – and one that can't be easily or humorously dismissed as in *The Pirates of Penance*.

Life *will* throw up moral or ethical paradoxes which are immensely taxing. How can you 'love thy neighbour' if your neighbour is threatening to kill you? How can you hold to 'thou shalt not steal', if steal is the only way to get food for your children in a war situation? Not every paradox has a ready solution. Such *is* the stuff of paradox. So there has to be an underpinning principle on which all else is based – even taxing, apparently insoluble paradoxes.

Might love be that guiding principle?
Might love inform all our ethical and moral decisions?
Will love matter above all else?

May 8 – Excuses

'If you don't want to do something,
one excuse is as good as another.'
Yiddish proverb

My secondary school in Fort William had a large catchment area. Some of us lived close by, so we walked or cycled to school. Others lived a long way away, so they boarded in the school hostel during term time. And there were those who stayed locally during the week and went home for the weekend. For them, transport was mostly by train and the early train on the Monday morning was not always the most reliable. Well, that's what we *thought* ...

All we knew was that, first thing on a Monday, someone was bound to be late and lateness meant a reasonable excuse had to be offered. Excuses were as creative as they were varied. 'Cows on the line, miss,' always got a few grins from rest of the class. 'The train-guard was sick, sir,' elicited knowing winks. 'Fog in the station, miss,' was always a winner. But the stand-out classic of all time was when two lads breezed into a Latin class half an hour late on a Monday morning announcing, 'Train had a puncture, sir,' and swanned off to their seats. Now, either the teacher was completely conned by such boldness and mock sincerity, or he was wiser than we thought and was storing up the misdemeanour for future ret-ribution. But it worked, and a made-up (and implausible ...) excuse had done its job.

Excuses are necessary sometimes, especially when we have some explaining to do. But if we were to put our creativity and variety of excuse-making into not having to make excuses in the first place, then we might not have to invent cows on the line or punctures in train wheels ever again.

George Washington once said:
'It is better to offer no excuse than a bad one.'

May 9 – Questions

'A prudent question is one half of wisdom.'
Attributed to Francis Bacon

There's a mantra I learned early on in debates and large public meetings where important decisions are being made – 'Questions are always in order.' I'm constantly worried, therefore, when I hear people discussing issues relating to faith or belief and it's clear that 'questions are *never* in order'. How can we grow in our understanding of anything if we are not open to exploration?

Questions, questions ... always some more questions,
Struggling with this and that, and whys and wherefores too ...
Questions, questions ... still a host of questions,
How? and when? and what? and where? and not forgetting who?

Questions, questions, overwhelming questions,
Never knowing when I'll say, 'I've asked enough for now ...'
Questions, questions ... will I have more questions
Even when I'm old and shouldn't care much anyhow?

Questions, questions? Yes, I like your questions ...
Come to me, and ask away, and show you want to learn.
Questions, questions? Please, ask all your questions ...
And you'll find you come to know what matters in return.

Questions! Questions! Never leave your questions
Out of sight from prying eyes or from true Wisdom's gaze ...
Questions! Questions! Find your Way with questions!
Grasp your Truth, fulfil your Life, with questions all your days.

From A Blessing to Follow *by Tom Gordon,*
Wild Goose Publications, 2009

May 10 – Perspective

'It is a narrow mind which cannot look at a subject
from various points of view.'
George Eliot, Middlemarch: A Study of Provincial Life

As part of the weekly pilgrimage on the island of Iona, there is often a visit to the Marble Quarry. It sits in a small inlet on the south-east of the island and intrepid pilgrims have a fairly strenuous hike to get to it. The quarry has a history going back to the late 1700s when it was opened by the Duke of Argyll. It quickly proved uneconomical because the marble was difficult to extract and transport was problematic. A failed enterprise followed in the 1800s, when the remote and rocky location proved too hazardous for the marble to be taken off by boat. A final attempt was made in 1907, but the quarry closed for the last time at the end of World War I. All that's left today is the rusted remains of old machinery, though the sharp-eyed pilgrim may still be fortunate enough to find a piece of the green-flecked marble.

However, the Marble Quarry is visited for more than just its industrial history. The rocks that surround it are among the oldest known in the world. George MacLeod, the founder of the Iona Community, invited pilgrims to ponder this: 'If the created world is represented by the height of Nelson's Column, put a penny piece on the top and it represents the length of time life has been on our planet. Place a postage stamp on top of the coin, and that's the time humans have been around.'

A postage stamp on top of a coin on top of Nelson's Column, and that's our place in the scheme of things – a small part of an amazing world. Looking at things from a different point of view at the Marble Quarry certainly helps to put our lives in perspective.

I need to remember how small I am in the great scheme of things.

May 11 – Bells

'We are his, to serve him nobly in the common cause,
True to the death, but not to be his slaves.'
William Cowper, The Task, Book V

One of the manses I lived in once had three servants. It was a detached Victorian villa in a grand part of Edinburgh, and though it had only been used as a manse since the 1920s, the minister in those days could afford servants in his home. Indeed, it was expected of him. So there was a live-in maid – accommodated in two rooms at the back of the house; a 'daily' who saw to the cooking; and a driver/handyman – who, among other things, looked after the minister's horse and trap. And, of course, in this ten-room house the servants were summoned by bells!

There were still wires in the attic which connected the bells in various rooms to what would have been a 'bell panel' in the servants' area so that someone could come when summoned. And although modernisation meant that most of the original bells had been removed over the years, there were still two brass-handled bell-pulls on either side of the fireplace in the drawing room as a reminder of a bygone age. Occasionally I would tug on one of the bell-pulls and live for a moment in a fantasy world where the door would open and in would come a servant who would bow and say, 'You rang, sir?' But no matter how hard I pulled, no one came, because, even if there *were* servants they couldn't respond, for no bells were connected at the other end.

Whatever help we need, what right have we to pull hard on a bell-pull to summon God's presence when we've never bothered to ensure that there is a connection in the first place? How distressed we are when God does not appear at our beck and call, when it was we who disconnected the bell *ages* ago.

To serve: 'To provide services that benefit or help.'

May 12 – True love

'How do I love thee? Let me count the ways.
I love thee to the depth and breadth and height
My soul can reach.'

Elizabeth Barrett Browning, Sonnets from the Portuguese

In his opera *Orfeo ed Euridice*, Gluck, in the words of his librettist, Ranieri de' Calzabigi, has Orpheus sing of his heart-rending grief.

Che farò senza Euridice, dove andrò senza il mio ben? Euridice, O Dio, rispondi. Io son pure il tuo fedele. Euridice! Ah, non m'avvanza più soccorso, più speranza, ne dal mondo, ne dal cel.

What will I do without Eurydice; where will I go without the wonder of my life? Eurydice! O God, answer! I am yours alone. Eurydice! Ah, I have no help any more, no hope, neither in this world, nor in heaven.

Gluck's opera is based on a Greek legend of a young musician, Orpheus, who falls in love with Eurydice, a beautiful nymph. Their marriage is idyllic, but Eurydice treads on a deadly snake and dies. The broken-hearted Orpheus takes his lyre and goes to Hades, the god of the underworld, to plead for the life of his love. Playing his lyre, he charms Charon, the ferryman, and is taken across the river Styx. And in the underworld he plays his lyre for Hades who eventually agrees that Eurydice can follow him out, but only if he does not look back to see her. Orpheus makes his way back to Charon, but with only a little way to go he looks round, and Eurydice fades and is pulled back … gone for ever.

*The pain of the loss when you have loved deeply is acute.
But would we choose never to love as a protection from grief?*

May 13 – Small

'Guid gear comes in wee bulk.'
(Good things come in small packages.)
Scots proverb

The Inn of the Sixth Happiness is a 1958 film based on the life and work in China of a young British Christian missionary, Gladys Aylward, during the years of turmoil before World War II. It stars Ingrid Bergman as Aylward, a role for which Bergman was nominated for a Golden Globe as best motion picture actress.

In China, Gladys Aylward settles in the town of Yang Cheng. There she works in an inn for travelling merchants where they can get a hot meal and hear stories from the Bible. After a time the local Mandarin appoints her as his Foot Inspector to ensure that the ancient practice of foot-binding is stopped.

When China is invaded by Japan, Aylward is encouraged to leave. She refuses, but finds that she has fifty orphans in her care. More orphans appear from a neighbouring town, so Aylward and her companion have no choice but to lead about a hundred children on a trek across the mountains. After a long, difficult journey, they all arrive safely. It's an amazing story.

As a teenager I had the privilege of hearing Gladys Aylward speak at a rally in my home town. Though her 1957 biography had been entitled *The Small Woman*, I'd only ever seen the film and so I expected Ingrid Bergman to appear, a tall, beautiful and imposing individual. But what I saw and heard that night was a small, gentle, humble and almost insignificant woman, who had, none the less, a remarkable presence, underpinned by a passionate faith. She had a profound effect on me as a young man. Small woman? I'm not at all sure ...

Even the smallest of people can achieve remarkable things
if their heart is in the right place.

May 14 – Lost

'A beautiful lofty thing, or a thing
Heroically lost, heroically found.'
WB Yeats, The Collected Poems

The parables of Jesus relating to something or someone being lost are among the most vivid, and most relevant, stories he told. The picture of a woman who has lost a precious coin turning her house upside down till she finds it, and then being ecstatic at its safe return, is a dramatic story no one can fail to relate to. Which of us has not had our frantic moments when we've lost something and rushed about, almost out of control, moving this and that in our desperate search to find what we need? And we can relate to the overwhelming sense of relief when the lost item turns up.

Through the story of the lost son – better known as the Parable of the Prodigal Son – we understand, from our own experience and from the reaction of others, the devastation of loss when a loved one dies. There is, for many people, a frantic sense of panic; a disbelief that this could be happening to them; often a rushing around trying to find the person, so that there is no loss. Don't we know people who are convinced they've seen their loved one on a bus, or heard their footfall on the stairs, or smelled their perfume? It's because they're still searching for what is lost in the frantic hope that their loved one will be returned.

Helping those who are bereaved begins with patience. We need to be patient with their behaviour, their frantic searching, their panic and disbelief. Their response to loss is not peculiar or out-of-the-ordinary. After all, didn't we all discover that we know what it's like to search for something that's lost?

How can we learn to live with loss
when what we search for is integral to our life?

May 15 – Found

'I have found the sweetest consolation.'
Christopher Columbus, Book of Prophecies

Loss can be devastating. When we've lost a *thing* and, despite our frantic searching, it hasn't been found, it's not the end of the world. Notwithstanding sentimental value, hassles with insurance companies and our own sense of stupidity and failure, losing something isn't a complete disaster. The loss of a loved one, however, can be so bad that it's as if there will never be a hopeful future. It feels as though the world has come to an end, and the only way life is going to make any sense again is for the loved one to be restored – 'found' to replace 'lost'.

We know in our heads that this isn't going to happen. But, with broken hearts, we feel that there is no worthwhile life to live. In time, of course, people adjust. In time. And if understanding and support for those who are bereaved *begins* with patience in the immediate response to the loss, so it has to *continue* with patience as adjustment to the loss gradually develops.

The dead person can't be 'found' like a lost coin or a son returning home. But, as one of the theories of grief reminds us, the dead person can be 'relocated' – found again, if you like, in a new way. Adjustment to bereavement happens because, in the remarkable way the body, mind and spirit are able to heal themselves, bereaved people find new ways of relating to the person who has died. The physical isn't available. But the relationship is as deep as ever it was. When this 'relocation' in loss takes hold, then 'found' can actually be the conclusion of our panic and our searching.

What we find after a loss
may not be what we've been looking for
but may offer a meaning we didn't expect.

May 16 – Live

'Human kind cannot bear very much reality.'
TS Eliot, Murder in the Cathedral

I was asked to take a friend's two boys to a football match. My friends aren't great football fans and going to a game would have been a bit of a chore. But their sons had been keen to go to a big game, and, being a devoted football follower, it needed no great persuasion for me to take them. We went to Tynecastle Stadium in Edinburgh – not the biggest football ground in the world – to watch Heart of Midlothian play Falkirk. It wouldn't be the biggest crowd in the world but it was just the right kind of game to give the boys an introduction to a real football match.

We got the tickets, bought the programmes, entered the ground, found our seats, opened our crisps and juice, savoured the atmosphere, dealt with repeated questions, felt the build-up of the excitement, cheered with the crowd when the Hearts players came out, watched with anticipation as the teams lined up for the kick-off, heard the referee's whistle start the game, saw the players kick off … and then the younger of the boys turned to me and, with a puzzled frown, enquired, 'Where's the commentary? I can't hear the man telling us what's happening?' Football for him had always been on TV, with a commentary to explain everything. Adjusting to a *live* game was quite another thing!

Someone once said that 'life isn't a rehearsal'. And that's true enough. It has to be lived while it's happening, and fully experienced while it's going along. But, equally, life isn't a broadcast, where someone else does the commentary and explains what's happening. Life is *live*, and, if there's going to be a commentary at all, we'll have to add it on ourselves.

'Carpe diem' – seize the day
Before the chance has gone away.

May 17 – Prayer again

'The fruit and the purpose of prayer
is to be one with and like God in all things.'
Julian of Norwich, Meditations

The Shoes of the Fisherman by Morris West was released in 1968 as a film starring Anthony Quinn. Set during the height of the Cold War, it tells the story of Lakota, the Metropolitan Archbishop of Lviv, who is unexpectedly released after twenty years in a Siberian labour camp. He is sent to Rome where he is elevated to the position of Cardinal by the elderly Pope. When the Pope dies, Lakota, as a compromise candidate, is surprisingly elected as the new Pontiff. The plot takes the new Pope Kiril into international politics and the threat of nuclear war. But the movie also sees Kiril consumed with self-doubt and struggling with his faith.

The evening after his election as Pope, dressed simply in the black cassock and berretta of the humble priest, he takes to the backstreets of Rome and finds himself taken by a doctor friend to the home of a dying man. Seeing the man *in extremis*, Kiril begins to recite the prayers for the dying in the Latin of his Roman Catholic tradition. The doctor points to a Star of David on the wall, for they are in a Jewish home. Without hesitation Kiril changes the prayer to Hebrew and begins to chant *The Kaddish*, the Jewish prayer of mourning. The doctor is clearly grateful for the sympathy shown to a grief-stricken family, but offers this insight: 'But Father, the dying is easy; it's the living that's hard.'

If religions and their prayers are to mean anything at all, they should speak to all of the human condition, to those from different religions and of none. After all, if the living *is* hard, then we need all the help that we can get.

When you don't know what to pray, pray anyway.
Your prayers will almost certainly be right.

May 18 – Beauty from brokenness

'Beauty of all kinds gives us
a peculiar delight and satisfaction.'
David Hume, Of Beauty and Deformity

Buried in the sand of Longniddry Bents on the East Lothian coast are the remains of a wooden boat. About thirty feet long, it rises from the sands at low tide when some of the ribs and part of the keel stand black and gaunt against the yellow of the unspoiled beach. I don't know the story of the wrecked boat. Was it beached because it was unwanted, abandoned to the ravages of the weather and the sea? Did it founder in a mist, so that it wasn't worthwhile putting it to sea again? Did it hit rocks further along the shore and reach safety here before it sank? Had lives been at risk or were sailors lost? And what had the boat been used for? Fishing for shellfish? Trips round the bay? And how long ago?

As I approached the boat one crisp, autumn day I saw a figure, lying prostrate on the sand with his head towards the ruined hull. As I drew closer, I realised that the man had a camera in his hand and was taking pictures of the boat's spars and ribs. I looked around, and on the far side of the Firth of Forth, over the hills of Fife, there was the most glorious sunset. I had no idea it was there, as I'd been walking away from it along the beach. The photographer, flat on his stomach, wasn't taking pictures of the boat alone; he was seeing the sunset through the outline of the wreck in the sand. Through the brokenness of the ruined boat he saw the beauty of an autumn sunset.

If he'd got stuck with the questions, as I was, he would have seen nothing else but the wreck. But now he'd found beauty from brokenness, *and* helped me see beyond what I'll never know or understand, to a new beauty that's just waiting to be viewed.

Can you see beauty beyond brokenness today?

May 19 – Marks

'Time doesn't heal any wounds;
it just leaves scars to look at later.'
Anonymous

I was three years old when I fell into a fire. I know I was *exactly* three years old because it happened at my third birthday at home. It was a simple, though dramatic, event. It didn't make the local paper or cause my parents to be questioned about child abuse or health and safety. But it has, in more ways than one, left its mark.

The birthday party was coming to an end and the open fire which heated our living room had died away to its last embers. As a result, my mother had removed the fireguard, on the assumption that there was no danger to anyone. She didn't reckon, however, on an exuberant version of 'Ring-a-ring-a-roses', with the 'ring' going round too fast and me letting go and shooting backwards into what remained of a *very* hot fire. I'm told there was much consternation. I'm told that my trousers were smoking. I'm told that my mother grabbed me and dunked my bottom in a basin of cold water in the kitchen sink. I'm told I cried. I'm told the birthday party broke up very quickly ... but I can't remember.

Did it happen? Yes, because my mother and father told me so in later years. But also .... I have a burn on an unmentionable place that's been there ever since! I have the mark to prove it.

Many events in life, good and bad, leave their mark. The mark can be physical, emotional, psychological or spiritual. But such marks are character-forming, shaping our understanding of ourselves and the world we live in. Marks are not bad things of themselves, but reminders of who we are and what we've come through to make us the individual people that we are.

'Mark this!' I was instructed.
'I don't have to,' I replied, 'for it has already marked me.'

May 20 – Comforters

'The comforter's head never aches.'
George Herbert, Jacula Prudentum

The sufferings of Job and his struggles to hold on to righteousness form the core of the Book of Job. And all of this is set in the context of a dialogue with 'friends' – 'Job's comforters' – Eliphaz the Temanite, Bildad the Shuhite and Zophar the Naamathite. Elihu the Buzite, who comes along later, also has a major part in the dialogue.

The bulk of the book is an uninterrupted contest between the cries of the much-afflicted Job and the reflections of his rational friends. The friends, as true thinkers, don't relate to Job and his specific sufferings. Instead they talk about the 'general', trying to find meaning and explanations for suffering itself, so that their friend can draw on their insights and find consolation. It's their job to help Job work it out and not to be 'infected' by his suffering. Job's 'comforters' are so intent on finding reasons that they fail to offer any reassurance; they are so focused on finding conclusions that they offer no consoling words; they are so tied up with lessons that no real love is shared with a friend in need.

Working in the hospice, I learned that suffering is a 'given' in life and no amount of explanations as to the reasons for it, theological, philosophical, or medical, will offer people healing and hopefulness. True comfort means entering into the world which suffering people inhabit, watching and waiting, often with nothing to say. Love can be shown without words and compassion without condition. Job needed true comforters, who could leave the 'general' behind for another time and be fully engaged with the circumstances of their friend and his real needs, here and now.

Comfort comes from the Latin 'cum fortis', meaning 'with strength'. Comfort, therefore, is much more than an added extra. It is a strong thing offered with purpose.

May 21 – Satan

'The devil keeps man from good
with a thousand machinations.'
Hildegard of Bingen, Letter to the Abbot

One of the motifs in the Book of Job is the role of the Devil. The story begins with a meeting between God and Satan.

The sons of God came to present themselves before the Lord, and Satan also came among them. And the Lord said to Satan, 'From where do you come?' Satan answered, 'From going to and fro on the earth and from walking back and forth on it.' Then the Lord said to Satan, 'Have you considered my servant Job, that there is none like him on the earth, a blameless and upright man, one who fears God and shuns evil?'

It seems odd that God and Satan would have a personal conversation about Job, or anyone else. But if it's seen as a metaphor for the struggles between what Job knew to be good and the evil he was experiencing, that's a struggle we all know. Job is everyone – angel on one shoulder, devil on the other. In Romans 7 St Paul has a lengthy treatise on this. In the NIV, this is how it is expressed:

I have the desire to do what is good, but I cannot carry it out. For I do not do the good I want to do, but the evil I do not want to do – this I keep on doing. Now if I do what I do not want to do, it is no longer I who do it, but it is sin living in me that does it … Although I want to do good, evil is right there with me. For in my inner being I delight in God's law; but I see another law at work in me, waging war against the law of my mind and making me a prisoner of the law of sin at work within me. What a wretched man I am!

May 22 – Reflection

'Grow brave by reflection.'
Thomas Paine, The American Crisis

In the vestry of one of my churches there was a black-and-white etching. No one knew where it had come from and I never discovered who the artist was. It depicts an elderly man, his age and countenance clearly designed to portray a scholarly figure. He is seated at a desk, and before him is an open Bible on which he is resting a bony hand. Beside his hand lie his spectacles, their thin, wired frames indicating they are from a bygone age. The man's bearded face is tilted slightly upwards; his eyes are wide open, gazing into the distance; his right hand rests against his cheek; his brow is clear and unfurrowed.

I have reflected on that picture many times for it communicates peace, serenity, thoughtfulness and depth. And the old man has spoken to me profoundly when I most needed his wisdom. He has been reading scripture, of that there is no doubt. But what is he doing now? Preparing to write something, a sermon, perhaps? Is he praying, even without clasped hands or tightly-closed eyes? Is he wrestling with some difficult Bible passage? Is he fed up with it and deciding to call it a day? Does he have doubts and fears, and will they overwhelm him?

It might be *any* of these. But for now it's just about stopping to think, pausing for reflection, not knowing where it will go or how it will work out. For now, I need to take time – and just be. Prayer? Maybe. Struggles? Perhaps. Decisions to make? Possibly. But mostly it's about taking it all in. And for *that* you need to pause and reflect for a while.

'The learn'd reflect
on what before they knew.'
Alexander Pope, *An Essay on Criticism*

May 23 – Greatness

'No really great man ever thought himself so.'
William Hazlitt, Table Talk

Arundel castle in Sussex is one of the greatest castles in England and the seat of the Dukes of Norfolk.

A story is told of a Duke of Norfolk of a bygone age who happened to be at a railway station when a little Irish girl arrived off the train carrying a heavy bag. She had come to be a housemaid at Arundel Castle. The castle was about a mile from the railway station, and the girl was trying to persuade the station porter to carry her cumbersome bag to the castle, for which she offered him one shilling, all the money she had. The porter refused with a sneer. Then the Duke stepped forward, unannounced and shabby in appearance, as was his usual style. Offering to carry the girl's bag to the castle, he took it and walked beside her on the road from the station, all the while talking gently with her about her journey, her home, her family and her new employment.

When they reached the castle, he gratefully accepted the shilling she offered him, never allowing her to know who he was. It was only the next day when she met her employer as she was going about her new duties that the housemaid knew it was the Duke of Norfolk himself who had carried her bag from the station to the castle, and that she had tipped him a shilling!

It is never safe to judge anyone by externals. Greatness lies not in status but in thoughtfulness. There is graciousness in receiving as well as in giving, as the Duke of Norfolk showed. To the truly great, no act of kindliness and service can ever be too humble.

Try swallowing your pride occasionally.
You'll find it's very non-fattening!

May 24 – Giving

'A hug is a great gift –
one size fits all, and it's easy to exchange.'
Anonymous

'What is love?' The meaning and nature of love, and how love can be described or explained, has exercised the greatest of minds through all the ages of history. But let me make this attempt to answer that searching question, and offer you the opportunity of finding in this piece which part of the answer works for you. The first two stanzas are by 'Anonymous', and the final two are mine.

What is love?

Love is giving, not taking; mending, not breaking;
Trusting; believing; never deceiving;
Patiently bearing and faithfully sharing
Each joy, every sorrow, today and tomorrow.

Love is kind; understanding, but never demanding;
Love is constant; prevailing, its strength never failing;
A promise once spoken, for all time unbroken;
Love's time is forever; eternal endeavour.

Love says, 'Sorry,' again when anger and pain
Would try to destroy both pleasure and joy.
Forgiveness it holds, more precious than gold;
With angels it sings as new pleasure it brings.

Love is drying the tears; and the calming of fears;
And healing and holding; with arms for enfolding;
Love is true to its word, its blessing conferred
On all who would say, 'I love you,' this day.

May 25 – Blame

'I praise loudly; I blame softly.'
Catherine the Great

My grandmother delighted in telling a story of a little boy who got the blame for something he didn't do. It came from the days when she worked as a milkmaid. When the milking was done, she would relate, a jug of warm, frothy milk was taken into the farmhouse kitchen to be used with the porridge for breakfast. When everyone was fed, the small boy of the house – who, of course, just loved the milk – was told not to touch it on pain of much retribution. However, when the family returned to the kitchen at lunchtime, there was a *lot* less milk in the jug than there should have been. No one else could have taken the milk. It *must* have been the small boy. So he got the blame! He insisted he hadn't stolen the milk. But, with no other culprit, he wasn't believed.

The boy's mother, however, detected some sincerity in the child, and, notwithstanding the scolding she felt obliged to give, she determined to investigate further. So, the next morning, after breakfast, she made sure that the boy was well away from the milk jug. But when the family returned to the kitchen this lunchtime, a lot of the milk had disappeared once again. It could *not* have been the boy after all. So, on the next day, when the boy was out of the way, his mother hid in the kitchen pantry to keep watch over the jug of milk. Imagine her surprise when she saw the kitchen cat slink into the room, jump up onto the table and dip its paw into the milk jug. Then, with obvious delight, the cat licked the milk from its paw. Once again the paw was dipped into the milk, and once more the cat savoured its delicacy.

Be careful who gets the blame.
And if blame is really necessary
make doubly sure it's pinned on the right person.

May 26 – Sunshine

'Keep your face always toward the sunshine –
and the shadows will fall behind you.'
Walt Whitman, Leaves of Grass

There is no doubt about the uplifting effects of sunshine. A shaft of sunlight through dark clouds; warmth on a summer's day; watery brightness after a rainstorm; the burning heat of a tropical sun; the myriad colours in a sunset; the sharp glint of light on crisp snow ... Sunshine brings us wonder and joy at every turn.

In 2005 a sci-fi movie was produced called *Sunshine*. The drama takes place fifty years into the future when the sun begins to die. A team of astronauts is sent to revive the sun, but the mission fails. Seven years later, a new team is sent to finish the task, the earth's last hope. I'll not spoil the plot, but clearly the sun *had* to be revived if people were to survive.

In 1999 a film, also called *Sunshine,* had been made by the Hungarian director István Szabó. It follows a Jewish family living in Hungary through three generations, from humble beginnings to positions of wealth and power in the decaying Austro-Hungarian Empire. The head of the family becomes a prominent judge, but is torn when his government sanctions anti-Jewish persecutions. His son converts to Christianity to advance his career but is caught up in the Holocaust. Finally, the grandson, after surviving war, revolution, loss and betrayal, realises that his ultimate allegiance must be to himself and his heritage. At one point one of the characters says, 'We believed we were going to make the world a better place for people, but ...'

We may not be able to switch the sunshine on again if the sun goes out, but we can, and do, bring glimpses of sunshine to people in the midst of their own turmoil.

We can go on to make the world a better place – with no buts!

May 27 – Joy

'And, e'en while fashion's brightest arts decoy,
The heart, distrusting, asks if this be joy.'
Oliver Goldsmith, The Deserted Village

When I was training for the ministry I played football for the college team. Every week the game was a genuine release from the rigours of theological study. The team was a mixed bag of personalities, theologies, countries of origin and football ability. But we were bound together in the camaraderie of representing the college, the love of the game and the desire to do well.

I played right full back, and in the days before overlapping Number 2s, wing backs, a back four, and the like, I stayed fully back on the right – my territory. Occasionally, *very* occasionally, I would venture over the halfway line, usually when we were playing against an inferior team, just to get more involved or get a kick of the ball. In one game I even ventured into the opposition penalty box. The ball was lobbed over from a corner, and, to my surprise, fell at my feet. I stuck out a boot, and the ball trickled into the net – a screamer from a yard and a half!

I was ecstatic! I'd scored my first goal *ever*. I shouted and waved my arms in the air as I ran back to my full back territory. Our goalkeeper came towards me. I was expecting a hug of congratulations, or at least a handshake and a 'well done'. Instead I was greeted with a stern countenance. He furrowed his brow and addressed me with words of admonition – and, I hope, only mock-seriousness. 'Too much joy,' he scolded, 'too much joy. This is a Presbyterian team. Joy? No place for that here.'

No joy for a Presbyterian? Not even when you score a goal? Oh dear, dear …

Joy is not in things, it is in people.
Joy is never transient; it has a lasting effect.

May 28 – Conscience

'There is no pillow so soft as a clear conscience.'
French proverb

Two pilgrims visited a holy man. 'We have done wrong,' they said, 'and our consciences are troubled. What must we do to be clear of our guilt?' 'What are your wrongdoings?' asked the old man. 'I have committed a great and grievous sin,' said the first. 'I have done quite a number of wrong things,' said the second, 'but they are all quite small and not at all important.' The holy man thought for a while. 'This is what you must do,' he said at last. 'Each of you must go and bring me a stone for each of your misdeeds.'

When the two men returned, the first was staggering under the weight of an enormous boulder which he dropped with relief at the feet of the holy man. The second arrived too, cheerfully carrying a bag of small pebbles. 'Now,' said the holy man, 'take all these stones and put them back where you found them.' The first man took his huge rock and struggled back to the place where he'd found it. But the second couldn't remember all the places where he'd collected his stones. After some time he came back complaining that the task was too difficult.

'You must know,' said the holy man, 'that sins are like your stones. If someone has done a great wrong, it lies like a heavy stone on the conscience. But if that person is truly sorry, then forgiveness means the load is taken away. But if someone does small wrong things over and over again, there is often no great load of guilt to be felt, and so there is no regret. Avoid little sins, my child, for they will ultimately weigh you down.'

Being troubled by your conscience
is your heart's way of reminding you
that something needs to change.
Why are you trying to rest on a lumpy pillow?

May 29 – Cheerfulness

'... to thy servant Columba,
the gifts of courage, faith and cheerfulness'
A prayer from the Iona Community

In Boswell's *Life of Johnson* there's a passage which relates how a Mr Edwards stopped Johnson on the way home from church. Fifty years before, Boswell tells us, Edwards and Johnson had been students at Pembroke College, Cambridge, and their paths had never crossed since. 'You are now a philosopher, Dr Johnson,' Edwards remarks. 'I have tried too in my time to be a philosopher, but – and I don't know how – cheerfulness was always breaking in.' *Cheerfulness was always breaking in.* Despite the seriousness of study and thought, cheerfulness always came back. Clearly Edwards considered all philosophers to be deadly dull.

In conversation with a friend recently I remarked that there were some ministers I knew who were far too serious for their own good, *and* for the good of their flock. 'Yes,' my friend replied, 'I know many of them too. There are even some who can perform the remarkable miracle of turning water into vinegar!'

One of the patients I worked with in the hospice had half her face taken away because of the ravages of cancer. Her face was swathed in bandages. The smell of decaying flesh was overpowering. It was hard to spend time with her. But what helped me to stay? The lady herself, who had no speech and none of the normal facial expressions, yet could smile with her eyes, a smile that simply lit up the room.

Despite it all, cheerfulness was always breaking in! I don't know how she managed it. But I know how remarkable it was.

*'I feel an earnest and humble desire, and shall till I die,
to increase the stock of harmless cheerfulness.'*
From *Speeches and Sayings of Charles Dickens*, GA Sala

May 30 – Tongue-tied

'I prefer tongue-tied knowledge to ignorant loquacity.'
Marcus Aurelius Cicero

There's a tongue-twister that originates close to where I live which goes as follows:

THE LEITH POLICE DISMISSETH US

Try it, if you've not done so before. It's a tough one, isn't it?

Tongue-twisters are fun, and they've been entertaining people for generations. You'll have your own favourites. What about 'Peter Piper' and his peck of pickled pepper; the one about the 'woodchuck' who chucks wood; the selling of 'sea-shells on the seashore'? Lots of enjoyment to be had …

However, while being tongue-tied is entertaining for others who listen to your stumbling attempts to get your words right, it can be embarrassing for the person who gets it wrong. Stuttering over your words when you're taking your wedding vows? Forgetting your lines in a play? Losing the place when you're making a presentation at work? We all get tongue-tied sometimes, and not just over tongue-twisters either. So, if we know what it feels like, can we not be more patient when it happens to other people?

So, now that we've got *that* sorted out and we're prepared to be more patient when folk get tongue-tied, it's back to more of the Leith police. Ready?

The Leith police dismisseth us; they thought we sought to stay.
The Leith police dismisseth us; they thought we'd stay all day.
The Leith police dismisseth us; we both sighed sighs apiece.
And the sighs that we sighed as we said goodbye
Were the size of the Leith police.

May 31 – Think

'A very great part of the mischiefs that vex this world
arises from words.'
Edmund Burke, Letter to a friend

My friend has a poster which reads, 'Before engaging your mouth, make sure your brain is in gear.' That goes for the written word too, as people who prepare church magazines so often prove.

This will be Father John's last Sunday with us.
The Choir will sing the anthem, 'Break Forth Into Joy'.

Please place donation in the envelope
along with the deceased person you wish to remember.

Our potluck supper will begin tonight at 5pm.
Music and medication to follow afterwards.

Our evening service will be held in the park across from the church.
Bring some blankets and come prepared to sin.

The youth group will lead the worship next Sunday
when they will teach us a new snog.

The weight watchers group will meet in the church hall at 7pm on
Wednesday. Please use the large double doors.

I wonder what tablets are available at 'Music and medication' and how many people aren't sure what a 'new snog' might be? It's amusing when words come out wrong. But damage can also result. And me? I have my blanket and I'm ready to sin!

When I speak today, help me to think first!

June 1 – Memories

'Remember tonight ... for it is the beginning of always.'
Attributed to Dante Alighieri

There are some memories from my early childhood which have obviously been implanted through family stories and access to old black-and-white photographs. I don't *remember* the coronation of Queen Elizabeth in 1953. But, clearly, it mattered – for there is a picture of me as a three-year-old in a fetching double-breasted coat with a velvet collar, waving a small Union Flag and standing beside my pushchair. I don't *remember* my first phone-call, but clearly I was committed to communication at an early age – for I am told that, when I was two, I was fascinated by a plastic toy phone from which, in the garden of my first home, I would call all the neighbours. I don't *remember* being in hospital when I was a toddler because I'd swallowed a safety-pin, but I was – and survived – and the story of how I told the surgeon that I'd 'shut it closed with my two fingers' is now part of the family folklore.

But I do remember *feelings* ... and you don't get that from family stories or any amount of old pictures. I remember feelings of security – I can put a word to it now, though at the time it was more about being safe. I remember feelings of enjoyment – I can call it that now, though at the time it was more about having lots and lots of fun. I remember the importance of family – that's clearly what it was, though at the time it was more about the familiarity of a mum and dad and an older sister. So I *do* remember things. And for *all* of that – even before memories are implanted in the mind – I am grateful for what's been implanted in the heart.

Remember how you felt as well as what you know,
for then you will have memories of what is true.

June 2 – Unity

'How good it is, how lovely
for brothers to live together in unity.'
Bible: Psalm 133:1

The original City of Edinburgh ran from Edinburgh Castle down to the Palace of Holyrood. When the city was expanding outwards from what is now known as 'The Royal Mile' but in older times was called the 'Kingis Hie Street', a series of wynds (lanes) and closes or entries (alleys) ran down the sides of the ridge. Merchants bought plots of land on these sloping sides, known as 'tenements', and the buildings erected were called 'lands'. On the north side of the Canongate, the lower end of the Royal Mile, there's a building known as 'Bible Land'. Above the door is a text from Psalm 133.

Behold how good a thing it is, and how becoming well,
Together such as brethren are, in unity to dwell.
IT IS AN HONOUR FOR MEN TO CEASE FROM STRIFE

The building was once occupied by the 'Guild of Cordwainers of the Canongate', skilled leather-workers (originally using goatskin from Cordoba in Spain, hence the name). The panel shows their trademark – a rounding knife placed between two cherubs. Did the cordwainers fall out so much that they needed cherubs to remind them how placid they *should* be, and were they so prone to strife that they needed a motto about the honour of living together in unity?

Perhaps we all need to create our own Bible Land, where cherubs are *our* role model too and we have a motto that reminds us of the honour of the unity we too need to create.

In unity, we have much to gain;
in disunity, we will always fall short.

June 3 – Love

'Love spends his all, and still hath store.'
Philip James Bailey, Festus

I wrote this based on the love I have for my wife, the pain one of us will feel when the other dies and the belief that love is eternal. Love *can* conquer all.

When love is rich,
Let me not be impoverished by its passing.
When love is bright,
Let me not be overwhelmed by the darkness of its going.
When love is joy,
Let me not be cast down by my sadness.
When love is full,
Let me not be broken by my emptiness.
When love is life,
Let me not be destroyed by dying.
When love is God,
Let me not be rejected by my doubting.
When love is good,
Let me not lose faith in love's own goodness.
When love is you,
Let me not lose love at your departing.
When love is me,
Let me not lose hope for all my living.

From New Journeys Now Begin *by Tom Gordon,*
Wild Goose Publications, 2006

'When love is ....'
Try filling in the blank.
Ponder your own definition of what love means for you.

June 4 – More influence

'Blessed influence of one true loving human soul on another!'
George Eliot, Scenes of Clerical Life

The poet John Masefield was born on June 1st 1878. When he was six, his mother died giving birth to his sister and he went to live with his aunt. His father died soon after, following a mental breakdown. After an unhappy education, Masefield left home to board the *HMS Conway* to train for a life at sea and to break his addiction to reading, an activity of which his aunt thought very little. Aboard the *Conway*, Masefield's love for storytelling grew, as did his desire to become a writer and storyteller himself. That urge, and the hopelessness of life as a sailor, drove him to desert ship in New York and live as a vagrant for several months doing various jobs, including as a barkeeper. Around Christmas 1895 Masefield read the December edition of *Truth*, a New York periodical, which contained the poem *The Piper of Arll* by Duncan Campbell Scott. Ten years later Masefield wrote to Scott: 'I had never ... cared very much for poetry, but your poem impressed me deeply and set me on fire. Since then poetry has been the one deep influence in my life, and to my love of poetry I owe all my friends, and the position I now hold.' In 1930 he became Poet Laureate. *The Times* said: '*His poetry could touch to beauty the plain speech of everyday life.*' By his wishes he was cremated and his ashes placed in Poets' Corner in Westminster Abbey.

John Masefield was undoubtedly a natural talent. But could Duncan Campbell Scott have known how one of his poems might set on fire such wonderful creativity? One poem, from one man, in one journal, altered the direction of John Masefield's life. What, then, might be the influence of our modest contribution on the talents and development of many others?

What, or whom, might I influence today?

June 5 – Weddings

'Love, as is told by the seers of old,
Comes as a butterfly tipped with gold,
Flutters and flies in sunlit skies,
Weaving round hearts that were one time cold.'
Algernon Charles Swinburne, Song

People love weddings – family weddings; the marriage of a close friend; a simple wedding; the grandest affair; a religious ceremony; a civil celebration. Talk will be of the style of the bride's dress, the beauty of the bridesmaids, the mother of the bride, the changeable weather, the quality of the meal, the success of the band, the cuteness of the flower girl, the best man's speech. But I wonder in all of that whether the love at the heart of a wedding is talked about as much as it should be. I fear sometimes love is squeezed out, or at least has a lower priority than it should.

Two weddings stick in my mind. The first was the biggest. I can't recall how many guests there were, but it was several hundred. I can't recall how many courses we had at the meal because I lost count. I never knew how much it all cost, but it must have been astronomical. And I remember a young, pretty bride, overwhelmed by it all. It was just too much for her. The meaning had been overtaken by the event. By contrast, the smallest wedding was, perhaps, the most beautiful. There were only the bride and groom, their two closest friends as the witnesses and I. We gathered in a small side-chapel in my church, and love was clearly at the heart of it all. I cherish that event to this day.

Love is why marriages happen. Love is what weddings are about. Let's not forget what should be at the heart of it all.

Forgot the purpose? Forget the meaning.
Forgot the meaning? Forget the love.
Forgot the love? Forget the future?

June 6 – Wealth

'The desire for wealth is nearly universal, and none can say
it is not laudable, provided the possessor of it accepts
its responsibilities, and uses it as a friend to humanity.'
PT Barnum, The Art of Money Getting

The pilgrim had reached the outskirts of the village and was set-
tling down under a tree for the night, when a man from the village
came running up to him. 'The stone,' the villager shouted. 'The
stone! Give me the precious stone.'

'What stone?' asked the pilgrim.

'Last night I had a dream,' the breathless villager continued.
'God spoke to me, of that I am convinced.'

'And what did your god tell you?' the pilgrim enquired.

'God told me to go to the outskirts of the village at dusk and
there I would find a pilgrim who would give me a precious stone
which would make me rich for ever,' the villager explained.

The pilgrim rummaged in his bag and pulled out a stone. 'He
probably meant this one,' he said, handing the stone to the villager. 'I have not had it for long, for I found it on the path by the
stream only a few days ago. You can certainly have it.'

The villager was overjoyed and gazed at the stone in wonder.
It was the biggest diamond he had ever seen, so big he could not
close his fingers around it. So, gripping the precious stone in both
hands, he walked away, returning to the village to share the news
of his riches. But that night he tossed and turned in bed, unable
to sleep. The next day, at the crack of dawn, he returned with the
precious stone to the outskirts of the village and woke the slum-
bering pilgrim. 'Give me the wealth,' he cried, 'the wealth you
must still have, that makes it possible for you to give away this
diamond so easily.'

What can we learn from an 'out of money' experience?

June 7 – What next?

'Our new Constitution is now established, and has an
appearance that promises permanency; but in this world
nothing can be said to be certain, except death and taxes.'

Benjamin Franklin, from a letter to Jean-Baptiste Leroy

One of the hardest things to grasp is life's impermanence. Our
intellect is all too aware that none of us will live for ever. Yet often
we live as if we, and our loved ones, were immortal. Among the
many unwritten sayings of Jesus from sources outwith the four
Gospels is this one: *The world is a bridge. The wise man will pass
over it, but he will not build his house upon it.*

In St Bede's *Ecclesiastical History of the English People* we find
an incident from 627AD. The elders of the ancient kingdom of
Northumbria meet to discuss whether they should embrace the
Christianity which Edwin, their king, had accepted. Coifi, a wise
counsellor, offers this picture of the nature of our living:

*So seems the life of man, O king, as a sparrow's flight through
the hall when you are sitting at meat in the wintertime, with
the warm fire lighted on the hearth, but the icy rainstorm outside. The sparrow flies in at one door and tarries for a moment
in the light and the heat of the hearth-fire, and then, flying from
the other, vanishes into the wintry darkness from whence it
came. So tarries for a moment the life of man in our sight; but
what is before it, what after it, we know not.*

The hope of an afterlife to combat the pessimism of the 'wintry
darkness'? Yet true wisdom begins by accepting the ancient knowledge that life is not a settled possession and that no one has a pre-
scriptive right to live for ever.

*Don't build a house on a bridge,
when the bridge is for crossing over to something new.*

June 8 – Death

'Death, in itself, is nothing; but we fear
To be we know not what, we know not where.'
John Dryden, Aureng-Zebe

I don't much like cats. I've had too many dubious experiences with recalcitrant moggies over the years to have any real affection for the felines of the animal kingdom 'Feed a dog and it thinks you're a god,' someone once said. 'Feed a cat and it *knows* it's God.' That just about sums it up. What use is a cat?

It was a *major* concession when our daughter, Kathryn, got a cat. To be honest, Kola, for that was he, wasn't really too much bother. Apart from depositing the odd dead bird on the back doorstep, he slept most of the time and actually had the good grace to purr contentedly when I tickled him under the chin. When Kathryn went to college she couldn't take the cat with her, so he stayed at home and we looked after him. All was well ... until the cat got sick. We kept Kathryn informed about the vet's diagnosis.

The cat got worse and the decision was made that he would have to be put down. My wife asked me if I wanted to come to the vet's. I thought she needed support. *It's only a cat,* I thought, but joined my wife on the sad journey to the vet's anyway. The vet was great. He comforted the cat as he held him in his arms. He gave the cat the final injection. *It's only a cat,* I thought. I don't much like cats ... and I broke down in tears on the way back to the car.

John Donne wrote, *Every man's death diminishes me, for I am involved with mankind.* I would go further. *Every* death diminishes me, because I am involved with life. A cat called Kola taught me that in his dying.

Death is an offence, and should fill us with horror.
Death is a gift, for through it we can see our mortality.

June 9 – Health

'From the bitterness of disease
man learns the sweetness of health.'
Catalan proverb

I spent fifteen years on the staff of a hospice. As a consequence, I am well aware of the value of good health and the devastation for patients and carers when health is compromised. Izaak Walton, writing in *The Compleat Angler* in 1653, put it this way:

Look to your health; and if you have it, praise God, and value it next to a good conscience; for health is the second blessing that we mortals are capable of; a blessing that money cannot buy.

'Look to your health; and if you have it, praise God.' Jesus has this to say on the subject in Matthew 6:19-21 *(NIV)*:

Do not store up for yourselves treasures on earth, where moths and vermin destroy, and thieves break in and steal. But store up for yourselves treasures in heaven, where moths and vermin do not destroy, and where thieves do not break in and steal. For where your treasure is, there your heart will be also.

It's a simple lesson. Health is very precious. It should be cared for and nurtured, as you would with a valuable treasure. When you lose it or find it corrupted, no amount of money can buy it back. And if 'earthly treasures' are our focus and good health is taken for granted, how much more devastating when it is endangered. Good health – 'a blessing that money cannot buy'.

*Why is it we toast the health of others
and often forget our own?*

June 10 – Education

'An investment in knowledge pays the best interest.'
Benjamin Franklin, The Way to Wealth

In *Nicholas Nickleby*, Charles Dickens offers insight into early 19th-century education. Nicholas Nickleby's father dies unexpectedly after losing his money in poor investments. Nicholas, his mother and his younger sister, Kate, move to London to their only relative, Nicholas's uncle, Ralph Nickleby. Ralph, a cold and ruthless businessman, hates Nicholas and gets him a low-paying job.

> *Mr Ralph Nickleby took a newspaper from his pocket, and ... read: 'EDUCATION – At Mr Wackford Squeers's Academy, Dotheboys Hall, at the delightful village of Dotheboys, near Greta Bridge in Yorkshire, Youth are boarded, clothed, booked, furnished with pocket-money, provided with all necessaries, instructed in all languages living and dead, mathematics, orthography, geometry, astronomy, trigonometry, the use of the globes, algebra, single stick (if required), writing, arithmetic, fortification, and every other branch of classical literature. Terms, twenty guineas per annum. No extras, no vacations, and diet unparalleled. Mr Squeers is in town, and attends daily ... one till four, at the Saracen's Head, Snow Hill. N.B. Able assistant wanted. Annual salary 5 pounds. A Master of Arts ... preferred.' 'There!' said Ralph ... 'Let him get that situation, and his fortune is made.'*

Have I missed out on important educational explorations in the fields of 'single stick', 'fortification', 'astronomy' and the like? If not, what is the nature of education that really matters?

Education, education, education ...
Good, good, good ...

June 11 – Regrets

'A ton of regret never makes an ounce of difference.'
English proverb

Edith Piaf, the French singer from the 1940s and '50s had the nickname *Parigot* – The Little Sparrow – because she was only four feet eight inches tall. I first heard her sing in my teens, and I was struck by how much power and passion was produced by this tiny frame. Songs such as *La vie en rose*, *Hymne à l'amour* and *Milord* are classics. But perhaps her most famous song is *Non, je ne regrette rien* – 'No regrets' – from late in her career.

During her life Edith Piaf was arrested as an accessory in the murder of her manager; her husband died in a plane crash in 1949; she herself was seriously injured in a car accident in 1960. She died of liver cancer at the age of 47, and was denied a funeral mass by the Archbishop of Paris because of her decadent lifestyle. How, then, could such a woman sing this?

Non! Rien de rien ... Non! Je ne regrette rien.
Ni le bien qu'on m'a fait ni le mal tout ça m'est bien égal!

No! Absolutely nothing ... No! I regret nothing
Neither the good things that have been done to me, nor the bad,
All this is much the same to me!

Piaf wasn't unaware of her frailties. But she was aware that the past can't be changed. It is what it is. We have to move on.

Avec mes souvenirs, j'ai allumé le feu;
Mes chagrins, mes plaisirs, je n'ai plus besoin d'eux!

With my memories I lit a fire;
My sorrows, my pleasures, I need them no more!

June 12 – God again

'The riddles of God are more satisfying
than the solutions of man.'
GK Chesterton, The Book of Job: An Introduction

I explored earlier the question 'What is God is like?' I tried in my confirmation classes to have the enquirers express something about their understanding of God in the form of a metaphor, a picture image which could define God for them without words. The picture of God as a blanket made from knitted squares is as vibrant and helpful as it was when I first heard it.

Another picture also stays with me. It was offered by a man who happened to work with a furniture-removal company. I didn't know that at the time, but it makes sense now. I share the picture with you as he shared it with me.

'God,' he said, 'is a strong, upright chair, old but well made, solid and dependable, unrestored but looking good, on which I can sit when I'm tired and know that I am safe and secure.' He paused before he continued. 'It's not an easy chair with soft cushions. That would be too comfortable, and I might like it too much and fall asleep. No, it's got a reasonably soft seat and a hard back. It makes me sit upright and know that I won't be there for long.' Another pause … 'And if I am inclined to linger too long, the chair gets tipped up and I have no choice but to stand up again and get on with things.' A final pause, and a beaming smile ... 'But I always know that my chair will still be there when I get back, doing its job, ready to support my big behind as I thump down unceremoniously on its seat at the end of a long, hard day.'

*'I sought to hear the voice of God
and climbed the topmost steeple,
but God declared: "Go down again –
I dwell among the people." '*
John Henry Newman

June 13 – Stigma

'I used to think that people with HIV were dirty
and deserved what they got.
I was devastated when I found that I had HIV.
I became one of those people.'

Anonymous

John died of AIDS when he was thirty-five and left behind an eight-year-old son. The cause of his death wasn't made public and the family was well supported at the time of the death. But rumours started about HIV. Hints about drug abuse and the gay community became whispered comments passed from person to person.

Ignorance was rife in the early days of HIV. People thought you could be infected sitting beside someone on the bus, or using a public toilet, or shaking hands. Soon, John's mother was stigmatised. People avoided her in the supermarket. They stopped talking to her when she took her grandson to school.

Even worse was the stigma John's son experienced. He was isolated in the school playground. Some children were excluded by their parents from the boy's PE classes. No one sat beside him in the dinner hall. The stigma was painful and cruel.

The headmistress decided something needed to be done. An educational programme was started to challenge people's ignorance and alleviate their fears. Leaflets were circulated and, slowly, attitudes changed. And it started when a headmistress went to a stigmatised little boy in the school playground, gave him a hug and carried him to his gran at the school gate, shook her hand and planted a big kiss on her cheek.

John died of AIDS when he was thirty-five and left behind an eight-year-old son. He'd been infected with HIV from a contaminated blood transfusion to help alleviate his haemophilia.

Stigma and bias bring shame on us all.

June 14 – Neighbours

'Borrow trouble for yourself, if that's your nature,
but don't lend it to your neighbours.'
Rudyard Kipling, The Kipling Reader: Cold Iron

It's hard to love your neighbour when he takes the last available parking place and you have to park two streets away and walk home in the rain. It's hard to love your neighbour when she takes 20 items into the 10 items or less (and it *should* be 'fewer') supermarket-queue – and cuts in front of you to get there. It's hard to love your neighbour when she not only talks during the movie but explains to her partner exactly what is going to happen next. It's hard to love your neighbour when he tosses an empty beer can into your carefully tended flower bed. It's hard to love your neighbour when he lets his dog poo in the park and doesn't clean it up. It's hard to love your neighbour when the 'music' from his car drowns out your conversation on the pavement. It's hard to love your neighbour ...

Well, OK. Maybe I could try harder to love *my* neighbour. *Yours* might be fine. But it's hard to love *mine* sometimes. And, to avoid any confusion, I'm not referring to *next-door* neighbours, who, in my case, are quite lovely. It's when I ponder neighbours in general that problems arise.

Jesus had something to say on the subject. He created a funny image of a man trying to take a speck of dust out of his neighbour's eye when he had a great 2-by-4 in his own! Think of your own faults, he said, before you criticise your neighbours for theirs. And, indeed, learn to 'love your neighbour as yourself'.

Of course it's hard to love your neighbour. But then, I'm someone else's neighbour, and maybe they're struggling to love *me* – with a great big beam in my eye, and all ...

Aren't neighbours just me on the other side of the fence?

June 15 – Start small

'No act of kindness, no matter how small, is ever wasted.'
Aesop, The Fable of the Lion and the Mouse

Here's a proverb offered in several variations over the years:

> *For the want of a nail, the shoe was lost;*
> *for the want of a shoe, the horse was lost;*
> *for the want of a horse, the rider was lost;*
> *for the want of a rider, the message was lost;*
> *for the want of a message, the battle was lost;*
> *for the want of a battle, the kingdom was lost.*
> *And all for the want of a horseshoe nail.*

A small, apparently insignificant error, overlooked, eventually leads, through a gradual worsening, to an absolute disaster. Look after the little things so that bigger things might be secured. But it's worth remembering that most of these chains of events are only seen in hindsight, and, as we know, hindsight gives us 20-20 vision. Did anyone lament the possible fall of a kingdom when they were faced with an unshod horse? So I prefer to look on the more positive side of this idea, to look forward, and know that what you do now can lead to *good* outcomes in the future. I was told regularly in a good, thrifty Scottish household:

> *Look after the pennies,*
> *and the pounds will take care of themselves.*

Or as the author's grandmother would advise a small boy:

> *Mony a mickle maks a muckle.*
> (Lots of little things can make a big thing in the end.)

June 16 – Mystery

'[We] never cease to stand like curious children
before the great mystery into which we were born.'
Albert Einstein, in a letter to Otto Juliusburger

'The Lewis Chessmen' were found close to Uig on the island of Lewis in the Outer Hebrides of Scotland. Products of late 12th-century craftsmanship, the chess pieces consist of elaborately worked walrus ivory and whales' teeth in the forms of seated kings and queens, mitred bishops, knights on their mounts, standing warders and pawns in the shape of obelisks.

Their discovery is shrouded in mystery. All that is certain is that they were found some time before April 11th 1831, when they were exhibited in Edinburgh at the Society of Antiquaries for Scotland, having been unearthed from a sand dune where they may have been placed in a small stone chamber. Who owned the chess pieces is also a mystery. And no one knows why they were hidden in the first place. Could they have belonged to a merchant travelling from Norway to Ireland? Might they be Icelandic in origin? Why were some of the pieces stained red when they were found? Would an original chessboard have been red and white, as opposed to the modern convention of black and white? Mystery upon mystery ....

Of the ninety-three pieces known to exist, eleven are in Edinburgh at the National Museum of Scotland, and eighty-two are in the British Museum. I have replicas of two pieces on the mantelpiece in my lounge. But do I lose sleep over the mysteries surrounding the Lewis Chessmen? No, I don't. I'm just pleased that through my Lewis Chessmen I have a living link to history and can foster admiration of the wonders of a bygone age.

*There is no greater mystery than love itself,
for there is nothing whatsoever that can explain it.*

June 17 – In disguise

'For thereby some have entertained angels unawares.'
Bible: Hebrews 13:2

Surfing the internet I came across a firm of private detectives in Milton Keynes called *Angels in Disguise*, advertising themselves as 'a professional, all-female team of investigators with a wealth of experience in private investigation'. I liked the snappy title. I wonder what a male equivalent company might be.

There's also a ministries' charity in the USA called *Angels in Disguise*. The aim of AID, as they call themselves, is simply to do good where good needs to be done, to be those 'angels in disguise' that people need and often never find. When we feel that there 'isn't much we can do' and end up doing nothing at all. AID suggests: 'Most of us have what it takes to meet at least one other person's needs. All of us see people we are capable of helping every day, and just walk on by without even taking notice.' So, when your elderly neighbour needs their path cleared of snow in the winter, where will an 'angel in disguise' come from? Or when the old lady in front of you in the supermarket queue is holding up the line because she can't pack her bags quickly enough, will an 'angel in disguise' appear? AID says, 'There are all kinds of simple ways to reach out into the community, ways to get more involved. Working together, we can change the world.'

Not for you? Well, maybe if you looked at it from the other end ... If you were in some difficulty and hoped and prayed that an 'angel in disguise' would come along, wouldn't *any* angel, female or male, from a charity or from Milton Keynes, *anybody* from *anywhere,* be just what you needed?

*Is it possible
that you might be the 'angel in disguise'
someone else needs today?*

June 18 – Proof

'For when one's proofs are aptly chosen
Four are as valid as four dozen.'
Matthew Prior, Alma

I used to be a runner. It's hard to believe now, but when I was younger I ran two marathons. I would think nothing of going on a training run for 10 or 12 miles. I wasn't the *best* marathon runner in the world. In 1983 I ran the Edinburgh Marathon in 4 hours 15 minutes, and the following year, having improved immensely, I ran the Glasgow Marathon in 4 hours *10* minutes. Yes indeed, I used to be a runner. But it's hard to convince my grandchildren of the truth of this. When grampa is seen puffing as he runs for a bus, or clearly enjoys sitting with his feet up reading the paper, how can they be persuaded that it's true? Easy! I have *proof*! For hanging in my study are two medals, clearly emblazoned with *The Scotway Marathon Edinburgh 1983* and *Scott's Porridge Marathon 1984 Glasgow*. If it's proof they want, they need look no further.

How often have we heard the challenge 'Prove it!' when someone hasn't believed what we're saying? Qualifications – where's the proof? Passport at an airport boarding gate – where's the proof? Buying a drink in an over-21 bar – where's the proof? Ran a marathon – where's the proof? But what about things that *don't* lend themselves to being proved? Can you prove that someone loves you, or that the God you believe in is real, or that you feel sad? Of course not. Sometimes we just have to believe what someone says. It's the quality of our relationships and the trust in each other's integrity that matter more than any proof. If I didn't have two medals hanging in my study, would my grand-sons believe me? I hope so, because the proof is really in me.

If proof is needed,
can you prove what goodness means by what you are?

June 19 – Revenge

'Life being what it is, one dreams of revenge.'
Paul Gaugin, Gaugin's Intimate Journals

Beside the A82 between Fort William and Inverness, on the shore of Loch Oich, there is a strange column topped by seven stone faces. It's known as 'The well of the seven heads' (in Gaelic, *Toban nan Ceann*, The well of the heads). The story behind the sculpture is one of revenge. In the grim days of 1663 when feuds between Scotland's Highland clans, and struggles for power within clans, were commonplace, Alexander MacDonald, the young Chief of Keppoch, and his brother Ranald were stabbed to death by rivals within their clan. There was turmoil and talk of avenging the deaths. Two years after the murders, the Privy Council in Edinburgh issued letters of 'Fire and Sword' against the murderers – a clear indication that they should be taken dead or alive. It fell to one Iain Lom (Bald John) to do the deed. He tracked down the seven murderers, killed them without mercy and chopped off their heads. Proof of the success of the 'fire and sword' enterprise was the presenting of the severed heads to the local clan chief. On his way to the chief's castle Bald John stopped at a spring to wash the heads and make them more presentable. From that day the spring was known locally as *Toban nan Ceann*.

A century and a half later a memorial was erected at the roadside to mark both the crime and the gruesome justice that followed. But for me the Well of the Seven Heads is more than just a memorial to crime and punishment. Could it be that Bald John's spring was a symbol of the need to have some place to wash away the evil that had been perpetuated by the revenge? After all, if hatred breeds hatred, and violence breeds violence, there are a lot of stains that need to be washed away.

Let the desire for revenge be the birth of forgiveness.
Let the birth of forgiveness be the beginning of trust.

June 20 – Gentleness

'A gentle hand may lead an elephant with a hair.'
Persian proverb

The Wind and the Sun had a quarrel. The Wind boasted that he was much stronger than the Sun. 'I'll show you I am stronger,' he said. 'Look at that man over there wearing a big coat? I bet you I can make him take his coat off quicker than you can.'

'OK,' replied the Sun. 'Let's see.'

So the Sun went behind a cloud, but left a little hole so that he could peep through and see what the Wind did. And, as he did, he saw the Wind blow and blow as hard as he could, causing a terrible storm. 'The stronger the storm,' the Wind surmised, 'the less likely the man will be to hold on to his coat.' But the harder the Wind blew, the tighter the old man wrapped his coat about him. In the end, the Wind was exhausted and had become so calm that he had to give in.

Then it was the Sun's turn. He came out from behind the cloud and smiled gently with sunshine at the old man. After a while, the man began to mop his brow, then, too warm for the sun's brightness, pulled off his coat. So the Sun's gentleness was victorious over the strength of the Wind.

St Francis de Sales wrote, 'He who can preserve gentleness amid pains, and peace amid worry and a multitude of affairs, is almost perfect.' We may not become as perfect as de Sales suggests, but gentleness can work, can't it? I'll remember that the next time I have to lead an elephant with a hair …

A harsh word can break a spirit;
A hard blow can cause much pain.
But a gentle word can soothe a troubled heart;
And a gentleness of spirit can heal a shattered soul.
So, lay aside your harshness, and let gentleness have its way.

June 21 – Birth

'High birth is nothing where virtue is not.'
Molière, Don Juan

In the early 1970s, during an Easter break, I took twelve teenagers to the Youth Camp on Iona. The hutted camp run by the Iona Community was, at that time, a rough-and-ready affair. But the youngsters were just happy that the week had been planned at all. None of them had been out of Edinburgh before, so the long journey north was a trial. 'Are we nearly there yet?' was the predictable question when the bus was just at the outskirts of the city. 'I'm still starving,' was the oft-repeated mantra, even though we'd already stopped for chips. 'Poxy boat,' was offered in a loud voice as we got on the ferry to Iona. 'What d'ya mean we have to *walk*?' was the moan as we left the jetty to head for the Camp.

I had settled the girls into their dorm and was taking the boys into their room next door, when I heard an ear-piercing scream. I turned to see one of the lads at the window at the far end of the dorm. 'Good grief. What the [expletive deleted] is *this*?' he cried. Within moments, six teenagers were wrestling for a place by the window to view the amazing sight ... of a sheep giving birth to a lamb. Soon we were joined by six girls. Not much was said, apart from the odd 'Ooohh!', 'Yeuch!' or 'Wow!' But the sense of amazement was palpable, and the effect on twelve teenagers on their first trip out of Edinburgh was profound.

New life became the theme of our week. It influenced the worship. It informed our nature studies. It suggested some ideas about what was happening back home. And a group of harum-scarum young people began a journey to new life that was more than just a trip out of their city for the first time.

There's no birth certificate when life begins again.
No proof is needed when your journey starts afresh.

June 22 – Great

'Are not great men the models of nations?'
Owen Meredith (Lord Lytton), Lucile

Have you ever wondered why Alfred the Great was labelled 'great' while other monarchs weren't? Maybe this will give us a clue. In the 9th century, when the Christian Gospel first arrived in Britain, our islands were inhabited by Celtic peoples. For four hundred years Anglo Saxons, Celts and Danes had struggled for dominance. Celtic missionaries from the north and Roman missionaries from the south did their bit to offer a healing and reconciling message.

Enter Alfred, the youngest of five sons of King Aethelwulf. In response to the Christian message he had wanted to become a monk. Events, however, contrived against him and when his father and his four older brothers were killed in battle he became king in 871. After defeating the invading army of Danes, he convinced their leader, Guthrum, and his nobles and chief warriors to convert to Christianity. Maybe they had little choice, yet, nonetheless, they welcomed Christian priests and missionaries into their communities. But Alfred wasn't finished. Able to lay aside his military leadership, he dedicated himself to repairing the damage that war had done to the cultural life of his people. He brought scholars from Wales and the Continent. Impressed by the provisions in the Law of Moses for the protection of the rights of the people, he ordered that similar provisions should be made part of English law.

Alfred was buried in the Old Minster at Winchester. He is the only English monarch to be known as 'The Great'. Great because of military conquests? Maybe so. But in my eyes, 'great' is a fitting title for any man who heals a nation and ensures that his people are properly valued, educated and supported.

Greatness is a label in our heart, not a medal on our chest.

June 23 – All for one

'It does me no injury for my neighbour to say
there are twenty gods, or no god.
It neither picks my pocket nor breaks my leg.'
Attributed to Thomas Jefferson

My oft-quoted and wise grandmother was fond of saying, 'We're a' Jock Tamson's bairns.' The wisdom of this familiar Scottish aphorism is simple: We're all members of the one human family. No one is better or worse than anyone else. Our humanity binds us together, and what we hold in common is more important than what divides us. We should, therefore, respect one another. As Thomas Jefferson points out, if another person takes a different view from ours in respect of religion, politics or attitudes, can't we continue to value our oneness rather than emphasise our differences?

But where does this wise phrase come from? For a start, it's Lowland Scots and Northumbrian English for *we're all John Thomson's children.* Some believe it's meant as a euphemism for God – 'We are all God's children.' A similar phrase, 'We're a' the bairns o' Adam', offers the same idea. Scottish Gaelic also has the shorter saying 'Clann MhicTamhais' – Thomson/MacTavish's children/clan. But the history of Duddingston Kirk in Edinburgh offers us a more personal explanation. It suggests that it refers to the Reverend John Thomson (Jock Tamson, or Thamson), a minister of Duddingston Kirk in the early 1800s. He called the members of his congregation 'ma bairns' (*my children*) and this resulted in folk saying, 'We're a' Jock Tamson's bairns,' to give a sense of belonging to a group with a common purpose.

Divine or human, my grandmother's wisdom still stands. We *are* one with each other, and anything that divides us will surely cause harm to some of Jock Tamson's bairns.

Which of 'ma bairns' do I need to be closer to today?

June 24 – Hidden

'Three things cannot be long hidden:
the sun, the moon and the truth.'

Buddha

I have a photograph in my hallway that dates from the 1920s. It's a studio portrait of my father's family. His father stands at the back with the children gathered round their mother who is sitting with her baby on her knee. Although it was taken before the two youngest members of the family were born, it's the best photograph we have of my father's family. My father was four when the picture was taken. There he is, looking straight at the camera, solid and still and bedecked in a fetching white polo-necked sweater. What the photograph *doesn't* show, however, is that my father is wearing his sweater back-to front. But why?

My father, by all reports, was a rascal when he was little. The children, in preparation for the taking of the photograph, had been warned that, wearing their Sunday Best, they should not under *any* circumstances get into mischief. But my father escaped and ended up in the street, fascinated by a tar-boiler being used for road-laying. The inevitable happened. The white polo-necked sweater got tar stains down the front. There was no change of clothes. There was nothing for it but to turn the sweater back-to-front. So there is my dad in the photo, looking resplendent, with the tar stains on his sweater hidden well out of sight.

What faces us head-on is not always the whole story. Maybe for good reasons, but sometimes for bad, the truth stays hidden. So beware of fetching white polo-necked sweaters worn back-to-front in a family photograph! There may be another story waiting to be revealed.

What you see may not be the whole picture.
What you think you know may not be the whole truth.

June 25 – Awareness

'Heavenly Father bless us, and keep us all alive;
There's ten of us for dinner, and not enough for five.'
Anonymous

St Paul's Cathedral in London contains the remarkable and famous 'Whispering Gallery'. Visitors can hear the guide's whisper travel around the whole dome of St Paul's, the sound bouncing back many times from the smooth wall. The gallery is 198 feet across, but if you put your ear close to the wall you can hear what is said on the opposite side of the dome, even when it is said very quietly.

There's a story told of a shoemaker and his young lady on a visit to St Paul's. His business was in trouble. He didn't have enough money to buy new leather to make more shoes, so he couldn't afford to get married. Confessing this in whispers to his betrothed, the news was responded to, not surprisingly, with quiet sobs and deep distress. But the conversation was overheard by a man on the far side of the Whispering Gallery. He decided to do something, and, finding where the shoemaker lived, had some leather sent to his shop so that the business could be saved. In time the shoemaker was able to marry the woman he loved. And the anonymous benefactor? None other than the Prime Minister of the day, William Gladstone.

The needs of others are seldom shouted. More often than not they come to us in whispered cries of need. It is our task to listen out for such whispers and respond in generosity and love.

Today,
let me be more aware of the needs of others;
where there is loneliness, let me offer friendship;
where there is rejection, let me offer my embrace;
where there is poverty, let me share my wealth;
where there is distress, let me share my comfort;
where there is need, let me practise my compassion.

June 26 – Walls

'I will tear down the wall ... and level it to the ground
so that its foundation will be laid bare.'
Bible: Ezekiel 13:14

When the Berlin Wall came down in 1989, it left us with iconic images of the destruction of a painful barrier which had stood for many years as a symbol of fear, restriction and division. It had been more than a symbol, of course, for it had been built as a physical barrier between the East and the West, separating opposing ideologies and dividing families. The Berlin Wall lay between different nation states, separated for all time, it seemed, by this massive, guarded, impregnable wall.

It's no surprise, therefore, that when the Berlin Wall came down there was unbridled celebration. People chipped away at the wall with hammers and chisels, venting their anger and frustration on the hated divide and trying to destroy it. Some tore at the concrete with their bare hands, sometimes alone, often with others, giving their all to remove the wall.

But for me the most iconic image was TV footage of people dancing on top of the wall. What had been a symbol of separation, pain and hatred had now become a platform for celebration and rejoicing; what had been a representation of fear and death had now become an image of freedom and hope; what had been the scene of tears and mourning had become a place where people could dance.

Let's believe that there will be more times when walls built to separate us will be broken down to create peace. Let us pray that mourning for the bitterness of sorrow and death will be turned again into dancing on the top of walls.

There is a time for breaking down, and a time for building up;
There is a time for mourning, and a time for dancing.

June 27 – More prayer

'Who rises from prayer a better man,
his prayer is answered.'
George Meredith, The Ordeal of Richard Feverel

When I was a probationer minister, I worked in Easterhouse in Glasgow. Like many of the post-war housing estates in the peripheral areas of our major cities, Easterhouse had its problems. And so did the church! In practical terms, the roof was a mess. The church dated from the early 1950s and it hadn't been well built. Damp had got into the roof and penetrated the compressed-straw (yes!) boards. The dampness had caused the boards to expand and the straw to sprout (yes!) and cause further damage. The whole roof had to be replaced. It took months, and there was much disruption. However, in time, it was done.

The day it was completed, I popped in to have a chat with the architect and the builder. They were surveying their handiwork. 'How are things?' I enquired. 'Pretty good,' came the reply. 'That's us done. All we need now is a heavy downpour of rain to test the roof. Any chance of you having a word with the Big Man to see if he can turn the taps on for a bit?' 'No problem,' I said, well used to such jibes. 'I'll have a quick prayer ...'

I opened the front door and the heavens opened with the biggest deluge we'd had in ages. Heading back inside, with the rain now battering noisily off the roof, I found the builder and the architect scratching their heads, clearly wondering what was going on. 'OK, lads?' I chirped. 'Seems like the Big Man's in a responsive mood today. That's prayer for you, eh?' I didn't wait around to hear a request for the winner of the 3.30 at Newmarket. I was just happy with the puzzled frowns on the faces of two men in our church pondering the effectiveness of prayer.

You can pray by who you are as well as by what you say.

June 28 – Human rights

'All human beings are born free and equal
in dignity and rights.'
UNO, Declaration of Human Rights, 1948

Rebecca's dad had been working hard all day. When he came home, all he wanted was to sit and relax. Rebecca, on the other hand, wanted her dad to play with her. Her dad had started reading his newspaper supplement and hit on a compromise. In his magazine was a full-page map of the world, in all its colourful glory. So he carefully tore the page out, found a pair of scissors and cut the map into different shapes round the outline of countries. He couldn't do *all* the countries, of course. Some of them were far too small, and anyway, he'd have had no time to himself.

Satisfied that the map of the world was now in enough pieces to keep a small child occupied for a reasonable time – *half-an-hour at least,* he hoped – he suggested that Rebecca take the home-made jigsaw over to the table and 'put the world back together', hinting that there might be a small, chocolate-type reward when the job was done. So a satisfied dad settled down to a time of quiet, while an animated Rebecca busied herself with her task. No more than *five minutes* had elapsed when a triumphant Rebecca announced that the job was done.

'How did you get it done so quickly?' an exasperated dad enquired as he examined the finished jigsaw.

'Easy!' Rebecca cried. 'I just turned the pieces over and on the other side there was a picture of a man. When the man was put together right, I knew the world would be OK too.'

*There are two important words in 'human rights' –
'human' and 'rights'.
If you're human, then you have rights,
and upholding these rights shows what matters to humanity.*

June 29 – Faith

'Faith is a recognition of those things
which are above the senses.'
Henry Ward Beecher, Proverbs from Plymouth Pulpit

Be Thou My Vision was my father's favourite hymn. The traditional Gaelic text goes back to the monasteries of 8th-century Ireland. Now sung in English to the Irish folk tune *Slane*, this hymn has sustained many people in trying times. My father didn't talk much about his faith. But in an unguarded moment while watching *Songs of Praise* on TV he told me that *Be Thou My Vision* had been very important to him during the war. That's all he said. Could it be these stanzas that sustained him through his own trying times?

> *Be thou my vision, O Lord of my heart,*
> *Naught be all else to me, save that thou art;*
> *Thou my best thought by day or by night,*
> *Waking or sleeping, thy presence my light.*
>
> *Be thou my battle-shield, sword for the fight;*
> *Be thou my dignity, thou my delight;*
> *Thou my soul's shelter, thou my high tower:*
> *Raise thou me heavenward, O Power of my power.*

Somewhere in the heart of a good Scottish Christian man, as uncommunicative about his beliefs as he was about his war experiences, there was the certainty of Faith. Whatever battle had to be faced, physical, emotional or spiritual, there would always be a guiding light and a shelter for his soul. He didn't need to explain. The words of the hymn communicated everything. We sang *Be Thou My Vision* at my father's funeral – because it said it all.

A vision above the senses; a faith beyond explanation.

June 30 – Redemption

'Though our works
Find righteous or unrighteous judgment, this
At least is ours, to make them righteous.'
Algernon Charles Swinburne, Marino Faliero

In an East Lothian church, hanging beneath the light above the chancel and communion table, there is the apparently out-of-place sign of a pawnbroker's shop – three brass spheres.

The three-sphere symbol has been recognised as the signage of the pawnbroker for generations. It is linked with the Medici family of Florence, Italy, and to the Italian province of Lombardy where pawnshop banking originated under the name of Lombard banking. The three golden spheres were a symbol medieval merchants hung in front of their houses, which may have originally been three flat yellow effigies of gold coins converted into spheres to better attract attention.

According to legend, a Medici employed by Charlemagne slew a giant using three bags of rocks. The three-ball symbol became the family crest. Since the Medicis were so successful in the financial, banking and money-lending industries, other families also adopted the symbol.

But why does it appear in a church? Not to indicate a concentration on money-lending, usury or banking of any kind, but because the symbol comes from the Church's understanding of redemption – fundamental to the pawnbroker's purpose and to the Church's message. In love, we are bought back, the Church believes – given a fresh beginning. No one is beyond redemption. Everyone, through love, has a second chance. We need no longer languish in the pawnbroker's, when there is always the offer of redemption.

*Let's throw all our bags of love
at the giants of judgement and rejection.*

July 1 – Unique

'I was not designed to be forced.
I will breathe after my own fashion.'
Henry David Thoreau, On the Duty of Civil Disobedience

In *Animal Farm* George Orwell offers an allegorical account of the animals taking over the farm. They dream of a world where all animals are equal and all property shared. But the pigs take control and one of them, Napoleon, becomes leader. There had been seven rules for a fair society. The seventh was, 'All animals are equal.' But, one by one, the principles of the revolution are abandoned until the animals have even less freedom than before. The pigs learn to walk upright; they carry whips and wear clothes. When the other animals begin to question whether they are any better off with this new hierarchy, they are told that the seven commandments have been reduced to one maxim: 'All animals are equal, but some animals are more equal than others.'

In our concerns for an equitable human society, we do well to hold to the animals' seventh commandment: 'All people are equal.' But how quickly is added 'but some are more equal than others', especially when we find that we may have to relinquish some of our power and control. However, if our mantra were to be, 'All people are unique,' then we might also add with justification, '... and some are more unique than others.' In other words, let's celebrate the diversity, colour and vibrancy of our communities. A friend who had cerebral palsy said to me, 'Let's stop talking about "dis-abled" people, and talk about "differently-able people". That way *everyone's* abilities are valued.'

'All people are equal.' Of course! But if we also remember that 'All people are unique', we might begin with valuing everyone in a healthier and fairer way.

What do you value most in your uniqueness?

July 2 – Child of the universe

'If we could destroy custom at a blow and see the stars
as a child sees them, we would need no other apocalypse.'
GK Chesterton, A Defence of Baby-Worship

In Latin, *Desiderata* means 'things that are desired'. In 1927 the American writer Max Ehrmann published a poem called *Desiderata*. Around 1959, Reverend Frederick Kates, rector of St Paul's Church in Baltimore, Maryland, included the *Desiderata* in a compilation of devotional material for his congregation. Such was its style and language that it was mistakenly thought that its origins went back several hundred years. But these beautiful words are Ehrmann's own. Adlai Stevenson, JF Kennedy's ambassador to the UN, had a copy of the *Desiderata* near his bedside. From the 1960s onwards the *Desiderata* has given inspiration and hope to many. You'll read the full text in a few days' time. But for now, think on this advice:

Beyond a wholesome discipline, be gentle with yourself.
You are a child of the universe, no less than the trees and the stars;
you have a right to be here.

In school I wrote my *full* address on my notebook:

99 Kilmallie Road, Coal, Fort William, Inverness-shire, Scotland,
United Kingdom, Europe, The World, The Solar System,
The Milky Way, Space, The Universe

Even aged seven something had been instilled in me that my place in the scheme of things was not confined to my own back yard or the limitations of my own surroundings. I was a child of the universe – a small but significant part of a wonderful whole.

If I am a child of the universe, that means you are too …

July 3 – Bending history

'We cannot escape history.'
Abraham Lincoln, Annual message, December 1862

'History-bending' is a concept that pops up from time to time in theological thinking. It's used as a snappy label on how a Christian should relate to the world around them. The Christian, it's said, is the one who can and should 'bend history', to create new possibilities in life out of the events, experiences and lessons of the past, to shape the opportunities yet to come. History-bending means history-making; history-making is about creating a new and wonderful future out of material from the past.

Well, that's as maybe. But if the Reverend Rowland Hill, pastor of Surrey Chapel in London, could say in 1844 'The devil should not have all the best tunes' (often *mis*quoted and variously attributed to Charles Wesley, Martin Luther, General William Booth, John Newton and Isaac Watts) I would suggest that, 'Christian theologians should not have all the best ideas.' Of course there are familiar concepts enshrined in Christian teaching – love your neighbour; turn the other cheek; feed the hungry; be fair in your dealings with others. But are these not universal truths all should live by if we are to have a just and equitable society – whatever our religious beliefs?

So it is with the concept of bending history. I have found myself on many occasions working with people who felt they were of no value, added nothing to society, left nothing behind. Time and again I shared with them the concept of 'bending history'. With the people around us, the family we share with, the community we are part of, we bend history every day – even in the smallest of ways. What an awesome responsibility; but what a wonderful opportunity.

You'll be bending history today. How best might you do that?

July 4 – Research

'As far as you can, get into the habit of asking yourself
in relation to any action taken by another:
"What is his point of reference here?"
But begin with yourself: examine yourself first.'
Marcus Aurelius, Meditations

In the mid-1970s I used some teaching material produced by the 'Ecumenical Institute' of Chicago in the USA. Enshrined in their material were the three concepts I've already shared – I am unique; I am a child of the universe; I bend history.

There's a story told of a researcher in the 1960s gathering some information around inner-city Chicago. He needs some kids to talk to and finds one lad swinging on a gate. 'Can I ask you some questions?' the researcher asks, clipboard in hand.

'Sure. Go ahead,' replies the kid.

'OK. First, your name. First name's fine.' No reply from the kid. He's thinking. 'Well,' the interviewer prompts, 'who are you?'

'I am unique,' the kid replies.

The researcher scribbles on his sheet. 'OK, then. Where do you live?' No reply from the kid. He's thinking again. Irritated, the interviewer probes, 'Well, are you from around here?'

'I am a child of the universe,' the kid replies.

The researcher scratches his head and decides to have one last go. 'Right, then. What about this? How do you pass the time in your neighbourhood?' No reply. The kid's back in thinking mode. 'Come on. I don't have all day. What do you do with yourself here?'

'I bend history,' the kid replies.

The researcher tears his notes into little pieces and stomps off. The kid continues swinging on the gate. He smiles. He's thinking about a researcher who still has a lot to learn.

If someone did research on you today, what might they find?

July 5 – Things most desired

'The desire accomplished is sweet to the soul.'
Bible: Proverbs 13:19

There's a statue of Max Ehrmann sitting on a park bench in his hometown, Terre Haute, Indiana. On a nearby walkway some lines from his poem, *Desiderata*, can be read.

Max Ehrmann knew his *Desiderata*, the 'things most desired' such as uniqueness, being a child of the universe and bending history. Here is the first part of this inspiring piece:

> *Go placidly amidst the noise and haste,*
> *and remember what peace there may be in silence.*
> *As far as possible, without surrender,*
> *be on good terms with all persons.*
> *Speak your truth quietly and clearly;*
> *and listen to others, even the dull and the ignorant;*
> *they too have their story.*
> *Avoid loud and aggressive persons,*
> *they are vexations to the spirit.*
> *If you compare yourself with others,*
> *you may become vain or bitter;*
> *for always there will be*
> *greater and lesser persons than yourself.*
> *Enjoy your achievements as well as your plans.*
> *Keep interested in your own career, however humble;*
> *it is a real possession in the changing fortunes of time.*
> *Exercise caution in your business affairs;*
> *for the world is full of trickery.*
> *But let this not blind you to what virtue there is;*
> *many persons strive for high ideals;*
> *and everywhere life is full of heroism.*

July 6 – Be yourself

'Abstinence sows sand all over
The ruddy limbs and flaming hair,
But Desire gratified
Plants fruits of life and beauty there.'
William Blake, Gnomic Verses

Max Ehrmann's *Desiderata* continues in this fashion:

Be yourself. Especially, do not feign affection.
Neither be cynical about love;
for in the face of all aridity and disenchantment
it is as perennial as the grass.
Take kindly the counsel of the years,
gracefully surrendering the things of youth.
Nurture strength of spirit to shield you in sudden misfortune.
But do not distress yourself with dark imaginings.
Many fears are born of fatigue and loneliness.
Beyond a wholesome discipline, be gentle with yourself.
You are a child of the universe,
no less than the trees and the stars;
you have a right to be here.
And whether or not it is clear to you,
no doubt the universe is unfolding as it should.
Therefore be at peace with God,
whatever you conceive Him to be,
and whatever your labours and aspirations,
in the noisy confusion of life
keep peace with your soul.
With all its sham, drudgery, and broken dreams,
it is still a beautiful world.
Be cheerful. Strive to be happy.

July 7 – Riding shotgun

'Who can hope to be safe, who sufficiently cautious?
Guard himself as he may, every moment's an ambush.'
Horace, Roman lyric poet

When my children were young, but old enough to ride in the front of our car, there always seemed to be an argument about who was to sit in the seat beside the driver. (*Both* parents together, of course, sat in the front. Well, it's one of the privileges of parenting, isn't it?) One day as I was taking the children somewhere on my own, the opening pitch to sit in the front seat came from my son – before we'd even left the house! 'Bags I ride shotgun!' he declared. *Shotgun*? What was this definition of riding in the front beside dad? Were we going to be ambushed at the Pass as we turned into the High Street? Did we need protection from a sharp-shooter as we parked in the shopping precinct? Of course not, but, nonetheless, it became common parlance in the family. There were even rules attached, like: 'You can't declare "shotgun" till the car is in sight.' Oh, the joys of family life …

The phrase 'riding shotgun' comes, of course, from the era when stagecoaches and wagons in the Old West were in danger of being attacked by bandits. Especially when there was bullion or cash aboard, the driver would have an armed guard who, with a rifle or shotgun, could provide a protective response if marauding bandits appeared.

'Riding shotgun' – synonymous with someone beside you in time of trouble or danger. I like that idea, because I'm happy to have my son beside me at *any* time – and not just in the car. He's just the kind of guy you need up front with you when times are tough …

Who rides shotgun for me today?
And who needs me to ride shotgun for them?

July 8 – Caring

'The only gift is a portion of thyself.'
Ralph Waldo Emerson, Gifts

How quick we are to judge people by appearances – the scruffy student; the posh duchess; the leather-clad biker ...

I watched an elderly lady trip and fall outside a supermarket. Her shopping spilled from her bags and rolled hither and thither. I was too slow to get there to help. I was beaten by a punk! He had more metal piercings than a hardware shop. You could cut yourself on his Mohican haircut. But he got there before anyone else. He helped the old lady to her feet, gathered up her shopping, sat with her on a bench until she'd regained her composure and carried her bags across the road when she was ready. Punks! What good are they? What good indeed?

You may not know me, but I have something to share...
You may not like me, but I have something so rare...
You may not want me, but I have something that's new...
You may not need me, but I have something for you.

For when you know me, you'll find the something I share...
And when you like me, you'll find the something so rare...
And when you want me, you'll find the something that's new...
And when you need me, you'll find the something's for you.

So, now you know me, you'll feel the living I share...
And when you like me, you'll find compassion so rare...
And if you want me, you'll know commitment that's new...
I know you'll need me, so I'll give my loving to you.

From A Blessing to Follow *by Tom Gordon,*
Wild Goose Publications, 2009

July 9 – Good health

'Greet one another with a kiss of love.'
Bible: 1 Peter 5:14

For those who might be puzzled by the obscure word which begins our thought for today, *Slainthe* is a Scots Gaelic greeting or toast. Pronounced *slanj*, it means 'health', and its expected response is '*slanj-a-va*', or 'good health', in return.

All cultures and languages have their usual form of greeting or toast. Some of us might be familiar with 'Cheers!', 'Bottoms up', 'Down the hatch'. But most toasts are like *Slainthe* and offer wishes of good health to the recipients. *Na zdravje* (Health) is used in Slovenia; *Prost* (May it be good for you) in Germany; *Egészségünkre* (For your health) is Hungarian; *Iechyd da* (For your health) is the Welsh toast; and so it goes on ...

Greetings are important. A toast or a simple expression of welcome or good wishes communicates that we want a blessing of health and happiness to come the way of those we meet. It shows that we are social beings, wishing for others what we would hope for ourselves.

I often think it's a pity that, social beings that we are, we pass one another as we go about our business and don't wish each other well. The dog-walker you pass in the park, who doesn't offer a simple 'good morning', and neither do you; the folk who stand with you waiting to cross the street, and not a word is exchanged; the work colleague you pass in the corridor with whom you don't even have eye contact. Are we too worried that we might be accused of invading someone's space, or breaking into their private world? But it doesn't need a full-blown *Slainthe*. Maybe a simple 'hello' might be a useful beginning.

Good health starts from the inside
and works outwards.

July 10 – Harmony

'Music is an agreeable harmony for the honour of God
and the permissible delights of the soul.'
Attributed to Johann Sebastian Bach

My wife is the musical one in our house. So when I asked her, 'What is harmony?' she handed me a book and suggested I look it up. Here's what I found in *The Grove Concise Dictionary of Music*.

Harmony is the combining of notes simultaneously to produce chords, and their successive use to produce chord progression ... Harmony is sometimes seen as the 'opposite' to counterpoint because it primarily operates vertically whereas counterpoint seems to operate horizontally.

Well, that may be right. But what I know from my musical ear rather than my musical knowledge is that harmony *sounds* good. It's comfortable on the ear. The balance between the tune and those notes above or below it just *feels* right. The tune's good on its own, of course. Melody matters! But when harmony is put around it, special things happen. Whether it's the close harmonisation of 'barbershop' or 'shape note' music, the free harmonies of Gaelic psalm singing or traditional African chants, or the full orchestration of a Tchaikovsky or a Beethoven, we know harmony works because it works. Our ear tells us it's right.

We know harmony works too in social relationships, community cohesion, tribal disputes and national tensions. When different voices feel only they have the right tune, and their tune is better than everyone else's, there is no harmony, only dissonance – uncomfortable on the ear, creating anger and aggression. But when relationships are harmonious and one 'line' listens to and complements the others, then everyone benefits.

*Why confine ourselves to the horizontal
when we can rise vertically as well.*

July 11 – Back-up

'Back up my computer? But it doesn't even have a
forward gear, far less a reverse ...'
From an IT helpline customer

I've learned about the need for back-up the hard way. In the early
days of word processors, I'd only just transferred from the
mechanical typewriter to the fancy 'computer' device. It suited my
writing perfectly. I could get material 'down on paper' before
editing it into its final form and printing it off. I had just finished
the first draft of a sermon when there was a power cut. I hadn't
backed up the material and in an instant I lost four hours' work.

You'd think I would have learned my lesson. Well, I did to an
extent. When I'm working on material nowadays on my PC, I back
it up as I go along. But what I *wasn't* prepared for was my computer
crashing! It got infected by a virus, and the whole thing 'went
down'. Fortunately, some very clever techie-people at my local
computer shop were able to rescue most of my work. But I'll never
forget the feeling of horror when I thought I'd lost everything. I'll
also never forget their salutary advice: 'Get a back-up system.'

Not everything can be backed up in that way, of course. Com-
puters are one thing, precious moments are another. One
approach is to ensure that at an important time in our lives, in a
significant place or at a special event, we make an effort to notice
things, to absorb the atmosphere, be aware of the surroundings
and people and recognise our own feelings and thoughts. Too
often we rush on without taking time for this. So why not create
your own back-up? You never know when you might need it.

If we pause and absorb what's necessary,
if we have all the back-up we need,
we can draw upon it when life's software has a glitch.

July 12 – Preparations again

'Be prepared.'
Motto of the Scout movement

'Measure twice; cook once,' my friend tells me. In her view preparation is *twice* as important as doing. Checking, measuring and clarifying properly before you cook anything at all is sound common sense and, no doubt, helps avoid culinary disasters.

I've not always been the best at preparations. When I was young, I did some running. One day, ready for a training run, I skipped my usual warm-up and off I went, pounding the pavements. I'd only gone about half a mile when I felt a twinge in my right calf. My training run had to be curtailed because I was in pain. I'd damaged my leg – because I hadn't prepared properly. It was two weeks before I could run again – and all because I'd skimped on my preparations.

When St Paul began working with a young evangelist called Timothy, he had a keen companion, and Timothy had a wise and experienced mentor and guide. When Timothy was let loose without supervision, could he do so without preparation? Not a chance! Imagine what damage Timothy could have done to the fledgling Christian communities of the early Church. 'Measure twice, cook once, young Timothy,' Paul might have said. 'Get your preparations right, and good things will surely follow.'

In his second letter to Timothy, he puts it this way:

Do your best to present yourself to God as one approved, a worker who does not need to be ashamed and who correctly handles the word of truth. Avoid godless chatter, because those who indulge in it will become more and more ungodly ... Flee the evil desires of youth and pursue righteousness, faith, love and peace, along with those who call on the Lord out of a pure heart.

July 13 – Evenings

'Good things of day begin to droop and drowse.'
William Shakespeare, Macbeth

The hymn 'The day Thou gavest, Lord, is ended' was written by the minister-poet John Ellerton. Seventy-six of his hymns were published in 1888 as *Hymns, Original and Translated.* Honesty, simplicity and reverence were Ellerton's hallmarks. It was said of him, 'No writer was ever more careful not to put on the lips of a congregation words which they could not make their own.'

> *The day Thou gavest, Lord, is ended,*
> *The darkness falls at Thy behest;*
> *To Thee our morning hymns ascended,*
> *Thy praise shall sanctify our rest.*
>
> *As o'er each continent and island*
> *The dawn leads on another day,*
> *The voice of prayer is never silent,*
> *Nor dies the strain of praise away.*

Originally a missionary hymn, Ellerton's words were later adapted for evening worship. Set to Clement Cotterill Scolefield's melody, *St Clement,* it has brought solace to many. Queen Victoria chose it to be sung throughout the land during her Diamond Jubilee in 1897. For me, it is the concept of perpetual praise and prayer that is the greatest encouragement. While I rest, others will offer praise; when I have no praise, others will sing for me; and if I'm in a barren place, others will say my prayers.

> *'The voice of prayer is never silent,*
> *nor dies the strain of praise away.'*
> *Thank God!*

July 14 – Dreams

'I have spread my dreams under your feet.
Tread softly, because you tread on my dreams.'

WB Yeats, He Wishes for the Cloths of Heaven

Some years ago I was puzzled by a recurrent dream. The details changed, but the core of it remained the same. It always had a beginning, middle and end. And I had no idea what it meant.

The scene is a street in the village where I was brought up, a winding street, with shops on one side and a green sward bordering the sea on the other. I'm driving a big car, a large version of a Morris Minor Estate, complete with wooden frame and doors at the back. As I'm negotiating the bendy road, I swing the car round a tight corner and the doors at the back burst open, spilling the contents onto the road. I pull the car over to retrieve the boxes. But instead of bundling them back into the car, I go through them one by one, keeping the things I want and discarding the rest. Eventually, what I need is packed into the car and I close the doors and drive off.

It wasn't disturbing. But I was puzzled. Then I got it! The car – the big, green estate car – was the one I learned to drive in. I wasn't *supposed* to be learning to drive – I was only fifteen. But the big car sat in the parking-lot of the petrol station where I worked on Saturdays. And the keys were in it, and the boss wasn't there at lunchtime ... The village? I was back where I'd grown up ... The boxes in the back? Stuff I'd accumulated through the years ... Things to leave behind? Clearly I had some sorting to do ...

I'm not a dream analyst, but figuring this one out has helped. I needed to make some decisions about what mattered to me and what didn't as I faced the future. And I still have some of that sorting to do ...

Dreams have a way of uncovering our hidden agendas.

July 15 – More sleep

'What means this heaviness that hangs upon me?'
Joseph Addison, Cato: A Tragedy

There's a story told of a little boy who went to church every Sunday with his grandfather, and every Sunday grandfather fell asleep during the sermon. The minister was concerned about this and the detrimental effect it would have on his reputation as a preacher. So he took the child aside one Sunday and whispered, 'When you come to church next week ... if I promise to give you £1, will you promise to keep your grandfather awake?' The deal was struck, and the next Sunday the minister slipped the boy £1 and, sure enough, grandfather was awake through the whole sermon. The next Sunday, £1 changed hands and grandfather was wide awake. The next Sunday, £1, and grandfather awake. The next Sunday, £1, and ... grandfather was fast asleep again. The minister was furious that the little boy was not doing his job and was now taking money under false pretences. So he took the child aside after the service. 'Listen,' he said, 'I thought we had a deal. I give you £1, and you keep your grandfather awake. Isn't that right?' 'I know,' replied the boy, 'but on our way to church today grandfather promised he'd give me a fiver if I let him sleep.'

There was a man in one of my congregations who fell asleep during every sermon I ever preached. I never asked him why. He might have said he was closing his eyes so that he could concentrate on my preaching. Maybe he thought my sermons were terrible, or perhaps he just needed his rest. In any event it probably did him the world of good. For, after all, does God not promise us rest and renewal, and the odd revelation of his word, even when the preacher is boring you to sleep?

'There is a time for many words, and there is also a time for sleep.'
Homer

July 16 – Pandora's Box

'Be careful what you wish for!'
Anonymous

The story of Pandora's Box originates from a Greek myth. Because of his anger at the trickery of Prometheus, Zeus, the chief god, devised an evil plan. He had the gods create an artificial woman, Pandora, who was so lifelike that Epimetheus, the brother of Prometheus, fell in love with her. Pleased that his trap was going well, Zeus gave Pandora a beautiful box as a wedding gift, with one condition – she was never to open it.

For a while Epimetheus and Pandora were happy. But Pandora began to wonder more and more what was in the box. She couldn't understand why someone would give her a box if she couldn't see what was in it. Finally she could stand it no longer and one day took the huge key, fitted it carefully into the lock and turned it. She lifted the lid to peep in but before she realised it the room was filled with terrible things: disease, despair, malice, greed, old age, death, hatred, violence, cruelty and war. She slammed the lid down and turned the key again ... keeping only the spirit of hope inside. Pandora's Box had been opened, but she had released into her world badness never experienced before. Zeus had got his way.

When Ernest Bevin was talking about the Council of Europe, he said, 'If you open that Pandora's Box, you never know what Trojan horses will jump out.' Bevin may have been guilty of mixing his metaphors – or even his Greek myths – but he offers an important warning about delving into Pandora's Boxes. Think about what might be in a Pandora's Box before you delve inside. You might not be able to control all that tumbles out. And the thing you need, hope for the future, might still be trapped inside.

If you open a box, make sure you can cope with what's inside.

July 17 – Silence

'Silence is one great art of conversation.'
William Hazlitt, Characteristics

I was in a public library recently for the first time in a while and I couldn't believe the noise. It wasn't *loud* noise like a pneumatic drill or a brass band, but it was noise nonetheless. A customer was talking *loudly* to the librarian, and not being told to 'Shush!' A mum was reading *loudly* to a child, next to where I was sitting. I moved seats, but two teenagers were discussing their homework – *loudly!* I looked around for big notices that insisted on SILENCE. But there weren't any. Libraries don't seem to demand that any more. And I'd only popped in for a bit of peace and quiet …

We seem to be surrounded by noise these days. Maybe I'm developing grumpy-old-man tendencies. But it seems to be getting worse – canned music in hotel toilets; the 'thump thump' from a passing car stereo; 'special offer' announcements in supermarkets. Oh, how I yearn for silence.

When the prophet Elijah was trying to work out what was right for him, he was having a bit of a struggle with God (1 Kings 19:11-13). At one point he finds himself on a mountain and he knows God is there. He just *knows* … But he can't work it out. There is a great wind and the rocks around him are smashed to bits – *loudly,* no doubt. But God's voice isn't in the wind. Then there is an earthquake, and the ground shakes – *loudly,* I suspect. But God's voice isn't in the earthquake. Then there is a fire, roaring *loudly,* for sure. But God's voice isn't in the fire. And then there is … silence. And Elijah hears God in 'a still, small voice'.

> *Could it be that when we crave for silence*
> *we are trying to listen to God?*
> *Could it be that when we eventually find it,*
> *God is waiting to speak?*

July 18 – Nnyyaaah!

'The good that I would, I do not:
but the evil which I would not, that I do.'
Bible: Romans 7:9

I was trying to find a parking space in one of those broad streets where cars are parked not only on the sides of the road but also in the centre, perpendicular to the traffic flow. It's all parking meters, of course, and although the limit is only an hour, finding a place as you drive along is like finding a fleck of gold on a sandy beach. I'd gone round the block, up and down, half a dozen times with no gold-dust appearing, when I saw a car pulling out of a space several cars away. I put my foot down and arrived at the vacated space just in time. Or, at least, I thought so … Because as I turned in from *my* side of the street, another driver was heading into the space *from the other side*. It was touch and go. There was no more than an inch or two in it. There was much eye-to-eye glaring. Who was going to blink first? It was the *other* driver, thankfully, who, shaking her head, backed down and reversed out of the space. I had done it! The space was mine! I was so elated, that all common courtesy, human sensitivity and Christian charity deserted me, and I mouthed, 'Nnyyaaah!' I think I pulled a face too, but as the car windows were closed and the other driver was too busy concentrating on reversing, my rudeness wasn't noticed.

What came over me? 'Nnyyaaah', indeed. And all because of a parking space. Yet badness took over even when I didn't want it to! Such is the way of things. St Paul knew that when he wrote to the Christians in Rome. Despite ourselves, 'Nnyyaaah' comes out when we don't want it to! A little bit more awareness next time maybe? Oh, *and* a sorry to the driver I did out of a parking place …

Might it be that the good I should do I don't do because …
I want to keep the good all to myself?

July 19 – Blessed

'Blessings star forth forever;
but a curse is like a cloud – it passes.'
Philip James Bailey, Festus

'Count your blessings' the old hymn tells us. Well, I do – often.
When I originally wrote what follows it was all about 'you' –
'You're blessed ...' and so on. But then I realised that it's actually
about *me*. If I know my blessings, shouldn't I count them too?

I'm blessed when I love,
and I'm loved when I'm blessed.

I'm healed when I'm blessed,
and I bless when I heal.

I'm blessed when I serve,
and I'm served when I'm blessed.

I'm forgiven when I'm blessed,
and I bless when I forgive.

I'm blessed when I seek peace,
and I know peace when I'm blessed.

I'm made new when I'm blessed,
and my blessings make things new.

I'm blessed when I'm great,
and I'm the greatest when I'm blessed.

Adapted from 'Blessed', *first published in* Welcoming Each Wonder
by Tom Gordon, Wild Goose Publications, 2010

July 20 – Commitment

'Never promise more than you can perform.'
Publilius Syrus

My mother and grandmother were converts at the Billy Graham rallies in the Kelvin Hall in Glasgow in the 1950s. It sounds dramatic now, especially to those who are familiar with those times and the work of Billy Graham. Actually, it is a moot point whether my mother and grandmother were converted at all! They both had a faith. My grandmother had learned her faith with her siblings from her own mother, and it had sustained her through tough times. My mother had been nurtured by my grandmother, and both of them found solace and comfort in a firm structure of beliefs and worship, and a support for one another in their shared Christian understanding.

Was going forward at an evangelist's rally a conversion to faith? It was certainly a new beginning, and a defining moment for both of them, one they talked of and drew strength from often as the years went by. But a conversion, as if nothing had mattered before? I don't think so. I'm more inclined to see their experience at the Billy Graham crusades for what it was – a moment of *re*commitment, an opportunity for public expression of what mattered, drawn from the past and projected into the future of faith. It was a definition of purpose from then on; an indicator of a possible direction in a journey of commitment. In that sense it really mattered to both of them. But it was one commitment among many, one moment of definition which took its place among others over the years, one expression of purpose which would be renewed again and again as life continued.

Commitment is important,
not just once in a while or once and for all,
but over and over again!

July 21 – Acceptance again

'Belief consists in accepting the affirmations of the soul;
Unbelief, in denying them.'
Ralph Waldo Emerson, Collected Works

'A friend is someone who knows all about you and still loves you.'
So ran a poster I had in my study for many years as a permanent
reminder of the true meaning of friendship. There are times when
we are, at the very least, puzzled and, at the very worst, repulsed
by what we get to know about people – from irritating habits to
disturbing personalities, from annoying character traits to mani-
festations of evil – so that it is genuinely hard to love some people
when we come know the whole person.

But which of us is perfect? Don't we all have faults that we hope
will be understood and accepted as part of who we are? If we are
judged only by our faults and failings, we won't have much of a
chance. But if we are accepted as we are, then there is a possibility
of finding what love means.

The German theologian Paul Tillich, a world-renowned writer
and teacher, sought to distil his beliefs into one idea. A chapter in
his *The Shaking of the Foundations* is headed 'I am accepted'. For
Tillich that was the crux of it. In relationships, the 'God' dimension, the purpose of living and the whole area of self-awareness,
'I am accepted' summed up everything.

If we come to know friendship because someone loves us as
we are, even when they know all about us, can we love ourselves
in the same way? If we can, don't we have a glimpse of a divine
acceptance as well?

Being at peace with yourself begins with
the balanced acceptance
of your present experience.
Why would you complicate it more than that?

July 22 – Understanding

'The aim of art is to represent
not the outward appearance of things,
but their inward significance.'
Aristotle

I went to collect my daughter from nursery school. The children had been doing their usual activities, and the final one had been at the painting table. I knew this because my daughter had multi-coloured fingers and a fetching green streak on her forehead.

This was confirmed by her excited squeal: 'Daddy, I've painted a picture for you.' 'Well done,' I replied, but she had already gone, rushing over to the painting table to retrieve her masterpiece. Within seconds she'd returned with a large, still-wet picture which was a riot of colour, but, to my eye, had no shape or form. Holding the picture at arm's length I studied it and with furrowed brow enquired, 'What's this?'

Just then, one of the nursery assistants – a good friend, as it happened – came over and, putting an arm round my shoulders, whispered, 'Can I have a word with you, Mr Gordon?' Taking me into a corner she offered me the best lesson in childcare I've ever had. 'Never ask a child "What's that?" ' she said, 'because that's a judgement and tells the child you don't understand. Better to say, "Tell me what's happening in your picture," or "What's the story of your painting?" Then you'll show that you want to learn more.'

I had nothing to say. So I went back to my daughter and, turning the painting towards her, said, 'What's happening in your painting today?' 'Oh daddy, it's a zoo,' she said excitedly, 'and there's the giraffe under the trees, and a lion in the bushes, and a penguin on the rocks ...' And she smiled the biggest smile you could imagine.

Ask 'What's happening?' and you might be interested in the answer.

July 23 – Peace

'The most disadvantageous peace
is better than the most just war.'
Erasmus, Adagia

The late Pope Paul VI wrote this:

*If we wish to have true peace, we must give it a soul. The soul
of peace is love. It is love that gives life to peace, more than victory or defeat, more than self-interest or fear or weariness or
need. The soul of peace is love, which for us believers comes
from the love of God and expresses itself in love for all people.*

Peace is not a decision of the head but an affair of the heart. When
heart speaks to heart – between nations, communities and individuals – how can peace not be found?

Thankfully, such sentiments are not new. There is much we
can learn from past wisdom. *In A Declaration from the Harmless
and Innocent People of God, Called Quakers,* presented to King
Charles II in 1660, there is this remarkably modern and admirable
sentiment:

*We utterly deny all outwards wars and strife and fighting with
outward weapons for any end, or under any pretence whatever;
this is our testimony to the whole world. The Spirit of Christ
by which we are guided is not changeable, so as once to command us from a thing of evil, and again to move into it; and we
certainly know, and testify to the world, that the Spirit of Christ
which leads us into all truth, will never move us to fight any
war against any man with outward weapons, neither for the
kingdom of Christ, nor for the kingdom of the world.*

July 24 – Co-operation

'We're all in this together.'
World War II English proverb

I met Nazar on a visit to Israel. He endeared himself to me and my colleagues through his ready smile, unfailing courtesy and willingness to engage in interesting discussions. Nazar was a Muslim, and, not surprisingly, conversations often turned to the tensions of Israel and Palestine, and the relationships among Jews, Muslims and Christians in the Middle East.

In a cafe one day Nazar told me of work he had done in his younger years. He had been a basketball-player who'd represented his country at under-21 level, but when injury prevented him from developing his career further, he turned to coaching. With obvious pride, he explained that he'd been instrumental in creating a team of talented young people, Jews and Muslims together, who, through sport and playing in the same team, could learn about co-operation, tolerance, reconciliation and much more that ran counter to the prejudice they experienced in their communities. It was a small thing, Nazar continued, but an important one. 'These young men could learn to work and play together and not hate each other. We travelled to Paris for a tournament. And we won the trophy,' he said, smiling broadly.

It is no small thing that this compassionate man did for the young people of his community and his country. They may have won a cup at the end of the tournament, but there were more trophies gained than that. And now I have a trophy too – the influence of a compassionate Palestinian Muslim on my own life.

Alone, we might struggle to achieve much.
Together, we can change the world.

July 25 – More achievement

'We judge ourselves by what we feel capable of doing,
while others judge us by what we have already done.'
Henry Wadsworth Longfellow, Kavanagh, A Tale

'She sells sea shells on the sea shore' is a well known tongue-twister. But it has its origins not just in a clever play on words but in the life of a remarkable Dorset woman. In 1811 a Lyme Regis fossil hunter, Mary Anning, then aged 12, unearthed, with her older brother Joseph, the skull of an ichthyosaur. The intrepid child spent a year extracting the 2m long dinosaur fossil from the 205-million-year-old Blue Lias cliffs. It remains one of the most famous of geological finds on what is known as the Jurassic Coast.

It began a remarkable legacy of pioneering work in fossil collection and identification – hence the 'sea-shells on the sea shore' rhyme – which still inspires many of today's experts. If she lived now, Mary Anning would be recognised as a world-renowned palaeontologist. Yet she was never credited as a scientist, for while she had great dedication and no little skill, this self-educated woman had two things which legislated against the recognition she deserved: firstly, she was a woman; and, secondly, she was a working-class child from the 'poor' side of town. Consequently, in a society dominated by wealthy men, her sex and social class prevented her from being accepted by the scientific community of Britain of the early 19th century.

Mary Anning was famous for the fossils she found and identified. What a tragedy that, even now, fossils of a different kind still prevent women being recognised for their full worth and value and also exhibit prejudice against those who are deemed to come from the 'wrong' strata of society. I know what fossils I value, and I know the ones I would throw back into the sea.

Value achievement, no matter the source.

July 26 – Instructions

'If everything else fails, read the instructions.'
Anonymous

I'm not particularly good with instructions. I'll unpack a box of self-assembly furniture, have a quick look at the instruction sheet, decide it's straightforward and bash on without much thought. Usually it's OK ... but sometimes it ends up taking *twice* as long as it should, and there are several screws and pieces of dowelling left over. If only I'd followed the instructions.

When my elder grandson was two years old, we were determined not to put all our ornaments out of reach just because some of them happened to be at eye level for a toddler. What happened? He picked up a porcelain bird and bashed it on the table – and broke the beak off! He'd been *told* not to touch! If only he'd followed the instructions.

We're surrounded by instructions all the time – do this; don't go there; cross now; open this end; type this password; press here; don't run; enter; push; danger ... and so it goes on. Our lives seem to be governed by instructions. Follow them, and all will be well; get them wrong, and you're in trouble.

Jesus said, 'Love your God with all your heart, and mind, and soul and strength; and love your neighbour as yourself.' There's an instruction! Love your God with everything you have. Give your *all* to what you believe in ... *And* love your neighbour. Give all you have to be at one with those around you, whoever matters most to you. Some instruction! But if we get it right, then all will be *very* well; and if we get it wrong, well, you can just imagine the trouble you'll be in ...

We should not only use the brains we have
but the wisdom we can gain from elsewhere.
That way, we might have double the success.

July 27 – God once more

'The best way of knowing God is to love many things.'
Vincent van Gogh, Letter to Theo van Gogh

I've already shared with you two images of God – the supportive chair and the blanket of knitted squares – which I learned from other people. The question, 'What is God like?' is one that, if handled in a creative way, can bring out new ideas which illustrate the richness of the God people seek to know. But how might I answer my own question?

To de-clutter myself from the complicated teaching I'd absorbed over the years, I learned to trust what I *feel* rather than what I know, and to work outwards from there. I've come to value my 'God moments', small moments of wonder, mystery, beauty, holiness, and much more, sometimes small in duration but huge in significance.

So, my picture of God? Well, it's as if God lives somewhere just over my shoulder, out of sight, and, if I'm honest, ignored most of the time. Then, when I least expect it – but, also, when I clearly need it – I feel a tap on my shoulder, a gentle, almost imperceptible touch, and I am aware of something there. So I turn, and I am reminded that I am still in the presence of wonder and mystery. I smile in recognition, and turn back to what I am involved with. It is enough. It is always enough!

> *May the road rise up to meet you*
> *and the wind be always at your back.*
> *May the sun shine warm upon your face*
> *and the rain fall soft upon your fields.*
> *And, until we meet again,*
> *may your God hold you*
> *in the palm of his hand.*
> Irish blessing

July 28 – Inspiration

'A breath of our inspiration
Is the life of each generation;
A wondrous thing of our dreaming
Unearthly, impossible seeming ...'

Arthur O'Shaughnessy, Music and Moonlight

As I shared with you earlier, the blind German social worker Sabriye Tenberken was so inspired by *Touch the Top of the World*, the account by the blind mountaineer Erik Weihenmayer of his conquering of Everest, that she read the book to the blind Tibetan teenagers in her care. She then wrote to Weihenmayer and said:

When I ended by saying: 'This man, who is blind like you, climbed the top of the world, not by holding the arm of a sighted friend, but with the help of some strings and two canes', they all proudly decided to walk on their own, without walking with the sighted. Stories like yours change their lives. Most of them now understand there is nothing to be embarrassed about. They can be proud little people and say: 'We are blind, so what? We can speak English and Chinese, we can find our way in the labyrinth of Lhasa's walkways, we are able to read and write in three different Braille scripts and we read and write without using light.'

The result was a remarkable expedition by the students to the top of the 23,000-foot Mount Lhakapa in 2006. These young people, although rejected and considered demon-possessed in their blindness, had been, in Tenberken's classroom, inspired to climb to unimaginable heights because someone believed in them. The impossible became possible before anyone set foot on a mountain.

'Stories like yours change their lives.' What's our story got to say?

July 29 – Temptation

'Get thee behind me, Satan!'
Bible: Matthew 16:23

I love the tune of the hymn 'Yield not to temptation' by Horatio R Palmer. Palmer was an American musician from the second half of the 19th century. While he was working on a music theory exercise one day, the idea for this hymn suddenly came to him. He wrote it down quickly and, with a few exceptions, the hymn has remained as it was written. Palmer also wrote the music, and called the tune 'Palmer'.

Now, I hope this isn't too disrespectful, but I don't like the words much. They're a bit too old-fashioned for me. So I've penned a few of my own. Keep Palmer's tune in your head as you follow my version of 'The temptation song'. After all, it's dealing with temptations that matters and not how it's expressed!

'Yield not to temptation!' That's easy to say!
Much harder to practise when you're led astray
By many temptations – some worse than the rest!
'Yield not to temptation!' Help, I'm failing the test!

'Yield not to temptation!' Please God, hear my cry –
I'm useless, no matter how hard I might try…
You know there is nothing (Here's a quote from the shelf …)
I cannot resist except temptation itself.

'Yield not to temptation!' I'm at my wits' end!
So, choose from your mercy some blessing to send
This poor, hapless sinner! Please help me again!
'Yield not to temptation!' Quick! I need you! Amen!

From A Blessing to Follow *by Tom Gordon,*
Wild Goose Publications, 2009

July 30 – Thin

'God grant that I may never live to be useless!'
John Wesley, How to pray: The best of John Wesley on Prayer

George MacLeod, the founder of the Iona Community, often described Iona as a 'thin place'. In a moment you could be taken from the mundane to the special, from the material to the spiritual. Perhaps it's because it's the cradle of Christianity from which St Columba took the Gospel message to Scotland and beyond, and the resting place of Scottish and Irish kings. Maybe it is the beauty of a Hebridean island, its fragility battered by the Atlantic breakers. Or it's possibly connected to the worship in the Abbey church, or the weekly programme of the Iona Community.

Whatever it is, or whatever combination touches the lives of those who visit or stay, there are countless people who have found a glimpse of holiness, who are taken through the tissue that separates the human and the divine, simply because of what Iona offers. They find the thinness takes them to depths of meaning they have never experienced before. That's why George MacLeod called Iona a 'thin place'.

But I recently heard a different slant on this image. A lady I met said there were people she knew – on Iona and elsewhere – who were 'thin people'. Through them she could see something deeper, beyond the ordinary, a glimpse of holiness, some understanding of the divine. These 'thin people' were vital for her journey of faith, she said, because through their transparency she could see beyond the mundane to something deeper and better.

When we judge people by their body image, and as a result give fat people a hard time, it's good to remember that 'thin people' matter – and not just on the scales.

Where are your 'thin' places,
and who are our genuinely 'thin' people?

July 31 – Ambition

'Most people would succeed in small things
if they were not troubled with great ambitions.'
Henry Wadsworth Longfellow, Driftwood

A small boy came home after playing his first ever game of cricket. His father, knowing how excited the lad had been in preparation for this great occasion, was keen to find out how things had gone.

'Well, how did you get on?' he enquired.

'Terrific, absolutely terrific,' the young boy replied.

'And how many did you score?' his father asked.

'Well, if I had scored another ninety-eight, I would have been the only one in the match to make a century.'

I have no doubt that the boy's ambition would be to score a century. But if he *never* managed to score a hundred, and, indeed, turned out to be a less than adequate cricketer, should his score of two be considered a failure? Ambition is a good thing. To reach high is a laudable quality. But we also need to recognise that we can do well with little things, even when we don't reach dramatic heights.

Edmund Burke was an 18th-century Irish statesman, author, orator, political theorist and philosopher who, after moving to England, was for many years a Whig party MP. In his *Letters on a Regicide Peace*, reflecting on Great Britain's relationship with France and the revolutionary French government, he wrote: 'Ambition can creep as well as soar.' There is nothing wrong with soaring ideals, whether that's to score a century at cricket or any-thing else. But when you have to creep, and score a meagre two runs, might that not be for some people an ambition fulfilled? As a poor cricketer, it would be for me!

It's ambition to reach for the stars.
To reach hearts is life-changing.

August 1 – Trickery

'The craftiest trickery are too short and ragged a cloak
to cover a bad heart.'
Johann Kaspar Lavater, poet and physiognomist

When we have boiled eggs for tea, even when there are no grand-children present, one of us is sure to take an empty eggshell, turn it upside down in the egg-cup and offer it as an uneaten egg. I've been doing it since I was a child. Everyone knows it's a trick, but they enter into the spirit of it anyway – just for a laugh.

Sometimes, however, trickery can venture into the realms of cruelty. In the *Peanuts* cartoons of the late Charles Schultz there are many accounts of the trickery of the bossy Lucy against the naivety of the hapless Charlie Brown. Charlie Brown regularly falls foul of Lucy's tricks. She holds the balls still for Charlie Brown to have a punt at goal. (Like a rugby-ball, a ball in American Football can be held steady to make sure that the punter has a better chance of kicking it well.) And as Charlie Brown runs up to kick, Lucy pulls the ball away and Charlie Brown falls on his bottom. The next time Charlie Brown is wise to the trick. 'You'll pull the ball away and I'll fall in the dirt,' he complains. 'No I won't,' Lucy assures him. So the trusting Charlie Brown has another go, only to find that Lucy tricks him once more and he's lying in the dirt once again. Charlie Brown never learns. He's on the ground more often than he's standing up. Lucy tells him she'll NEVER pull the ball away EVER again. But she always does. Trickery is in her nature as much as trust is in Charlie Brown's.

No one cares much for trickery. Playing tricks for a laugh might be OK. But trickery which is perpetrated to 'do the dirty' or gain an unfair advantage is never acceptable.

Bread of deceit is sweet to a man;
but afterwards his mouth shall be filled with gravel.
Bible: Proverbs 20:17

August 2 – Free?

'What is bought is cheaper than a gift.'
Portuguese proverb

'There's no such thing as a free lunch' is advice worth heeding. What *appears* to be a good deal, especially if 'free' appears in the invitation, will no doubt have a catch in it somewhere. On the internet, it's called 'phishing' – an unsolicited email which seems to offer something for free and almost certainly is a scam: the Nigerian businessman who informs you that you've inherited a large sum of money, and all you have to do is ...; the American soldier who promises you will profit greatly if you respond immediately, and all you have to do is ...; the bank that makes contact with the absolute assurance that there is a windfall coming your way, and all you have to do is ...

There's no such thing as a free lunch. If something seems too good to be true, it probably is too good to be true! It should be avoided at all costs.

But what about 'BOGOF', the 'buy one get one free' deals in the supermarket? Or the 'three for the price of two' offers? Surely all you're doing is buying something and the extra is *actually* free. But beware! The 'cost' of the 'free' part is built into the profit margins of the store. 'Free' to you here and now means that it's paid for by a cost built in somewhere else. Didn't I tell you that there's no such thing as a free lunch?

Is *anything* free then? Does everything have a catch to it? Is there a scam behind every offer? I don't believe so. When someone loves you, isn't that love given away freely, with nothing expected in return? When you love someone, do you do so because you expect to be paid?

You have many gifts you can give away today.
The more you give, the more will be available to you.

August 3 – Laughter

'Laughter – the best medicine!'
Reader's Digest *joke page*

When my first grandson was four years old, he started telling jokes. He never really *understood* the jokes he was trotting out. He just repeated what he'd been told by his mum or his dad – or, indeed, his grandfather. But it was clear that he enjoyed the reaction of the adults to his 'jokes', and that made it worthwhile.

Him: 'What's purple and lives at the bottom of the sea?' Me: 'I don't know. What's purple and lives at the bottom of the sea?' Him: 'Moby Plum.' Me: Laughter … Him: A huge grin …

Him: 'A man went into the doctor's and said, "Doctor, doctor, I don't know what's happening. I feel like a pair of curtains." "Oh, for goodness' sake," the doctor replies. "Just pull yourself together."' Me: More chortles … Him: A bigger grin …

Him: 'Knock, knock.' Me: 'Who's there?' Him: 'Abyssinia.' Me: 'Abyssinia who?' Him: 'Abyssinia tomorrow when you come round.' Me: Unable to speak for giggling … Him: Visibly delighted!

There are more where these came from and I suspect they will be added to as he gleans jokes from TV programmes, school pals, joke-books, Christmas crackers and the like. He doesn't understand the language, and certainly has little grasp of the subtleties of what he's engaged with. But he *does* know he can make people smile, or laugh, or chortle, or giggle. And he already knows, at the age of four, how important that is. He'll probably never end up as a stand-up comedian or even be the best joke-teller in the world, but if he goes on remembering what it feels like to make people smile and laugh, then he won't be doing too badly.

Martin Luther suggested,
'You should have as much laughter as you have faith.'

August 4 – Grief

'A time to weep, and a time to laugh.'
Bible: Ecclesiastes chapter 3

As I shared with you earlier, the Marble Quarry on the island of Iona has been defunct for decades. Yet no one visits the Marble Quarry without trying to find a small piece of marble to carry home. Pick up a piece of the white marble flecked with green and you have a precious memento. But plucked from the ground or, in past days, chiselled from the rock, the marble fragment is uneven and sharp. Squeeze it in your hand and you can feel the roughness. Tighten your grip, and the jagged edges will be hard to hold.

Our grief at a loss is like that. It has to be held, of that there is no doubt. It is ours and cannot be discarded. But it is rough and sharp when we pick it up and hard to hold. As we grip it, the edges cut and stab, and the holding of our grief is hard to bear.

Further round the south-west coast of Iona is St Columba's Bay, sloping from a grassy sward to a pebbled beach, where the stones become smaller and smaller as you near the water's edge. Legend has it this is where Columba landed when he left Ireland. Search carefully among the stones and you might find smoothed fragments of Iona marble, which, rounded by the tides over centuries, are almost translucent in their beauty. These are 'St Columba's teardrops' and, we're told, if you find one you will be blessed with love and happiness.

Our grief is like that too. Grip it tight at the beginning and it is sharp to hold. But over time the edges become smooth, the pebble more rounded, and you can hold it with less pain. It's still yours, and can't and shouldn't be discarded. But, as you hold it over time, who knows what healing is yet to come in place of pain?

No one can hold your grief for you, so you will hold onto it tightly. But this is the truth – the more you hold it, the easier it is to do so.

August 5 – Responsibility

'Lord, make me to know mine end, and the measure of my days,
what it is; that I may know how frail I am.'
Bible: Psalms 39:4

I had decided that in the preparation of this book I wouldn't include anything that was current in my own life. Reflections on the lives of others, stories remembered and tales with a helpful message would suffice. And if, perchance, some autobiographical reflections were included, they would be from past events which had been well processed as time had moved on.

Today, I break that promise. Towards the conclusion of the text for the book, I lost a dearly loved aunt, the last to survive from my father's generation. She was 87 years old, had been widowed for some years, had no children of her own and had been cared for in a nursing home for four years. I loved her deeply. She gave me the privilege of caring for her. It was never a chore or a duty. And I miss her with profound sorrow. This book is dedicated to her memory.

With my father and his seven siblings all gone, I and my cousins are now the senior generation of our family. I'm not sure I want that kind of responsibility. But it is there, given to me by the death of a lovely lady. I am not, of course, responsible for the future of humankind – not even for the survival of my own family. It's not *that* kind of responsibility. But it's the weight of expectation that I might be looked to, from time to time, for wisdom and guidance, character and strength. Can I handle that? Yes, I believe I can. If my father and his little sister, my much mourned aunt Kit, can do it for me, I will surely be able to do it for those who come after me. That, too, will be my privilege.

Am I ready for responsibility?
I have to be – that's the responsible approach.

August 6 – Hope

'Hopes; what are they? – Beads of morning
Strung on slender blades of grass;
Or a spider's web adorning
In a straight and treacherous pass.'
William Wordsworth, Hopes, What are They?

Hiroshima Day commemorates the dropping of the first atomic bomb on the Japanese city of Hiroshima on August 6th 1945. More than 80,000 died in Hiroshima, 60,000 more dying as a result of radiation poisoning. Sadako Sasaki was two when the bomb fell.

On August 6th 1954 Sadako's family went to a remembrance gathering at the Peace Park. As the sun went down the people took paper lanterns to the river, to let it carry out to sea the names of relatives who had died. To Sadako they looked like little stars on the dark water. In 1955 Sadako was diagnosed with leukemia, 'the atom bomb disease'. Her best friend brought her a piece of gold paper which she folded into a crane, telling her of an old Japanese legend that anyone who folds a thousand paper cranes would be granted a wish. Sadako began folding a thousand paper cranes. Her wish was for good health, but she died at the age of twelve on October 25th 1955 before completing her project. She'd folded 644 cranes. Her friends folded another 356 so that she would have 1000 cranes buried with her. Hope mattered to Sadako, and matters still.

Hope bears him into life in her arms,
She flutters around the boy's young bloom,
The soul of youth with her magic warms,
Nor rests with age in the silent tomb;
For ends man his weary course at the grave,
There plants he Hope o'er his ashes to wave.
Friedrich Schiller, *Hope*

August 7 – Peace again

'While you are proclaiming peace with your lips,
be careful to have it even more fully in your heart.'
St Francis of Assisi

Sadako Sasaki, a victim of the Hiroshima atomic bomb, died before she'd made a thousand paper cranes in her commitment to peace. In her memory her friends completed the task. In a letter written eight months after Sadako died, her mother, Fujiko, wrote:

Sadako! Listen! Can you hear your friends' strong voices for peace? As the mother of a child who passed away when she was only twelve and a half years old, I'd like to appeal to mothers not only in Japan but all over the world that I don't want such a horrible thing to happen again. So many children are looking for peace.

The local children began to dream of building a monument to Sadako and all of the children killed by the atom bomb. Young people all over Japan helped collect money for the project. In 1958 a statue of Sadako holding a golden crane was unveiled in Hiroshima Peace Park. Inscribed at the bottom of the statue is the children's wish:

This is our cry. This is our prayer. Peace in the world.

Each year in Japan, people fold paper cranes to express their hope for world peace and they are placed at the foot of the Children's Monument in the Peace Park in Hiroshima.

We shall find peace. We shall see angels.
We shall see the sky sparkling with diamonds.
Anton Chekov

August 8 – Bullies

'Perhaps it is only human nature to inflict suffering on anything
that will endure suffering, whether by reason of its genuine
humility, or indifference, or sheer helplessness.'

Honoré de Balzac, Père Goriot

The twelve labours of Heracles in Greek legend, set for him so he
could atone for his madness in slaying his six sons, are remarkable
in their intensity. For any ordinary mortal, they're more than body
and soul could bear. In the middle of the tasks, the labour set by
the severe King Eurystheus was for Heracles to capture the wild
Erythmanthian boar. This creature was so savage that nobody
could get near it. But Heracles killed it and after tying its feet
together dragged it back to the king. The king was so terrified of
it that he jumped into a brass jar and hid until the coast was clear.

I was bullied at school. I was set upon by a bunch of bigger
boys on the way home one day. I didn't know how to handle it. I
didn't tell anyone. But somehow my big sister found out. Big sisters? They're not supposed to tackle 'wild boars' and fight battles
for their little brothers. Well, this one did, and, whatever she did,
I was never bullied by that gang again.

People who are bullies, be they kings or gangs, don't like it
when someone stands up to them. I don't know if the kids who
bullied me hid in a brass jar to get away from my sister, but, like
King Eurystheus, they didn't like it when the tables were turned.

Bullies are usually cowards. They will pick on the weaker ones
because they can get away with it. It's never a good idea to fight
violence with violence. It makes things worse. But bullies have to
be challenged. Maybe it would be good to have another brass jar
ready – just in case it's needed ...

'*I would rather be a little nobody, than to be an evil somebody.*'
Attributed to Abraham Lincoln

August 9 – Help!

'It is the greatest of all mistakes to do nothing
because you can only do little. Do what you can.'
From The Wit and Wisdom of Rev. Sydney Smith

One of the hardest things I've had to learn is to ask for help. It's not that I'm good at everything, and don't need any advice and guidance. I'm aware enough that there are people who can do things better than I can. But for a long time I simply didn't know how to ask for help. It was, I thought, a sign of weakness and that I would be a bother to other folk. I had to *learn* to ask for help, and to come to believe that there were people who were more than willing to offer something to me.

The labours of Heracles in Greek mythology offer us a fascinating account of the trials and tribulations of life's journey. But, for Heracles, they were a good deal more dramatic than most of ours! One of the tasks set for him by the king was to kill the Stymphalian man-eating birds. Athena had to help him this time because the tasks were verging on the impossible. The birds were terrifying, with great long claws, sharp beaks and feathers like spears. But Athena was clever and gave Heracles some castanets especially made by Haephestos. When Heracles crashed them together the birds rose up in fear and Heracles killed them with his arrows.

I've never had anyone make castanets for me. But I now know that I need people like Athena to stand with me in a fight; to tend my wounds when I'm broken; to listen when I'm at my wits' end. I had to learn to ask for help. But, having done so, I know there are lots of Athenas waiting to offer their castanets ...

*The help you offer in quiet
will shout loudly to the people who need to hear.*

August 10 – Cheat!

'I would prefer to fail with honour than to win by cheating.'
Sophocles, ancient Greek tragedian

I love to play tricks on my grandsons – like making a longed-for sweet vanish into thin air and then 'magically' reappear from behind an ear; turning a gent's handkerchief into a little mouse and making it jump unexpectedly, and then transforming the animated mouse back into a hankie in a flash. Abracadabra! We're even learning a card game called 'Cheat!' It's fun – and all the more so now that the boys are beginning to see through my attempts at trickery. But cheating 'for real' is not fun at all. Grandsons are learning that too, especially when we play board games together. 'Read the rules!' is a cry often heard.

No one likes being cheated, especially when they have been done out of what is rightly theirs. That's because cheating is hurtful, damaging and often painful. TV programmes such as 'Rip-off Britain' and 'Saints and Scroungers' are ample evidence that there *are* cheats out there, ready to prey on unsuspecting victims.

There are charlatans around – internet scammers; unscrupulous telesales people; cowboy builders. We know that. So, be careful. But be careful, too, of your own actions – we all have it in us to cheat, to go beyond having fun with our grandsons, to get one over on an innocent victim for our own ends.

'People in glass houses shouldn't throw stones' we are told. 'Let him who is without sin cast the first stone,' Jesus said. 'Cheats never prosper,' my granny often intoned. Well, I don't know about that. But the best way to stop any possibility of their prospering is not to get involved in the cheating at all. Sophocles' advice from centuries ago is still valid. Failing with honour is better than winning by cheating.

Cheating is a choice, not a mistake.

August 11 – Gratitude

'Your bounty is beyond my speaking;
But though my mouth be dumb, my heart shall thank you.'
Nicholas Rowe, Jane Shore

Among the many end-of-life conversations I've had the privilege of being involved with there is this one. It was with an elderly man who, in all measurements, had lived a good and godly life, and was coming to the end of his days with peace and dignity.

One day our conversation turned to his service in the Second World War. He had been a merchant seaman, one of the brave sailors who had served on the ships of the North Sea convoys. Within moments he started to cry, not unusual during reminiscences of war service. So I let the silence offer him space to regain his composure. When he did, he told me a simple but remarkable story. He had been on shore-leave before a convoy was due to sail. Two days before he was expected to join his ship in the Orkney Islands, he took ill, ended up in hospital and was told by his doctor he was unfit to travel. During his recuperation, he learned that his ship had been sunk with only a few survivors.

Through tears he asked two questions: 'Why was I spared when others died?' and 'Have I been thankful enough for the life I've been given?' We concluded that, whatever we believed, his living while others died was no more than random chance. 'But,' I said, 'have you been thankful enough? I would reckon you have – and that's been amply shown by your goodness and godliness, the values you've lived by and what you've done for others.'

An old sailor knew that 'his bounty' was beyond his speaking. But when *his* mouth was dumb, his heart, and his life, had shown gratitude enough. That's what made an old man smile a little through his tears as the end of his life drew close.

'Thank you': two small words worth a massive amount.

August 12 – Persecution

'The religious persecution of the ages has been done under what was claimed to be the command of God. I distrust those people who know so well what God wants them to do to their fellows, because it always coincides with their own desires.'

Susan B Anthony, A Defense of Elizabeth Cady Stanton
against a motion to repudiate her Woman's Bible *at a meeting of the National-American Woman Suffrage Association 1896 Convention*

George MacLeod, founder of the Iona Community, was fond of thought-provoking epithets. 'The anagram of Presbyterian 'is "Best in prayer". The anagram of Episcopal is "Pepsi Cola".' But he also claimed: 'The trouble with Christians today is that we're never persecuted.' I didn't know what that meant till I went on a pilgrimage to the Holy Land. Though I was familiar with the persecution of the Palestinian people and the minority Christian community, I had no idea what it meant in practice.

'For 2,000 years,' a young man told us, 'Christian families have lived and worshipped in the land where Jesus lived. We're not converts, immigrants or foreigners. We are the descendants of the first followers of Jesus. But through lack of opportunity, poverty and increased persecution, the Christian population has gone from 18% of the population to less than 1.5% in the past 60 years.'

Going through security at the Western Wall in Jerusalem, I had my Bible taken from me. While it was returned to me later, I was deeply affected by the incident. My distress was put into perspective, however, when our pilgrimage leader suggested, 'Now you have a glimpse of what the Palestinians have to endure all the time.' And I understood for the first time what George MacLeod's epithet about Christians and persecution was about.

Beware of religious persecution that justifies itself
as nothing more than over-zealous piety.

August 13 – Pacifism

'They will beat their swords into ploughshares and their spears
into pruning hooks. Nation will not take up sword against
nation, nor will they train for war any more.'

Bible: Isaiah 2:4

Pacifism, especially as a Christian position, is a theological and ethical stance which is the subject of much debate. Those who are pacifists consider any form of violence to be incompatible with the Christian faith. If Jesus was a pacifist, they argue, his followers must be too. There are others who consider this unrealistic. Yet we surely cannot fail to be moved by the lives of such pacifists as Martin Luther King Jr or Mahatma Gandhi and be challenged by the integrity, consistency and dedication of their position.

In 1914, at the outbreak of the First World War, two Christians – Henry Hodgkin, an English Quaker, and Friedrich Siegmund-Schultze, a German Lutheran – made a pact that as Christians they were one in Christ and could never be at war. To take that pledge forward a conference was organised in Cambridge in 1915 where Christians of all denominations agreed to found the Fellowship of Reconciliation, pledged and committed to non-violence and linking people from all over the world who took a similar stance. They set out the principles that had led them to do so in a statement which became known as 'The Basis', which I shall offer in full tomorrow.

Is pacifism a valid Christian position? One can only look at those who have taken that stance to know the sincerity of their cause. If more people took a pacifist stance, who knows what wars might have been avoided and conflicts ended in their infancy?

'Blessed are the peacemakers,
for they shall be called the children of God.'
Bible: Matthew 5:9

August 14 – Fellowship of Reconciliation

'Be kind to one another, tender hearted,
forgiving one another, as God in Christ forgave you.'
Bible: Ephesians 4:32

The Fellowship of Reconciliation, which I mentioned yesterday, set out their principles of non-violence in a statement known as 'The Basis'. Here is what it states:

That love as revealed and interpreted in the life and death of Jesus Christ, involves more than we have yet seen, that is the only power by which evil can be overcome and the only sufficient basis of human society.

That, in order to establish a world-order based on Love, it is incumbent upon those who believe in this principle to accept it fully, both for themselves and in relation to others and to take the risks involved in doing so in a world which does not yet accept it.

That therefore, as Christians, we are forbidden to wage war, and that our loyalty to our country, to humanity, to the Church Universal, and to Jesus Christ our Lord and Master, calls us instead to a life-service for the enthronement of Love in personal, commercial and national life.

That the Power, Wisdom and Love of God stretch far beyond the limits of our present experience, and that He is ever waiting to break forth into human life in new and larger ways.

That since God manifests Himself in the world through men and women, we offer ourselves to His redemptive purpose to be used by Him in whatever way He may reveal to us.

August 15 – Pride

'Only connect. That was the whole of her sermon.'
EM Forster, Howard's End

We decided the lounge needed decorated. Of the several men who came round to 'cost for the job', the final one was the most intriguing. He called to give us an estimate at the time arranged, and when we showed the middle-aged man with his tape-measure and notebook in hand into the lounge, he stood at the door and fell silent. Without a word he moved into the centre of the room and looked this way and that, up and down. Then, going over to the far wall, he stopped and ran his hand carefully over the wallpaper. Standing back he looked at the wall once more from floor to ceiling, before moving to another part of the room and beginning the strange ritual again.

Then the painter/decorator spoke to us for the first time. 'My father did this,' he said, almost in a whisper. 'I checked my records before I left the shop. My father papered this room forty-eight years ago. There's even a sample of the wallpaper in his invoice book.' He smiled, and gazing fondly round the room once again concluded, 'This is my father's work. I can almost hear him speaking to me from these walls.'

We would hope that a father would be proud of his son. But to hear how much pride a son got from his father's work was quite inspiring. And that mutual pride was clearly a lasting bond between them.

Today, will I have time to pause
and ponder my connections with those I love?
Will I say that I am proud of them
and hear them respond with words
of pride for me?

August 16 – Ready

'If I always appear prepared,
it is because before entering an undertaking,
I have meditated long,
and have foreseen what might occur.'

Attributed to Napoleon Bonaparte

The flamboyant King George IV visited Scotland in 1822, the first monarch to do so since Charles II in 1650. Famous as the Prince Regent who had built the Brighton Pavilion, the king did everything he could to make a favourable impression in Edinburgh. When he appeared at the royal residence of Holyrood, his more than ample figure was bedecked in tartan, though historians tell us his legs were modestly concealed in pink tights! Worship had been arranged in St Giles' cathedral, the heart of Scottish Presbyterianism. The preacher was Dr David Lamont, the Moderator of the General Assembly of the Church of Scotland. Everything needed to be right, so Dr Lamont was reminded that the king would expect the Lord's Prayer to be said. But the Lord's Prayer had not been used in the Scottish Church for many years and Dr Lamont wasn't used to saying it in public. So, mindful of the slight of omitting the prayer in the presence of the king or the embarrassment of getting the words wrong, a fellow minister took him into a tenement entrance and made him repeat the prayer over and over again until he was word perfect.

I'm sure that Dr Lamont, like the king himself, always appeared prepared. But this time he needed to be properly ready, for appearances were never going to be enough.

*'It is not genius which reveals to me suddenly and secretly
what I should do in circumstances unexpected by others;
it is thought and preparation.'*

Napoleon

August 17 – Boring

'Society is now one polished horde,
Formed of two mighty tribes, the Bores and Bored.'
Lord Byron, Don Juan

I'm a great lover and user of Facebook. From time to time something will circulate round the social media community which invites you to list your 'top five' or 'top ten' of something or other. Like your 'eight desert island discs', it's interesting to ponder what might be your five all-time favourite movies, or your top ten pieces of music, or your list of favourite places. Recently the emphasis went the other way, and people were invited to think of their 'top ten worst books' or their 'top five most boring stories'. I could list my top hundred most boring *people* without any problem, but I'm not going to risk sharing *that* on Facebook or anywhere else.

If you are in the habit of praying, might God have you in his list of several million 'most boring people'? I once heard of a vicar who'd been invited to a royal palace to dine with the Queen. Being a vicar, he was invited to say grace before dinner. The grace was more long-winded than was needed and went on for several minutes. One of the footmen was heard to remark to a colleague, 'We thought he was never going to stop. All we needed was a blessing on the meal, not a forerunner of the Sunday sermon!'

In the 2nd century AD, we're told, a Roman official was rewarded by having his name on a memorial because he rescued an entire town from boredom. How or why is lost in the mists of time. But the point is well made. Perhaps those who pray might try to rescue God from boredom. Maybe that will be *our* lasting memorial, and save us from being accused of offering a forerunner of *our* Sunday sermon instead of a simple prayer!

Do not speak unless you can improve on the silence.
Anonymous

August 18 – Words again

'His speeches to an hour-glass
Do some resemblance show
Because the longer time they run
The shallower they grow.'

Anonymous

One of my favourite films is *Amadeus*. A 1984 period drama directed by Miloš Forman and written by Peter Shaffer, *Amadeus* was adapted from Shaffer's stage play of the same name and tells how the composer Antonio Salieri recognises the genius of Wolfgang Amadeus Mozart but seeks to thwart him out of pride and envy. The film received a host of awards. It was voted best picture at the Academy Awards. F Murray Abraham won an Oscar for best actor as Salieri. Tom Hulce's portrayal of Mozart is quite remarkable. Early in the film there is an encounter between the young Mozart and Emperor Joseph II, a musical patron of considerable significance. Mozart has played for the Emperor without impressing him much, and they have this exchange:

Emperor Joseph II: *My dear young man, don't take it too hard. Your work is ingenious. It's quality work. And there are simply too many notes, that's all. Just cut a few and it will be perfect.*
Mozart: *Which few did you have in mind, Majesty?*

Mid-way through a long Communion prayer, I once heard Emperor Joseph II speak to me too. But not about notes ... Instead he said: 'My dear young man, there are simply too many words,' and, there and then, I resolved to cut what wasn't actually needed.

Do we offer too many words in our prayers?
If so, which ones matter and which ones can be cut?

August 19 – Homes

'Home is a name, a word, it is a strong one; stronger than
magician ever spoke, or spirit ever answered to.'
Charles Dickens, Martin Chuzzelwit

There's a house in my street which has its name, *Shangri-La*, over
the front door. I'm tempted to ring the doorbell to ask, 'Why?' But
I don't really need to. The name says it all. Here's a place where a
family, a couple or an individual has found a glimpse of their personal paradise. Or it could be that someone *hopes* they will one
day – and the house-name communicates that to everyone who
passes by.

Dunroamin does the same thing. It says something about the
wanderlust of the occupants being at an end, replaced with a settled life, and if not now, then hopefully soon. 'No more roaming
for me, folks. I'm done with that.'

The house my wife and I live in is called *Swallow's Nest*. It's
what we called the first flat we bought and we've taken the name
with us to our present home. It comes from Psalm 84:

> *How lovely is your dwelling place, Lord Almighty! My soul*
> *yearns, even faints, for the courts of the Lord; my heart and my*
> *flesh cry out for the living God. Even the sparrow has found a*
> *home, and the swallow a nest for herself, where she may have*
> *her young ...*

What do we want the name of our house to communicate about
our home? The hope that it will be a 'dwelling place' of love; a
yearning to offer a home where meaning and purpose matter; a
place where one can search for deeper things.

'Swallow's Nest'
Domesticated sparrows and passing swallows always welcome

August 20 – Affirmation

'What passion cannot Music raise and quell?'
John Dryden, St Cecelia's Day

When my wife Mary was a student at Glasgow University she sang in the Trinity College Choir under the guidance of William Barclay, the professor of New Testament in the university. The ministry of the Church of Scotland having been a male province until the 1970s, the Trinity College Choir had been a male-voice ensemble. But with the advent of women training for the ministry, and courses being offered to students for whom ordained ministry wasn't the primary focus, female students were included. Mary enjoyed her time with 'Willie Barclay's choir' enormously.

In 1985, CL Rawlins edited a collection of William Barclay's correspondence, *Ever Yours*. Imagine Mary's surprise when she discovered the following in one of the letters the Professor had written to a former choir member.

> *Life is full of changes. There is the shattering change of girls in the choir. Fortunately they are good. This year we have an ex-D'Oyley Carte tenor and a marvellous girl soprano, and to hear them sing 'Ah leave me not to pine alone' from 'The Pirates of Penzance' is an experience.*

My wife knew that the 'marvellous girl soprano' was her. Imagine her pleasure at the comment. A letter written to a friend, commenting on someone else, and, through time and circumstance, the 'someone else' getting to read it …

How enriching and encouraging when affirmation gets back to the person being affirmed.

> *How vital that we say the right things,*
> *about the right people, at the right time.*

August 21 – Equality

'No one has yet been found resolute enough in dogmatising
to deny that Nature made man equal;
that society has destroyed this equality
is a truth not more incontrovertible.'

Percy Bysshe Shelley, Letter to Elizabeth Hitchener

The Gospel Train's a-Comin' is part of the rich heritage of song from the slave trade. It was used to alert other slaves that a group was preparing to escape and travel north to freedom. 'Gospel train' was code for the underground railroad. It has other meanings too – a belief in heaven, the ultimate promise of freedom. Plantation owners would be unaware the slaves were planning an escape and would simply hear the biblical and religious references.

The Gospel train's a-comin'; I hear it just at hand;
I hear the car wheel rumblin' and rollin' thro' the land.
Get on board little children; get on board little children;
Get on board little children; there's room for many more.

I hear the train a-comin'; she's comin' round the curve;
She's loosened all her steam and brakes and strainin' ev'ry nerve
Get on board little children ...

The fare is cheap and all can go; the rich and poor are there;
No second class aboard this train; no difference in the fare.
Get on board little children ...

Even in the midst of oppression and fear there was this truth – everyone deserves a ticket to freedom.

There's no difference in the fare to hope and freedom.
Everyone matters. Everyone counts.

August 22 – Colours

'There are moments when our passions speak
and decide for us.'
George Eliot, Romola

The first time I took my son to a big football match he was eight years old. He'd been pestering me for ages to take him to a 'big game' and I relented. We chose a quieter game as his introduction – Heart of Midlothian versus Falkirk in the Scottish Premier League. The crowd would be manageable; the banter genial and non-threatening; the match-day atmosphere exciting but not over-whelming. Neither Hearts not Falkirk were teams I supported so I was a 'neutral' at the game, taking pleasure from my son's day out. In time, I expected my son to follow the same team as his dad (I've been a Rangers supporter all my life). Neither Hearts nor Falkirk would get in the way of *that*! How wrong I was ...

On our way home we were passing stalls selling team colours. Being close to the Hearts ground the colours were predominantly the maroon and white of 'The Jambos'. 'Can I have a scarf, Dad?' my son asked. 'It's not cold,' I replied. 'I know, Dad,' he pleaded, 'but it's a Hearts scarf, Dad ... for my team.' I couldn't believe my ears. *My* team! I tried to ignore the pleas, but it was no use. So my son walked home proudly bedecked in a Hearts scarf and hat. He was hooked! He's been a Jambo ever since.

Every football fan is proud to wear their team's colours – to identify their allegiance; show what side they're on; give them a bond with others. Are there colours we can wear too? ... To iden-tify our value systems; to show what lifestyle we follow; to create bonds with like-minded people? What colours can we proudly wear that really show who we are and what we stand for?

Choose what and whom you follow with great care.
And then be pleased to wear your colours with pride.

August 23 – The long view

'Glories, like glow-worms, afar off shine bright,
But look'd too near have neither heat nor light.'
John Webster, The White Devil

Lord Northcliffe, the newspaper magnate from the beginning of the 20th century, was gifted with very long sight. It is said that he could read the prices of articles in shop windows while he was sitting in a taxi cab driving down the street. But, as an avid reader and with a passion for current politics, affairs of state and the people of his day, he spent most of his time reading books and newspapers. At one time, Northcliffe was threatened with blindness. A London eye specialist took the view that only an operation could save the great man's sight. But Northcliffe was unwilling to undergo an operation and sought another opinion. He went to a German eye specialist and the verdict was that the patient was suffering from extreme weariness of the optic nerve.

And the cure? Northcliffe was informed that he must, at least for a time, stop peering only at things that were right under his nose and look instead at things in the distance.

We like to do both. Often we need to study and absorb what is close at hand, to look at the detail and understand all that's important. But if that keeps us from taking the long view and from trying to understand the bigger picture, then we won't have things in a proper balance. Like Lord Northcliffe, before we do ourselves damage, we have to take the long view as well. Sometimes there is much to learn by looking into the distance.

How can we know what might be possible
when we only see what's under our nose
and never look beyond what's familiar?

August 24 – What lasts?

'Time ... thou ceaseless lackey to eternity.'
William Shakespeare, The Rape of Lucrece

Do you wonder whether you'll be remembered when you're gone?

'What lasts?' we ask, when pondering
the worth of what we've done.
What will the world remember
when each one is dead and gone?
What impact will remain to show
the difference we've made?
And will we be remembered as
the ones who've made the grade?

Will generations yet to come
recall what we've achieved?
Might they rejoice and marvel at
the tapestry we've weaved?
Can signs remain forever showing
we've been past this way?
Will changes we have made outlive
the passing of our day?

Will what we thought was special be
remembered by the rest?
Might we be singled out for praise
reserved for just the best?
Will what we have accomplished mean
a plaque can mark our fame?
Will people talk of eminence
when mentioning our name?

From A Blessing to Follow, *Tom Gordon, Wild Goose Publications, 2009*

August 25 – This is what lasts

'I have the most ill-regulated memory.
It does those things which it ought not to do
and leaves undone the things it ought to have done.'
Dorothy L Sayers, Gaudy Night

In 1968 Martin Luther King reflected on what his funeral might contain. 'If you get somebody to deliver a eulogy,' he said, '... tell them not to mention that I have a Nobel Peace Prize, that isn't important. Tell them not to mention that I have three or four hundred other awards ... I'd like somebody to mention ... that Martin Luther King, Jr. tried to give his life serving others [and] tried to love somebody ... And all of the other shallow things will not matter ... I won't have the fine and luxurious things of life to leave behind. But I just want to leave a committed life behind. And that's all I want to say.'

O, child, you'll be remembered not by things that will not last,
Like merit, style or prominence, or kudos, rank or class,
Or accolades that make you seem august and grandiose,
But by your help for others who have needed you the most.

Where love has changed a life, then you'll be worthy of our praise;
Where brokenness found healing, a voice in thanks we'll raise;
When poverty was challenged, then you'll be recalled with pride;
If justice was your watchword, then your worth can't be denied.

The things of time will soon decay and crumble into dust;
For transience can never offer substance we can trust;
If you want immortality, kiss things of time goodbye,
And grasp what is eternal – then your love will never die.

From *A Blessing to Follow*, Tom Gordon, Wild Goose Publications, 2009

August 26 – Headlines

'Headlines twice the size of the events.'
John Galsworthy, End of the Chapter

According to legend, the headline of *The Aberdeen Press and Journal* on April 16th 1912 was: *Titanic sinks. Aberdeen man lost at sea.*

Even though the headline has turned out to be a myth, people still sometimes make fun of the parochial nature of *The Press and Journal* and its alleged limited understanding of the world outside its circulation area of Aberdeen, Inverness and NE Scotland. *The Press and Journal*, often called the *P&J*, was established as *The Aberdeen Journal*, a daily regional newspaper, in 1747, making it Scotland's oldest daily newspaper. It's occasionally criticised for its regional perspective on global events, though it prides itself on serving a local community and offering relevant, local news.

Whatever the truth is, in the *P&J* or anything else, headlines are eye-catching and important. No matter the news story, the headline is designed to 'make you want to read more'.

This headline from a UK tabloid grabbed the attention: *Freddie Starr ate my hamster.*

Whatever the importance of Freddie Starr or the fate of the hamster is for the readers to decide! But, again, headlines are eye-catching as a foretaste of what's to come.

What headlines would others see in us? What would be designed to draw people in to know us better, to explore our values, faith or concerns? And, after we've offered the headline, will they find a true and interesting story that follows?

What might the headline be for your story?

August 27 – Gates

'They have their exits and their entrances.'
William Shakespeare, As You Like It

The Cowgate in Edinburgh runs from the Grassmarket, under George IV Bridge, to the foot of the Pleasance. Something to do with cows – cattle going through a gate, perhaps? Maybe a toll-gate into the city where cattle were counted and taxes paid? Close – but no cigar. In fact, cows *were* herded down it for Edinburgh's market days in centuries past. But 'gate' (or *gait*) was a Scots name for a street and *not* an entrance in a wall or fence. So 'Cowgate' simply means 'Cow Street', and that's the end of it.

Jesus spoke of a 'gate' in Matthew's Gospel (7:13-14):

Enter ye in at the strait gate; for wide is the gate, and broad is the way that leadeth to destruction, and many there be which go in thereat: because strait is the gate, and narrow is the way which leadeth unto life, and few there be that find it.

One of the children in a Sunday school asked what 'strait' meant. The teacher replied, 'It means that Jesus had a sense of humour ...' She went on to explain that strait means narrow and that there was a narrow gate in the walls of Jerusalem through which merchants would enter the city. If they were very wealthy and had over-laden camels, the beasts would be too wide to get through the narrow entrance. So the merchant would have to unload every camel and carry his possessions through the gate one by one. Often things would have to be left behind before the gate was closed for the night. The idea of a fat camel trying to squeeze through a narrow gate was funny. Jesus *did* have a sense of humour. I think he would have laughed at 'Cow Street' as well!

Strait gates are only workable if we travel light.

August 28 – And yet more words

'We know not what we do
When we speak words.'
Percy Bysshe Shelley, Rosalind and Helen

During my time as hospice chaplain, I conducted a wedding for one of the patients. Olivia was a 44-year-old divorcee who had lived with Allan for twelve years. She had no children to her first marriage, and she and Allan had no children together. They had fallen in love and had had twelve happy years together, not contemplating marriage because of the deep scars Olivia carried from her earlier experience. But now that she was dying, the issue of marriage came into focus. There were practicalities for Allan after Olivia died – a shared house, bank accounts, the benefits system, and the like. But, more than that, there were the emotional issues – the need for a definition of what twelve years of love had meant and the value of thanksgiving in the face of death.

A wedding was arranged in the hospice. Though aware and awake, Olivia was unable to get out of bed. So her room was decked out with balloons and streamers, the champagne was on ice in the corner and two of the nurses were the witnesses. It was moving and meaningful. But, because of the nature of her cancer, Olivia couldn't speak. There was to be no 'I do' in response to Allan's spoken commitment to her. Instead, it was my words and her assent, my questions and her response, my expression and her affirmation. Olivia spoke with her eyes. There was a silent mouthing of the vows, the nodding of her head, even, at one point, a glorious thumbs-up with both hands, and, of course, a shared kiss with her new husband. Without words, so much was said.

*How important it is to listen to what's behind the words,
and to make sure that our words don't get in the way
of what we really mean.*

August 29 – Truth

'Truth is rightly named the daughter of time,
not of authority.'

Francis Bacon, Novum Organum

I worry about the desire for purity in the Church. 'I have the truth,' some say, 'and you live in ignorance if you do not accept the truth as it has been revealed to me.' Others add, 'Doctrine is pure. If you are unable to accept that purity you do not have a complete faith.' I do not agree. Faith for me is a changing, growing and developing entity. We must never stop searching and exploring. We are always on a quest for a deeper knowledge and a clearer understanding. If we believe we have arrived at the truth and our knowledge is complete then faith becomes a static thing and we cease to grow.

One of my lecturers in divinity college, the late Canon Roland Walls, suggested that we should put all the books of dogma in a bin, put a lid on the bin, and all sit together on the lid so that the dogma doesn't get out again. I like that. I don't want my faith to be complete. I want it to grow and develop. Purity doesn't allow for that.

Mohandas Gandhi wrote in his autobiography:

I worship God as Truth only. I have not yet found Him, but I am seeking after Him. I am prepared to sacrifice the things dearest to me in pursuit of this quest. Even if the sacrifice demanded my very life, I hope I may be prepared to give it.

Like Gandhi, I am fearful that if I were ever to find the Truth and to believe my faith was pure as a result, I would lose the very nature of the God I believed I'd found.

Truth and justice are lovers who walk hand in hand.

August 30 – Hardship

'The very greatest things – great thoughts, discoveries,
inventions – have usually been nurtured in hardship,
often pondered over in sorrow,
and at length established with difficulty.'

Samuel Smiles, Happy Homes and the Hearts that Make Them

A woman had a phone call from a friend who pleaded, 'There's
been a power cut and the heating's gone off. And we're *freezing*.
Can we come round to your house for a warm?' 'But,' she
responded, 'our power's off too, so unless we're going to have a
group hug for the rest of the day, you're out of luck.' 'Oh well,' was
the sorrowful reply. 'I'll just have to phone John. He's got a coal
fire in his house. That'll be just the ticket.' 'See you there, then,'
the woman suggested, while looking up John's phone number at
the same time.

An emergency? Yes, of course. But *freezing*, actually freezing?
I don't think so. Yet how quickly we complain about inconveniences and how ready we are to construe them as hardships. Of
course we are bothered when things go wrong. We like our home
comforts and we take for granted our electricity supply and other
forms of power for our homes. But *freezing*?

And how often have we said, 'Goodness, I'm starving,' when
we're not? Of course we complain about inconveniences, for they
are what they are. But spare a thought for those who are *actually*
starving because they are deprived of nourishment on a permanent basis, and who have little prospect of it being any better. And
ponder the homeless teenager who is sleeping rough in freezing
temperatures because they have no home to stay in or bed to lie
on. *That's* hardship, isn't it?

The causes of poverty and injustice are worth complaining about
and not our minor inconveniences.

August 31 – Marked

'I am a part of all that I have met.'
Alfred Lord Tennyson, Ulysses

The Old Testament story of the twin brothers Esau and Jacob in the book of Genesis is filled with intrigue, failure, evil, reconciliation and hope. The core of the tale is that Jacob, the second of the twins to be born and, therefore, having no claim on the first-born's inheritance, cheats his brother out of his birthright. Jacob inherits everything, and, not surprisingly, there is a major fall-out between the two boys. For years they live apart, Jacob being fearful of Esau's wrath. But, as time goes on, asking for forgiveness becomes Jacob's primary focus.

On his way to the reconciliation with his brother, Jacob has an encounter with his God – if that is what we are to take from the story. The account has him wrestling with 'a being', variously described as a man, an angel, or God. It's a story of a real struggle – with faith, conscience, self-doubt, fear, and who knows what else? But it is significant for Jacob for two reasons: first, his name is changed – from Jacob to Israel; and, second, he walks away from the encounter with a limp. He is struck in 'the hollow of his thigh'. And whatever the interpretation of that might be, Jacob leaves this momentous event marked for life.

Nothing in life is wasted. Whatever we go through – success or pleasure, tribulation or pain – we are formed a little differently because of it. We are changed, 'marked' by life's events. We have little choice in what happens to us and we all have our times of struggle. But even if we are marked, and, like Jacob, walk away with a limp, we can go forward to reconciliation and hope and carry with us the lasting mark of a formative experience.

No life is free from influence.
Every life can have a positive influence on another.

September 1 – Helpfulness

'No one is useless in this world
who lightens the burdens of another.'
Charles Dickens, Our Mutual Friend

I knocked a sugar bowl from a table in a cafe recently. I moved my coat too quickly and caught the bowl with my sleeve. Crash! The bowl smashed on the concrete floor and shards of glass and glistening sugar were scattered everywhere. People were looking at me. There were whispered comments. Someone giggled. And I went scarlet with embarrassment.

Just then, a young woman appeared at my shoulder. 'Who's a clumsy clot, then?' she enquired. But instead of giving me a hard time for the accident, or, indeed, writing out a bill for the damage, it was clear that she had come to help. She had a dustpan and brush in her hands, and in seconds was down on the floor clearing up the mess. *How did she get over here so quickly?* I wondered. *Was she hovering behind the counter eyeing up a potential clumsy clot so that she was ready, like a superhero, to be there in an instant?* Whatever it was, I was immensely grateful for her help, for the dissipation of my embarrassment and for the consequent restoration of an appropriate complexion to my reddened cheeks.

Helpfulness! What a joy! How easy it would have been to criticise my clumsiness – as if I would have caused the accident on purpose. How quick she might have been to add to my embarrassment by creating a scene; how effective her instant offer of helpfulness, and the calming and healing effect it had on the whole situation – and on me.

*It's a great mistake to do nothing to help
because you think it's not going to be enough.
Do what you are able. It matters.*

September 2 – Possibilities

'It is natural to develop prejudices.
It is noble to rise above them.'
Anonymous

Erik Weihenmayer climbed Everest despite being blind. His story
was an inspiration to a classroom of blind Tibetan students whose
teacher, Sabriye Tenberken, had read them Weihenmayer's book,
Touch the Top of the World. Weihenmayer was invited to come to
Tibet. Tenberken's letter of invitation said:

*After I had told your story, the boys were walking together with
some of our sighted colleagues through the inner part of Lhasa,
not the blind-friendliest city in the world. There are holes in
the street, sometimes meters deep. Construction sites are never
protected. You can step in huge puddles of dirty water or even
excrement. Most of our children know their way through this
chaos. I teach them mobility and they are confident in using
their canes. They always think that if I could find my way they
also have to try. The problem is that they are sometimes embarrassed to show their canes since nomads and pilgrims ... make
fun of them. They call them 'blind fools', imitate them and
laugh at them. One of the boys, however, once said: 'You cannot
talk to me like that, I am blind but I am not a fool! And did
you ever go to school, do you know how to read and write? Can
you find the toilet in the middle of the night without a torch?'*

The real 'blind fools' can't see possibilities because of their prejudice.

*The blind fools aren't those who can't see with their eyes,
but those who can't see what's possible.*

September 3 – Keep going

'Life is like riding a bicycle.
To keep your balance you must keep moving.'
Albert Einstein, in a letter to his son Eduard

Two months before my son – the youngest of my three children – was born, I wrote my car off in an accident. I can *honestly* say it wasn't my fault. A car coming towards me skidded on a bad corner of a country road and hit me side-on. My car was thrown off the road and smashed into a massive gatepost. With the car crushed on one side by the crash and on the other by the gatepost, I ended up in the little space left in the middle. All I had was a cut on my forehead from a piece of windscreen glass. But my minor injury was nothing compared to the psychological effect of the accident.

Many reading this will have had greater traumas to survive or will know others who have struggled after a major tragedy. So I won't parade my process of recovery. But I will share three thoughts. The first thing I did was to ask for a cigarette, ruining the benefit of having stopped smoking some months before. Secondly, I knew how slender the thread of life is. An inch or two either way, a greater impact, and I would have been dead. How much life is to be appreciated! How much more did I love my son when he was born. But what I remember most is that, the following day, I had to drive home. I was terrified, shaky and *very* careful. Thirty years later I still get apprehensive when I see a car coming towards me on a hill, on a wet day, on a country road. But if I *hadn't* got on with it, it would have been all the harder.

I don't belittle the trauma and I'm not special. But I've learned about the fragility of life and about getting on with things. I still draw on these lessons. And, yes, before you ask, I *did* manage to stop smoking some years later as well.

Keep on carrying on – no matter what you're carrying.

September 4 – Changes

'He only is a well-made man who has a good determination.'
Ralph Waldo Emerson, An Essay on Culture

A friend found a diary among the belongings of an old relative who'd died a few months before. It wasn't a 'private' diary, but it contained a fascinating record of her relative's earlier years ...

January 28
Sold Ford Anglia. Sorry to part with old girl. Bought new Mini. Excellent deal. Hope to go on long run with new car in few days.

January 29
*Saw Partick Thistle v Rangers in Cup. Terrible weather. Jags awful. Rangers worse. 0-0 draw. Had drink with Albert after game.
He has new job. Good ho!*

January 30
Attended church. Poor sermon. Got engaged to Agnes.

January 31
*Two new starts at work. Both from out of town, but OK. One went to same school as cousin Robert. Will get along fine.
Met Aggie's parents.*

February 1
*Not working. Took car for run up country. Good mileage. Comfortable. Stuck behind sheep on loch-side. Ham sandwiches/flask tea for lunch. Home tea time.
Drink with Albert tonight. Late back.*

An example of Emerson's 'good determination' perhaps? But what place for the lovely Agnes in such a full and varied life?

September 5 – Priorities

'A change came o'er the spirit of my dream.'
Lord Byron, Childe Harold's Pilgrimage

Here's another few days from the diary found by my friend and belonging to an old, recently-deceased relative:

May 3
Had bump with car. Lorry in High Street. Not my fault. Distressed at damage. Insurance will cover. Love my car. Needs new front wing.

May 4
Skipped football to paint gate. Too wet. Went pub. Albert off work – bad back. Pain eased with several pints. Pie & mash. Home late.

May 5
Went to church. Poor sermon. Fixed date for wedding.

May 6
Trouble at factory. Boss on rampage for shoddy work. Think might look for new job. Maybe change car. TV on blink.

May 7
Off work with cold. Had planned to discuss wedding with Aggie's parents, but gave it a miss. Rumour minister leaving church. No loss. Met Albert at Pub.

And an entry a month later tells us this:

June 5
Married town Registry Office. Wet.

Priorities? What would you note down as being important today?

September 6 – Listening

'In listening mood she seemed to stand
The guardian Naiad of the strand.'
Walter Scott, The Lady of the Lake

We have two ears and one mouth, and we should use them in that proportion. I don't know where I got that advice from, but it's been a mantra I've tried to live by. And it's a lesson I've imparted to students when I've been teaching the importance of good communication skills.

If you've already learned that lesson, don't be complacent. There's more ... for non-verbal communication offers a great deal too. We should listen to more than just the words. Non-verbal communication is the process of sending and receiving wordless messages between people – through gestures and touch, body language or posture, facial expression and eye contact. Social psychologists tell us that non-verbal communication makes up about two-thirds of all communication between two people or between a speaker and a group of listeners. The wrong message goes out if the non-verbal signals don't match the words.

We're told that we have less than ten seconds – and more realistically close to four – to make a good impression on those we meet. When communication is being absorbed, the recipient is taking in clues in lots of different ways, using all five senses in the interaction. Eighty-three per cent of the impact on the brain of information from the senses comes from visual stimuli. Only 11% comes from hearing.

So when you ask someone how they are, and they say, 'Fine!', what non-verbal clues are they offering that might confirm or challenge their spoken response?

Listen more than you speak.
And be aware with more than your ears.

September 7 – Goodness

'Whatever any one does or says, I must be good.'
Aurelius Antoninus, Meditations, Chapter VII

Status, achievement, success, money, accolades, celebrity, and much more besides, are too often the measurements that are used to define a person's worth and value. Let's have a think about what might be a better measuring stick. Goodness, perhaps?

It's not your social standing that's the meaning you still seek.
It's what you choose to stand up for that makes your life unique.
It's not what you'll be known for that will make our eyebrows raise,
But what you show of goodness all your days.

It's not how you're rewarded by the trappings of success,
But what rewards you offer those whose lives you're called to bless.
It's not enough that people sing your name in hymns of praise –
It's what you show of goodness all your days.

It's not the riches of the world that make your treasure store,
But what enriches those who know your love, and need still more.
It's not how you present yourself that will your friends amaze –
It's what you show of goodness all your days.

So stand up for the righteousness that peace and justice brings;
And value the rewards that give you greater wealth than kings;
And measure out true worth that sets the fires of love ablaze –
And seek to show your goodness;
Make the most of goodness;
Go and share your goodness all your days.

Revised from A Blessing to Follow *by Tom Gordon,*
Wild Goose Publications, 2009

September 8 – Suffering again

'It is an easy thing for those whose foot is on the outside
of calamity to give advice and rebuke the sufferer.'

Aeschylus, Prometheus Bound

The Book of Job in the Bible is about suffering. It's the story of Job, his trials at the hands of the Devil, his discussions with friends on the origins and nature of his suffering, his challenge to God and, finally, God's response. The question asked in the book is the universal one, 'Why do the righteous suffer?' It's the kind of question that lies behind the title of Rabbi Harold Kusher's 1981 book, *When Bad Things Happen To Good People.*

Bad things a-plenty *do* happen to the good Job: all his possessions are destroyed; 500 yoke of oxen and 500 donkeys are carried off by his enemies; 7000 sheep are burned; 3000 camels are stolen; the house of his firstborn collapses; all of Job's offspring are killed … all apparently to test this good man. But Job does not curse God. Instead he shaves his head, tears his clothes and says, 'The Lord has given, and the Lord has taken away; blessed be the name of the Lord.' It's a remarkable testimony by a suffering man of true resilience and character.

I do not believe suffering is divinely inflicted or devil-inspired. God does not send pain because of wrongs we have done. Of course people ask, 'Why do the innocent suffer?' 'What have I done to deserve this?' 'Why would God make bad things happen to good people?' But I believe the 'God' part of Job's story is no more or less than a metaphor for the suffering – the random, arbitrary, 'it makes no sense' suffering – which is part of life. Job's story is our story. It's not about faith, but about life and how we cope with and move forward from pain and sorrow. It's about character. Isn't there much to admire in Job's resilience?

Suffering: the furnace in which character is formed.

September 9 – Counting your chickens

'Every path has its puddle.'
The author's grandmother

Here's another of Aesop's fables ... Patty the Milkmaid was going to market carrying her milk in a pail on her head. Such was the way of things, and, as it was a long way to the market, she had plenty time to think. So as she went along she began calculating what she would do with the money she would get for the milk.

'I know,' she thought, 'I know just the thing. I'll buy some hens from Farmer Brown. For he has good hens and they are good layers. And they will lay eggs for me every morning.'

She had gone no more than a few steps further, thinking about her hens, when she was struck by another thought. 'I know. When they lay their eggs each morning, I will collect them and sell them to the parson's wife. She will pay me well for my eggs.'

A few steps more and she thought, 'And then, with the money I get from the sale of the eggs, I will buy myself a new frock and a fine straw hat.'

She smiled at the picture she had of herself and said out loud, 'Ah yes. And so when I go to market, won't all the young men come up and speak to me? Annie Shaw will be *so* jealous. But I don't care. I shall just look at her and toss my head like this.' And, with that, the actions matched her words and she tossed her head back. But in her musings she had forgotten the pail she was carrying on her head. So it fell off it, and all the milk was spilt. And then she had to go home and tell her mother what had happened.

'Ah, my child,' said the mother, 'you have much to learn. And you would do well to begin with: "Do not count your chickens before they are hatched." '

Don't run too far ahead of yourself,
for you never know what obstacles will slow you down.

September 10 – Hidden things

'Nothing is secret that will not be made manifest.'
Bible: Luke 8:17

I live in a village where the people take pride in the appearance of their community. There's a local 'Amenities Group' who are largely responsible for the tubs and boxes, borders and hanging baskets which bring colour and beauty to the village at different times of year. It's more than just doing well in the 'Scotland in Bloom' competitions – though there's been success there too. It's about pride in the village and creating a better neighbourhood, with some committed people working very hard so that the rest of us get a lot of pleasure.

For people like me who aren't avid gardeners it's worth remembering that the plants and shrubs, the colour and blooms that brighten the whole village don't appear out of nowhere. It's not a case of 'one day they're not there and the next day they are'. *Voilà! Abracadabra!* Someone, somewhere, has prepared a greenhouse; planted seeds; nurtured little plants; chosen the best blooms; prepared the tubs and boxes; planted the flowers; arranged the displays; placed them in position; watered them carefully ... and all before I've noticed they're there at all!

The hidden work and careful preparations that lie behind the floral displays bring pleasure to my streets. And I don't even know the folk who are involved. They just get on with what they do, deriving enjoyment from giving pleasure to others.

Remember the hidden things and the work done in secret, for, in its own way, it is already touching the lives of a lot of people.

[We pray that] hidden things may be revealed to us
and new ways found to touch the lives of all.
Iona Community prayer

September 11 – 9/11

'Speech is of time, silence is of eternity.'
Thomas Carlyle, Sartor Resartus

'9/11' is now etched on our minds. It is, of course, the American way of defining a date with the number of the month coming first, and, at the start, sounded strange to those whose dates are written the other way round. But 9/11 has stuck, and now defines a dreadful moment in history – the terrorist attacks on the twin towers of the World Trade Centre in New York City on September 11th 2001. I was horrified watching the live pictures, and deeply confused because of what I had to deal with later that evening.

In 2001 I was the Moderator of Edinburgh Presbytery with the honour of presiding over monthly gatherings of ministers and lay people to deal with Church of Scotland business affecting the churches and the people of the city. On September 11th I was to officiate at the annual Presbytery Communion service, attended by nearly 300 people. But as the day went on, the sermon I had prepared seemed less and less appropriate. I abandoned it before the Communion. I trusted my ability to say the right thing, but remained consumed by an overwhelming sense of sadness. When it came time to preach, this was my sermon: 'In the light of today's events, I have nothing to say. So I suggest we will sit prayerfully together and silently commit the whole thing to God, believing he can make more sense of this than we can.'

The celebration of Communion later was as deep and meaningful as I can remember. At the end an old churchman took me aside. 'Thank you for your sermon. It's the best I've heard someone preach for years. The silence said it all.'

The only prayer that says it all
is when the heart, devoid of words,
in depth of silence calls.

September 12 – Decisions

'Decide not rashly. The decision made
Can never be recalled. The gods implore not,
Plead not, solicit not; they only offer
Choice and occasion, which once being passed
Return no more. Dost thou accept the gift?'
Henry Wadsworth Longfellow,
Masque of Pandora – Tower of Prometheus on Mount Caucasus

It's hard to make decisions sometimes. My son has two dice in his pocket. When he's out with his mates and they can't decide what to do next, they allocate numbers to their choices, throw the dice and the decision is made. My wife sometimes flips a coin when there's a choice to be made – heads, it's one way; tails, it's another – or so you might think. But instead, it's not just the way the coin comes down, but the way you *feel* when the coin comes down that makes the decision. I recently went for a meal with some colleagues. 'I'll decide last,' one of them said. He waited till we'd all ordered before he chose. And even *then* he was struggling to make up his mind. 'Anything more than two items on the menu and I'm toiling,' he confessed.

Some folk don't get stressed with decisions while others have steam coming out of their ears; some can decide quickly and others take an eternity; some worry after they've made their choice, while others will just go with the flow.

Of course it's hard to make decisions sometimes. Yet decisions are part of our living. Let's hope we have some principles on which to base our *important* decisions, and don't just leave it to chance. After all, there are some things that are worth more than the throw of dice or the random toss of a coin.

When we've decided what we shouldn't do,
then we might give our all to what ought to be done.

September 13 – Redeeming qualities

'William Gladstone has not a single redeeming defect.'
Attributed to Benjamin Disraeli

There are two men called Mephibosheth in the Bible. The first was the son of King Saul by his concubine, Rizpah, who, sadly, met a violent end. But the second, the son of Jonathan and grandson of Saul, has a story worth the telling. Mephibosheth was five years old when his father and grandfather died in the Battle of Mount Gilboa. Hearing of this calamity, his nurse fled with him from Gibeah, the royal residence, and in her haste stumbled, dropping him on the ground and beginning a paralysis that disabled him for the rest of his life. He was carried to the land of Gilead where he found refuge in the house of Machir, who brought him up. Some years later, when King David had subdued all the adversaries of Israel, he recalled the family of Jonathan and discovered that Mephibosheth was staying with Machir. So he sent royal messengers there and brought Mephibosheth, and his infant son Micah, to Jerusalem, where they stayed in the royal palace.

There are many twists and turns to the story thereafter, but there is something in David's action that is worthy of note. David had a chequered career and made some questionable moral decisions during his life. But here he is showing reconciliation where he need not have done, and succour and hospitality to a disabled man when it would not have been normal to do so – an offer of reconciliation against the odds, an offer of refuge and protection against expectations. Mephibosheth isn't remembered much for himself, but his name is a sign that even the worst of sinners can do the right thing even when no one expects it.

Even the most questionable of people
can show redeeming qualities.
There's surely hope for us all!

September 14 – Babies

'Sweet babe, in thy face
Soft desires I can trace,
Secret joys and secret smiles,
Little pretty infant wiles.'
William Blake, A Cradle Song

I've learned as a grandparent how much I had forgotten about bringing up my own children. Being a grandfather allows me to be aware of more things, to stand back and be amazed at what's going on.

I was playing with my second grandson when he was six months old, bouncing him gently on my knee and singing to him. And then I realised that he was mirroring my facial expressions. When I smiled, he smiled back, watching me intently. When I opened my mouth wide, he did the same; when I screwed up my eyes, he tried to do it too; I even stuck my tongue out at him – and I haven't dared tell his mother what he did back to me.

We're told by child psychologists that children can mirror our behaviour from a very young age – some suggest it starts at a few weeks. That was emphasised on a poster I had on my wall when I was a student which said: 'Children learn as they live.' So from infancy and as they grow up children learn from what they see in the adults around them, and I could see it happening in front of my eyes as I played with my grandson.

Adults do the same. How much better it would be if we remembered that people around us are affected by our behaviour – all the time – and that when we are close to them they can copy good things from us. How much we still have to learn ...

Out of the mouth of babes and sucklings
you have gained your strength.
Bible: Psalm 8:2

September 15 – Emphasis

'So the unwanting soul sees what's hidden,
and the ever-wanting soul sees only what it wants.'
Lao Tzu, Tao Te Ching

In Khartoum in the Sudan there is a famous statue of the great soldier General Gordon. It shows Gordon mounted on a camel. A small boy is taken by his father to see the statue of General Gordon. Not surprisingly the enthusiastic father tells the boy, 'This is Gordon, General Gordon, my boy. Take a good look, lad. Gordon is very, very special.' At the end of the day the father asks the boy, 'Well, you saw Gordon's statue today, didn't you? Something worth seeing and remembering wasn't it? 'Yes,' replies the child. 'Thank you, Father. I liked seeing it very much. But tell me, Father, who was the man sitting on Gordon's back?'

It was the camel that had caught the boy's imagination. The camel was well worth remembering indeed. To this child it wasn't the statue of a man on a camel that stood in Khartoum; it was a statue of a camel with a man on it.

The poem by Robert Burns called 'Tae a Louse' was prompted by his fascination with a small insect crawling on the hat of a fine lady in front of him in church. Of course the louse provided inspiration for a clever and evocative poem, and we are grateful for that. But might the concentration on a louse not have deflected Burns from the value of the sermon, or some concern for his own soul?

Sometimes we get the emphasis wrong. At times like these, we might be the better for changing our focus and seeing the bigger picture, or at least noticing that there are other important things that are also worth our concentration.

I think I see all that there is to see till I change my perspective
and find that there's much that was hidden
that is yet to be revealed.

September 16 – All nations

'Seid einig – einig – einig.'
'Be united – united – united.'
Friedrich von Schiller, Wilhelm Tell

The Church of All Nations stands near the foot of the Mount of Olives in Jerusalem. In front of the altar is a flat outcrop of rock which Christian tradition identifies as the Rock of Agony where Jesus prayed the night before he was crucified, which is why the church is also known as The Basilica of the Agony. The church and the adjacent Garden of Gethsemane, with its eight ancient olive trees, provide an evocative place for meditation. It was built in 1924, and its architect, Antonio Barluzzi, responsible for many of Jerusalem's churches, evokes the night-time of the Agony by leaving the interior in semi-darkness, relieved only by subdued natural light filtered through violet-blue alabaster windows.

The basilica is called the Church of All Nations because many countries contributed to the cost of construction. National symbols of twelve donors – Argentina, Belgium, Brazil, Canada, Chile, the UK, France, Germany, Italy, Mexico, Spain and the United States of America – are inside the ceiling domes. The mosaics in the apses were donated by Hungary, Ireland and Poland. Australia gifted the wrought-iron wreath around the Rock of Agony.

On the one hand, the Basilica of the Agony, the agony of separation, religious tensions, a fragmented Church, a broken world; on the other hand, the Church of All Nations, co-operation across national boundaries, the sharing of beauty and worship. In one place, a symbol of all our shame and hope, fears and dreams.

Pray with those in the Garden of Gethsemane
that Church and world will move from agony to beauty,
from separation to reconciliation, in Jerusalem and beyond.

September 17 – Nonsense

''Tis the privilege of friendship to talk nonsense,
and have her nonsense respected.'
Charles Lamb, Letters to Coleridge

The writings of Edward Lear from the second half of the 19th century are best known for their sense of the ridiculous. *The Owl and the Pussy-Cat* and *The Jumblies* are the most famous of his works, but *Incidents in the Life of my Uncle Arty, The Duck and the Kangaroo* and *The Pobble Who Has No Toes* offer even more from the imaginative musings of this remarkable writer. In *The Courtship of the Yonghy-Bonghy-Bó*, Lear offers us this description of the origins and circumstances of the title character:

> *On the coast of Coromandel*
> *Where the early pumpkins blow,*
> *In the middle of the woods*
> *Lived the Yonghy-Bonghy-Bó.*
> *Two old chairs, and half a candle; –*
> *One old jug without a handle; –*
> *These were all his worldly goods.*

Nonsense? Well of course. Fun? That too. So why is it that we smile at and are entertained by the ridiculous writings of a man like Edward Lear? I like to think it's because in this adult world of ours, with all its demands for logic and common sense, responsibilities and seriousness, we can still be in touch with the imagination and fun of our childhood, and enjoy simple nonsense. After all, aren't there times when these ridiculous things help us make sense of all the rest?

Appreciating nonsense is a serious business
and shouldn't be taken lightly.

September 18 – More gratitude

'We thank with brief thanksgiving ...'
AG Swinburne, The Garden of Proserpine

An African proverb reminds us: *A river that forgets its source will dry up.* When the source of goodness is remembered, the river will continue to flow ...

I was thinking about this when I was driving through town. I was slowing down as the traffic in front of me stopped at a pedestrian crossing. Cars were waiting to join the queue from the side-street on my left. But the first one couldn't get into the line because there was no space. So, for once feeling in a beneficent mood, I held back, left a space, beckoned the car to join the line and slowly moved on behind it. The irritated driver behind me tooted his horn and flashed his lights. In contrast, the driver of the car in front waved her hand out of the driver's window with a thumbs-up – a sign of gratitude if ever I saw one.

The traffic inched its way down the street till it was stopped again. Then I really saw the effect of my small act of kindness, as the driver of the car in front let two cars out of a street on the right to join the line, on both occasions being responded to with a cheery wave. And then, when a bus was allowed to pull out from its stop and continue on its way, another grateful thumbs-up was the result.

The effect of this spreading courtesy didn't do much for the blood pressure of the driver behind me. But there were at least another two car drivers and a bus driver who knew there was a source of goodness somewhere, because the goodwill just kept on flowing ...

From too much irritation I pray to be released,
For once I'll show I'm grateful – well, it's a start, at least!

September 19 – Balance

'Happiness is not a matter of intensity
but of balance and order and rhythm and harmony.'
Thomas Merton, from 'Being and Doing'
in No Man is an Island

On the north side of the Abbey Church on the island of Iona there
is a stairway running from the Abbey transept to a heavy wooden
door at the top. Go up the stair and through the door and you
enter the living quarters of the Abbey complex, where guests and
staff, volunteers and visitors mix and mingle. There's a library and
a telephone-box, toilets and bedrooms, cleaning-cupboards and
the refectory. The beauty and tranquillity of the Abbey and the
vibrancy and challenge of a week in community – with the stairs
as a link between the two.

It was no different when the medieval Abbey was in its heyday.
For these 'night stairs', as they were known, were the link for the
monks between the world of community and the world of worship. In the early hours of the morning they would descend the
night stairs, coming straight from their living space to enter the
Abbey for prayer. And when their devotions were over they would
return to their work and their community, and the link would be
used again. Perhaps that's why, high up on the sides of the arched
window by the south side of the Abbey chancel, there are two
medieval carvings, one of a monkey and the other of a cat – the
active and the passive, the busy and the reflective, the energetic
and the tranquil, the two sides of the medieval life. Work and worship, community and church, activity and reflection, each in balance with the other, and always with the link between.

Today I strive for a life in balance.
If I'm too busy to find time to reflect,
I need help to reflect on why I'm too busy.

September 20 – Necessity

'Teach thy necessity to reason thus:
There is no virtue like necessity.'
William Shakespeare, Richard III

In his *Fables*, Aesop offers us this simple tale with an important message for us all:

In a field one summer's day a Grasshopper was hopping about, chirping and singing to its heart's content. An Ant passed by, bearing along with great toil an ear of corn he was taking to the nest. 'Why not come and chat with me,' said the Grasshopper, 'instead of toiling and moiling in that way?'

'I am helping to lay up food for the winter,' said the Ant, 'and recommend you to do the same.'

'Why bother about winter?' said the Grasshopper. 'We have got plenty of food at present.'

But the Ant went on its way and continued its toil. When the winter came the Grasshopper had no food and found itself dying of hunger, while it saw the ants distributing every day corn and grain from the stores they had collected in the summer. Then the Grasshopper knew: It is best to prepare for the days of necessity.

'Necessity is the mother of invention', the old proverb tells us. But it might also be good to remind ourselves of the importance of preparation too.

John F Kennedy once said, 'The time to repair the roof is when the sun is shining.' Prepare for the days of necessity. For you never know what will come along.

If necessity is necessary and can't be neglected
Then timely preparation should always be expected.

September 21 – More responsibility

'You cannot escape the responsibility of tomorrow
by evading it today.'
Abraham Lincoln, Letter to Edwin Stanton

We learned earlier of the chance meeting recorded by Boswell in his *Life of Johnson* between Dr Johnson and Mr Edwards. The two men had not seen each other since they were students in Pembroke College, Cambridge, fifty years before. Boswell relates how Mr Edwards embarks on a litany of failures, regaling Johnson with all the things he regretted not having done as the years had gone by.

'I wish I had continued at college,' he moans. 'But why do you wish that, sir?' Johnson asks. 'Because,' answers Edwards, 'I think I should have had a much easier life than mine has been. Why, I should have been … a parson, yes, a parson, a parish clergyman, and had a good living … and lived comfortably.'

'Sir,' replies Johnson, 'the life of a parson, of a conscientious clergyman, is not easy. I have always considered a clergyman as the father of a larger family than he is able to maintain. I would rather have Chancery suits upon my hands than the cure of souls. No, sir, I do not envy a clergyman's life as an easy life, nor do I envy the clergyman who makes it an easy life.'

Being conscientiousness means we also have a burden of responsibility. If we, then, have our responsibilities, as a parson, or in our own work, commitment or passion, let us discharge them with equal conscientiousness. And if we are conscientious, let's pray that we find equal fulfilment.

Some are born with responsibilities.
Some choose responsibilities.
Others have responsibilities thrust upon them.
But we all have to get on with things as well as we are able.

September 22 – Truth again

'Truth never lost ground by enquiry.'
William Penn, Some Fruits of Solitude

An engineer, physicist, mathematician, statistician and computer scientist are on a train journey heading north. The engineer, looking out of the window, spots a black sheep in a field and says, 'Look! All sheep in Scotland are black.' The physicist exclaims, 'No! All we can say is that *some* Scottish sheep are black.' The mathematician shakes his head and pronounces, 'Wrong again! The truth is there is at least one field in Scotland, containing at least one sheep, of which at least one side is black.' The statistician smiles and announces, 'Sorry, chaps! This one sheep is not significant. We're only working with one sheep, and within a + or – 3% margin of error, we can't extrapolate sufficiently from a sheep sample from Scotland that's this small.' And the computer scientist furrows his brow and affirms, 'I think it's a special case.'

Who told the truth? The travellers could write a series of manuscripts for scientific journals to make their points. The statistician could author a paper on 'Sheep spotting on trains: inadmissible assumptions about sheepskin colours.' The physicist could prepare a treatise on 'The practicalities of human judgements about the colour of sheep.' They could also choose to discuss their points of view during their journey northwards.

We can only hope that they respected each other's understanding of the truth, continued their discussion in an amicable fashion and reached their destination without falling out. Such is the nature of truth, and such is the necessity to ensure that we don't come to blows over different standpoints.

A family were travelling in a car when they had a puncture. When the little boy saw what the problem was, he said, 'Don't worry. It's only flat at the bottom.' Was he right?

September 23 – Revelation

'’Tis Revelation satisfies all doubts.'
William Cowper, The Task

When I was young the only kind of revelation I knew was in a strange book of the Bible, the last in the New Testament, 'The Revelation of St John the Divine'. From my adult perspective the strangeness has somewhat dissipated. Given my understanding of the context of the book, the time of its writing, the story of St John the Divine, the symbolism of the contents, the purpose of the message, and much more, I can now rationalise a lot of the peculiarities. But when I was young the Book of Revelation was just *weird*, with its beasts and horsemen, angels and scrolls, dragons and plagues, trumpets and 144,000 of the 'elect'.

The trouble with revelation – and not just Revelation with a capital 'R' – is that it's *usually* considered strange, and by more than just children. After all, isn't *all* revelation kind of weird – prophecies of doom; odd visions; communications from the afterlife? Isn't revelation only for oddballs? How wrong I have been.

When the sun rises in the morning, is that not a revelation of a new day, with all its promise and wonder? When I get a hug from my grandson and he tells me he loves me, is that not a revelation of the nature of love, right there, holding onto my leg? When I read something that resonates with my whole being so that I want to shout 'Yes!', is that not a revelation of a truth that I've glimpsed for the first time?

Revelation is always there,
waiting to be revealed,
and hoping someone's going to pass by
who will notice.

September 24 – Heroes

'I want a hero: an uncommon want,
When every year and month sends forth a new one.'
Lord Byron, Don Juan

Role models are important for our young people. In adult life too
we need those we can look up to, who will challenge us and make
us better human beings. 'Heroes' we might call them – not only
those who have done great things or are in the public eye, but
people who set examples of goodness in quiet, unassuming ways.

I have a little hero; her name is Sarah Jane.
She comes on Friday nights and stays for tea.
She knows I can't get out because I'm still in too much pain.
So she's promised now that she will come to me.

She's always bright and cheery; she gives me all her news,
She makes me feel I matter while she's there.
She listens to my stories; she never yawns or frowns;
She doesn't rush; she takes the time to care.

We need our little heroes; we need them every day;
Like Sarah Jane – or maybe you and me;
They're not in stained-glass windows, or found in history books;
They're the here and now; the current crop, you see.

The ones who're bright and cheery; the ones who lift us high,
Who help us reach from darkness to our sun.
We know them when we see them; we thank them as they come;
Yes, let's hear it for the heroes, everyone!

From With an Open Eye, *by Tom Gordon, Wild Goose Publications, 2011*

September 25 – Stormy seas

'God moves in a mysterious way his wonders to perform;
He plants his footsteps in the sea and rides upon the storm.'
William Cowper, Olney Hymns

Above the doors to the two aisles in an Edinburgh church there are wrought-iron designs in black metal – one of a fish, an early symbol of Christ; and the other, a bold cross in a small fishing boat, a traditional symbol of the Church tossed about on stormy seas. A fish and a boat ... modern depictions of ancient symbols. But a different kind of meaning was created when a priest, on seeing the wrought-iron symbols for the first time, remarked, 'Isn't it great we can come to worship in a fish and ship shop!'

I once had a girlfriend who had family in the north east of Scotland. One day we were down by a village harbour chatting with a fisherman who was baiting his lines in a small boat. 'Want a spot of fishing?' he asked. 'I'm going out for an hour to fish for cod.' Not wanting to appear wimpish in front of my girlfriend, I agreed, as she did, and off we went. Negotiating our way out of the harbour was fine. Moving across the gentle swell outside the harbour bar was OK. But facing the choppiness of the open seas was not, and fielding the breakers in the middle of the Moray Firth was absolutely terrible. Any pretence of being macho in front of my girl rapidly disappeared over the side with my lunchtime fish-and-chips. Stormy seas? I thought my life was coming to an end.

Did an experienced sailor know something I didn't, that small boats *can* make it through stormy seas? Yes he did. Did the relationship with my girlfriend last long? You can work it out. Did I have a lot to learn? Yes, very much indeed ...

'O God, be good to me;
The sea is so wide, and my boat is so small.'
Irish fisherman's prayer

September 26 – Loving kindness

'Help thy brother's boat across, and lo!
thine own has reached the shore.'

Hindu proverb

There's a passage in *The Talmud* which reads:

> *There are ten strong things. Iron is strong, but fire melts it. Fire is strong, but water quenches it. Water is strong, but the clouds evaporate it. Clouds are strong, but the wind drives them away. Man is strong, but fears cast him down. Fear is strong, but sleep overcomes it. Sleep is strong, yet death is stronger. But loving kindness survives death.*

The evangelist and preacher John Wesley was travelling in a carriage with, among others, an army officer. Their conversation was lively and interesting, but the officer's contribution was regularly punctuated by swear words and blasphemies for which he never once apologised. The gentle Wesley was understandably disturbed by this language but never showed his displeasure.

When eventually they stopped to change the coach's horses, Wesley seized the opportunity to have a word with the officer. 'I wonder if I might ask you a favour,' Wesley asked. The officer, pleasantly surprised, agreed. 'We will yet be travelling some distance together,' Wesley said. 'And if I should perchance forget myself and use a swear word in front of the ladies, perhaps you would kindly correct me.' The officer took the point and the implied rebuke, and the journey continued without another swear word being heard.

I chastised a man, and he argued back.
I was kind to another, and he was kind to me.

September 27 – Guilt

'No one who is guilty is acquitted
at the judgement seat of his own conscience.'
Juvenal, Satires

In Greek mythology, Heracles was born to a mortal woman but had the god Zeus for his father. To protect his son, Zeus gave him the gift of great strength. But Hera, Zeus's wife, was jealous and plotted revenge. Heracles grew into a tall, strong man. He married and had three sons and led a very settled, peaceful life with his family. But Hera's plot involved giving him a dreadful dream. In that dream he killed his family. Heracles was devastated. What did this mean? Was he really a bad person with evil within him? In confusion, Heracles went to the Oracle to ask the gods what he had to do to be released from this mental anguish. The solution was that he had to go as a slave to serve King Eurystheus who set him twelve labours which would free him from the burden of his family's death. If he completed all the tasks he would once again be a free man.

Whether it's in the mind or in reality, created by a dream or a vivid memory, we are so often tortured by the guilt of past mistakes that we find it hard to move on. The guilt of things done or left undone; the guilt of promises made and promises broken; the guilt of things said or that we never had the chance to say; the guilt of unsaid goodbyes and unforgiven wrongs. Guilt cannot be dismissed. Whatever the Oracle did or said, it was clear that the guilt of Heracles – unjustified, as it would appear – had nonetheless to be accepted and understood for what it was, the torture of an anguished soul. Before we move on from guilt, we have to begin from where we are and not from where we or others would like us to be.

No one who is guilty can be acquitted by his own conscience.

September 28 – Hypocrisy

'Don't do as I do; do as I say.'
Anonymous

The poem *Holy Willie's Prayer* is a satirical masterpiece by Robert Burns. It was written to mock William Fisher, an elder and leading light in the church in Mauchline in Ayrshire. Fisher was a hypocrite who spied on people and reported their wrongdoings to the minister, while at the same time living a far from blameless life himself. The poem is a biting satire based on this hypocrite's life and the title 'Holy Willie' is now rooted in the Scots language as a description of someone who is humourless, ultra-religious and hypocritical. Robert Burns had his own problems with the Church, and was called on more than one occasion to account for his moral misdemeanours. But he remained a God-fearing man. So his poem is not a 'dig' at religion, but is a fierce condemnation of religious hypocrisy and self-righteousness.

> *Yet I am here a chosen sample,*
> *To show Thy grace is great and ample;*
> *I'm here a pillar o' Thy temple,*
> *Strong as a rock,*
> *A guide, a buckler, and example,*
> *To a' Thy flock.*

'There is none like me,' William Fisher is saying. Yet the whole Mauchline community knew what Holy Willie was *really* like and how much of his life was worthy of the condemnation he was quick to throw at others. 'Beware of wolves in sheep's clothing,' Jesus said. Watch out for hypocrisy!

> *Beware of the beautiful house*
> *which hides decay and disappointment inside.*

September 29 – Common ground

'We are already one. But we imagine that we are not.
And what we have to recover is our original unity.
What we have to be is what we are.'

Thomas Merton, Asian Journal

In 2007 I attended a Europe-wide gathering of healthcare chaplains in Tartu, Estonia. The long and tiring journey to the conference was quickly forgotten as chaplains from all over Europe met and learned from each other, ate and prayed together, renewed old friendships and forged new ones.

The Estonian chaplains were delighted to welcome us and show us something of their country. One afternoon on a bus tour we stopped at a little church in a run-down village. The doors of the church were chained. There was no sign of life. But within a few minutes, roaring down the road in a cloud of dust on the back of a beat-up scooter, came an Estonian Orthodox priest, complete with black cassock and long, grey beard flapping in the wind. Greetings were exchanged, chains were removed from the church door and a group of pilgrims was ushered inside. And there we found the most beautiful, holy and tranquil Orthodox sanctuary.

There was a deep silence as we absorbed our surroundings. Then someone began to sing a beautiful Latin chant from the Taizé Community in France. One by one the others joined in, Catholics, Presbyterians, Orthodox and Pentecostals, till the church was filled with the harmonies of many voices from diverse traditions. We'd found what we had in common – an appreciation of holiness and love, and of beautiful, reflective singing.

Ubi caritas et amor,
Ubi caritas, Deus ibi est.
(Where you find charity and love, God is there.)
The Taizé Community

September 30 – True friendship

'Nothing but heaven itself is better than a friend
who is really a friend.'
Titus Maccius Plautus, Roman playwright

Two men, travelling together, found that their pathway took them deep into a dark wood. Fearful of any dangers that might be lurking there they stuck close together, each warning the other when any strange sound might indicate impending danger. But, despite all their care, they turned a corner, and there, to their surprise and terror, they were confronted by the biggest bear that either of them had ever seen.

One of the men ran for his life, climbed quickly into a tree and concealed himself in the branches. The other, seeing that he was likely to be attacked, fell flat on the ground and lay absolutely still. The bear, puzzled by the happenings on his path, came up to the man lying on the ground, felt him with his snout and smelt him all over. The terrified man held his breath, trying not to move a muscle, not even the smallest twitch. He feigned the appearance of death as much as he could, for he had been told that a bear will not touch a dead body. It worked, for the bear soon left him.

When the traveller was sure the bear had gone, he breathed at last, and, now shaking with relief, pulled himself to his feet. He was dusting himself down when his companion climbed down from the tree and jocularly remarked to his friend that it looked as though the bear had been whispering in his ear. 'What did the bear say when you were lying on the path?' he enquired.

'He gave me this advice,' his companion replied. 'Never travel with a friend who deserts you at the approach of danger. For is it not true that misfortune tests the sincerity of friends?'

Friendship isn't really a big thing;
it's the combination of a million little things.

October 1 – Coping

'Grief tears his heart, and drives him to and fro,
In all the raging impotence of woe.'
Homer, The Iliad

It's hard for people to manage after a death. How will they cope?

I wonder how I'll manage in the processes of change,
As I contemplate what's steady and what must be rearranged;
When I feel a bit bewildered, and I don't know why or how …
I wonder how I'm managing just now.

I wonder how I'll manage – or perhaps I'm going mad
As I ride the roller-coaster of the bad, then good, then bad;
When I feel I'm coping better, and the whole world turns to grey …
I wonder how I'm managing today.

I wonder how I'll manage on those special days again,
As I cope with celebrations, but I can't get past the pain;
When I put a happy face on, then it soon will disappear …
I wonder how I'm managing this year.

I wonder how I'll manage as the time goes on and on,
As I lay a new foundation to build future dreams upon;
When I know it will be different, but just how I've not a clue …
I wonder how I'm managing what's new.

Yes, I wonder how I'll manage … so I'll go on wondering still
As I ask 'Can I go forward?', then I answer, 'Yes I will!'
When I know the future's out there, a new picture to be drawn …
Yes, I wonder how I'll manage; yes, I'm going to have to manage;
So I'm trying hard to manage moving on.

From A Blessing to Follow *by Tom Gordon,*
Wild Goose Publications, 2009

October 2 – Forgiveness

'He who cannot forgive breaks the bridge
over which he himself must pass.'
Edward Herbert, The Life of Edward Lord Herbert of Cherbury

I have a permanent burn mark under my chin. The event that caused it was traumatic at the time, though it is now no more or less than an interesting family story from my childhood. But it's left not only a physical mark, but a character-shaping one as well.

I was about seven and my sister and I had been told to take the hot-water bottles upstairs to warm the beds before bedtime. We had an argument and my sister threw her hot-water bottle at me. It hit me on the side of the head and burst open, the scalding water pouring down over my face and neck. I screamed, and my mother came running, pulled my jumper over my head and doused me with cold water. The shock was traumatic, and, according to what I am now told, I was very ill for a time. My face was covered in blisters and I had to get special treatment. I was in bed for ages. But, thankfully, through good family and medical care, I recovered.

I actually remember little of the event – apart from getting new toys to cheer me up and it wasn't even Christmas! But I now have a permanent burn mark under my chin as a reminder that it *did* happen. In her rush to pull off my jumper, my mother hadn't unfastened the popper-buttons along the shoulder and the metal tore my skin. It's never healed properly. Wearing a beard helps to cover it, but it's a permanent part of me.

I don't hold it against my sister, nor do I blame my mother, though I do get fed up when I'm shaving and nick myself under my chin. It's about forgiveness. And, whether I was conscious of it as a small boy or not, that's just what had to happen.

Despite how we are marked,
forgiving and moving on is just simply part of what we are.

October 3 – Hypocrisy again

'Of what benefit is it to say our prayers regularly, go to church, receive the sacraments, and maybe go to confessions too; pray, feast the priest, and give alms to the poor, and yet lie, swear, curse, be drunk, covetous, unclean, proud, revengeful, vain and idle at the same time?'

William Penn, Some Fruits of Solitude

In Luke's Gospel, Jesus tells a tale of two men going to the Temple to pray – a vivid and colourful piece of biting satire. Into the holy Temple comes a Pharisee, obsessed by his own virtue. During the 1st century, Pharisees were well known for their strict adherence to the Law of Moses. But this Pharisee goes *beyond* his fellows, fasting more often than is required and giving a tithe on all he receives, even when the rules don't require it. The Pharisee parades his goodness before God – and everyone else too.

In contrast there is a publican. Such men were despised for being collaborators with the Roman authorities. Best known for collecting tolls or taxes, they were commonly described as tax collectors. But there is no condemnation in Jesus' parable of the publican's occupation. Instead, the man is held up as an example of humility, because he recognises his state of unworthiness, and confesses his need for reconciliation.

In the Eastern Orthodox Church the *Sunday of the Publican and the Pharisee* commemorates the parable and begins the three-week pre-Lenten season. It warns against the hypocrisy of the Pharisee and provides an example of the humility which should be practised during the Lenten period. This is one of the prayers said at the time:

Let us flee from the pride of the Pharisee!
And learn humility from the Publican's tears!
Let us cry to our Saviour: have mercy on us, only merciful One!

October 4 – Choices

'Betwixt the devil and the deep sea.'
Erasmus, Adagia

One of the reasons people struggle to make choices is that they know that when they've made up their mind they are automatically ruling out the thing they've chosen to reject. They'll tell you it's a no-win situation. You make the choice, and that's hard enough. Then you have to live with missing out on something.

When children are in their developmental stages they need help with that kind of pressure. 'Do you want to go to the park or to watch a DVD?' Impossible choice! They may want to do both. Choosing the park means no DVD, and *vice versa*. So one way to help children is to give them 'practice choices', decisions that are 'win-win'. 'We're going to the park today and we can watch a DVD. Which one would you like to do first?' Success! 'There's a banana and an apple. I know you like both. So, which one would you like now, and which one shall we keep for later?'

I'm not sure whether this technique will make any child more adept at making choices in adult life, but it does flag up two important things. First, don't rush into choices; take your time to consider your options. 'Marry in haste; repent at leisure' we are told. Well, I'm not sure about that. But if it were to be 'Decide in haste; repent at leisure' I know exactly what that means.

And, second, it's possible to live with most choices, even if they don't turn out to be the right option or you wish you'd chosen differently. Choices are no more or less than changes in direction, where at least you had more than one option.

I will not choose what many men desire,
Because I will not jump with common spirits,
And rank me with the barbarous multitudes.
William Shakespeare, *The Merchant of Venice*

October 5 – Failure

'Don't be discouraged by failure.
It can be a positive experience.'
Attributed to John Keats

Operation Market Garden took place between September 17th and 25th 1944 and was supposed to end the Second World War by Christmas. It was unsuccessful and the war continued well into 1945. 'Market' was the name given the airborne forces, while the troops on the ground were the 'Garden' part. The goal of Field Marshal Montgomery, who had dreamed up the plan, was to force an entry into Germany and over the Rhine, securing the bridges and allowing a rapid advance by armoured units into northern Germany. Initially the operation was successful and several bridges were captured. However, at Arnhem, the British 1st Airborne Division encountered far stronger resistance than anticipated. In the ensuing battle, only a small force managed to hold one end of the Arnhem road bridge and after the ground forces failed to relieve them they were overrun on September 21st. The rest of the division, trapped in a small pocket west of the bridge, had to be evacuated on September 25th.

The code-name 'Operation Market Garden' is often replaced by 'A Bridge Too Far', the title of a well-known film about the whole event. But how was such an innocuous name chosen in the first place for such a dangerous and audacious operation? We may never know. But this I *do* know: where once the phrase 'Market Garden' was, and is still, for me synonymous with fruit and veg stalls in a farmers' market, it's also associated with waste and suffering, destruction and failure.

Behind the most innocuous of names
can lurk danger and death.
It just depends how we look at it.

October 6 – Rest

'Sleepe after toyle, port after stormie seas,
Ease after warre, death after life, does greatly please.'
Edmund Spenser, The Faerie Queene

'The Rest and Be Thankful' is a section of the A83 road in Scotland which runs from Tarbert on the west shore of Loch Lomond to Campbeltown at the south end of the Kintyre peninsula. 'The Rest and Be Thankful' – known locally as 'The Rest' – is so named because the climb out of Glen Croe is so long and steep at the end that it was traditional for travellers to rest at the top and be thankful for having made it. As a result, *Rest and be thankful* are the words inscribed on a stone near the junction of the A83 and the B828, placed there by soldiers who built the original military road in 1753, now known as the *Drovers' road.* The original stone fell into ruin and was replaced by a commemorative stone at the same site.

I discovered recently that there's an organisation called, 'The Friends of the Rest'. They're a group of enthusiasts who are interested in restoring the old Rest and Be Thankful road as a motoring heritage site. The Rest and Be Thankful featured prominently in Scottish motor sport for many years, especially in the '50s and '60s, helping launch the careers of some of the greats of the international sport, such as Sir Jackie Stewart.

'Friends of the Rest.' A wonderful idea! And wouldn't it be good if that idea were utilised for other kind of 'rests' too? How I wish I'd known how to be a Friend of the Rest when I worked too many hours doing too many things, and missed out on important family time, space for myself and time for prayer as a result?

Because I now value my times of rest and renewal, and I'm all the more thankful when they come along, this is my prayer:

Dear God, today, for a time, I'm going to be a friend of the rest.

October 7 – Appearances can be deceptive

'Things are seldom what they seem,
Skim milk masquerades as cream.'
WS Gilbert, HMS Pinafore

I'm not a great *Doctor Who* fan, but I've always been fascinated by the amazing Police Box that has remained central to the *Doctor Who* stories over several decades. On the outside it's a plain, blue, uninteresting Police Box. But on the inside it is transformed and becomes a massive space of lights and control panels, switches and levers, drama and activity. The writers of the early *Doctor Who* scripts named it 'The Tardis' (Time And Relative Dimension in Space) and 'tardis' has slipped into common parlance to describe a place that looks plain and small on the outside but on the inside seems much bigger and grander.

As well as not being a *Doctor Who* fan, I'm not a lepidopterist either! That's a person who studies and collects butterflies – and I'm definitely not one of those. But I *do* know that a butterfly emerges from a chrysalis. When a caterpillar is ready to change into a butterfly, it forms a pupa, a hard shell of protein which protects the changing life-form inside. That's a chrysalis.

I once held a chrysalis in my palm. That was OK for me, because the chrysalis didn't move. If it had still been a caterpillar I wouldn't have let it near me. I'm not good with little crawly things! But the chrysalis just looked dead, as dull and uninteresting as an old Police Box. But a chrysalis is a tardis! There's more going on inside than the hard, dull, exterior shell of the pupa would ever indicate. And, of course, in time, the wonder that is a fully formed butterfly emerges, in all its amazing delicacy and glorious colour.

Things are often judged more by how they look than by what they are.
A person, too, may be judged only by their appearance,
when they might actually be a tardis,
with amazing things inside ready to be shared.

October 8 – Parents

'Children begin by loving their parents; as they grow
older they judge them; sometimes they forgive them.'
Oscar Wilde, The Picture of Dorian Gray

Someone once said that when they were a teenager, their parents
knew nothing, but by the time they'd turned twenty their parents
had learned a great deal. I expect I thought that of my own parents
too. And my children will certainly have said something like it.

I have a black-and-white photograph of my father on an Ayrshire beach. He has his trousers rolled up ready to paddle in the
sea. It's a lasting image for me of security and strength. My dad
died when he was old, but I remember him always being solid and
dependable. I love him deeply and I miss him every day. My
mother died when she was fifty-eight. But the image I have of her
now is not of a fifty-eight-year-old, but of a young woman, aged
about thirty-five. I would have been about ten or so – a very
impressionable age. I have no photograph. It is simply etched in
my mind.

I don't know how troublesome a teenager I was or how much
my parents managed to learn by the time I turned twenty. But they
have clearly left me images of dependability, love and happiness –
and that's good enough parenting for me.

*You that are parents, discharge your duty; though you cannot
impart grace to your children, yet you may impart knowledge.
Let your children know the commandments of God. 'Ye shall
teach them your children.' You are careful to leave your children
a portion; leave the oracles of heaven with them; instruct them
in the law of God. If God spake all these words, you may well
speak them over again to your children.*

Thomas Watson, from Josiah Hotchkiss Gilbert's
Dictionary of Burning Words of Brilliant Writers

October 9 – Marriage

'I have always considered marriage as the most interesting event
of one's life, the foundation of happiness or misery.'
George Washington, Letter to Burwell Bassett

Two people who love one another making their relationship public
and permanent – marriage! The foundation of happiness, we
hope, rather than misery. So what is the secret of a marriage that
lasts four or five decades or more? A lot can happen over the years.
Personalities change, bodies age, romantic love waxes and wanes
and no marriage is free from conflict. What enables a marriage to
endure is how a couple handles those changes.

I've been married about four times. I say *about* four times
because I've lost count. All these marriages have been to the same
person, but my wife and I have changed, and so has our relationship
and the things we enjoy together. We've learned again and again
what we mean to each other, and we've fallen in love several times.

Tom Paxton sings a song for his wife, Midge, to whom he's been
married for many years. It's called 'Marry Me Again'. What a wonderful sentiment! Because it's just how I feel.

Here's a blessing for marriage from the Native American culture, from the Apache tribe:

Now you will feel no rain;
for each of you will be shelter for the other.
Now you will feel no cold;
for each of you will be warmth for the other.
Now there is no loneliness for you;
you are two persons, but there is only one life before you.
Go now to your dwelling place,
to enter into the days of your togetherness;
and may your days be good and long on the earth.

October 10 – Little by little, once again

'Nothing can be done except little by little.'
Attributed to Charles Baudelaire

A church building had been closed in Edinburgh. In the restructuring of the Church's life and work in the city, this small congregation had been united with another to make a stronger unit. The new congregation had to decide what would happen to the redundant building. Imaginative suggestions and creative options were pursued with enthusiasm and purpose. While this book is being written, all of that is still being done.

While these decisions were being explored, there were the church's artefacts to dispose of. What was to happen to pews and stained-glass windows, hymnbooks and pew Bibles, Communion table and Font, all the accoutrements familiar in any church? Some were used by the new congregation. Others were relocated in local churches. And a few items were offered to anyone who might be interested. When I heard about this, I asked if I could have an item that meant a lot to me. Now I am the proud custodian of a simple wooden offering plate.

A former minister of that church had been a good friend. He'd died several years before, and this offering plate is in memory of him. I can now hold something my friend has lovingly taken, placed on the Communion table and said prayers over. It is a tangible link to someone I love. And an offering plate is also a reminder of generations of offerings, gathered in by the faithful people of God. Little by little, Sunday by Sunday, people put their offerings in this plate. It's not about money alone, but about years of giving of time, talents and other gifts to the glory of God.

Little by little, offerings make a difference. Little by little, faithfulness and commitment matter. Little by little, day by day.

What are the offerings you might drop into an offering plate today?
And when you've given today, what about tomorrow?

October 11 – Permanent

'I shall never transform anything permanent ...
All I ask is that good things also have their place.'
Attr. to Richard Wagner, Cosima Wagner's Diaries

When I was twenty-two I went camping for the first time. I wasn't into camping at all, but I'd been persuaded that it would be a good way to have a cheap holiday with the minimum of organisation. So I borrowed a 'one-man-tent' from the local Scout troop, a sleeping bag from a mate and a rucksack from our next-door neighbour. I'd worked out what I needed to take with me, clarified my destination and arranged my transport. It was going to be the best adventure ever, a holiday I'd always remember.

Yes, it was a great adventure. And, yes, it is a holiday that is firmly fixed in my memory. And yes, I did enjoy it in lots of ways. But there are three reasons why my first camping holiday has had a lasting and permanent affect on me. The first is – I forgot to take sugar with me! And, there being no shops within walking distance, I had to endure two weeks of no sugar in tea and coffee or on my cornflakes. I've never used sugar in tea and coffee or on cornflakes ever since. It's permanent ...

The second is – I forgot my razor! And, there being no shops ... I'd never really liked shaving, so it was no great hardship. But, there again, I'd never been unshaven for two weeks before. But I liked it! And I've had a beard ever since. It's a permanent part of who I am and how I look.

And the third one? Easy – I've never been camping since! I hated it. I have a lifelong aversion to holidaying under canvas! It's permanent! And I have a beard and sugarless coffee to prove it!

What is permanent is there for a reason.
What the reason might be is for us to ponder.
What we ponder might give us answers to who we are.

October 12 – Well done!

'When I'm not thank'd at all, I'm thank'd enough,
I've done my duty, and I've done no more.'
Henry Fielding, The Life and Death of Tom Thumb the Great

A friend told me a story recently that made me think. Her little girl had come home from school while her aunt was visiting. The child liked her aunt – her mother's sister – and always had fun with her. Aunt Megan was a teacher, and lots of the activities shared with her were teaching-orientated. But that was OK, because Aunt Megan was Aunt Megan and you just got used to that.

However, the little girl wasn't interested in Aunt Megan *right away*, because she had something really exciting to tell her mum. So, bounding into the kitchen, she announced, 'Mummy! Mummy! I got the result of Friday's test.' 'Oh,' her mum replied, 'and how did you get on?' The beaming child answered, 'I got 98%.' Before her mother could respond Aunt Megan had come into the kitchen and asked, 'You got *how* much for your test?' '98%,' the child repeated, with an ever-broadening smile. 'Oh,' Aunt Megan replied, 'and what happened to the other 2%?' The little girl's smile disappeared in an instant.

It doesn't take much to work out that what she heard from a well-meaning aunt was disappointment and a sense of failure. I'm sure that's not what Aunt Megan meant. But that's what was communicated. The child *knew* she wasn't perfect, but it didn't need an Aunt Megan or anyone else to reinforce that. A simple 'Well done!' would have been better. Leave the lost 2% to another time. Concentrate on what's been done well. People receive too many negative signals throughout their lives without the Teacher-Aunt-Megan in us making it worse.

A 'Well done!' to someone
might make all the difference to them today.

October 13 – Counting

'Count your blessings.'
Johnson Oatman Jr, Count Your Blessings

The home in which I was brought up had a living room, kitchen, hallway and toilet on the ground floor, and three bedrooms on the first floor. So, logically, it had a staircase. The stair had fourteen steps – seven to a small landing; two on the turn of the stair; five up to the hallway outside the bedrooms ... one, two, three, four, five, six, seven; one, two; one, two, three, four five. The house I live in now has twenty-one stairs ... twelve to a half-landing; three from there to the back of the house; six from the half-landing to the rooms at the front. So, using the upstairs toilet at night means one, two, three, four, five six downwards; then one, two, three up to the loo. I know it so well I can do it in the dark.

For as long as I can remember, I've counted the steps of every staircase I go up or down. A behaviour therapist might have a field day with this. It might even be a condition defined by a label – I don't know. But, you see, I thought *everyone* did it.

We are what we are. We do what we do. Wherever it comes from, such behaviour is part of our make-up. We don't *need* to know why we do things. If we accept the idiosyncrasies of our own make-up, we can give thanks for the uniqueness and individuality that is our part of amazing and wonderful humanity.

'One, two, three, four, five,
once I caught a fish alive.
Six, seven, eight, nine, ten,
then I threw it back again.'

I wonder whether that was done every time.
But then, who's counting?

October 14 – Memory again

'When time who steals our years away
Shall steal our pleasures too,
The mem'ry of the past will stay
And half our joys renew.'
Thomas Moore, 'Song', from Juvenile Poems

'The Great British Bake Off' has become a TV institution in recent years, highlighting skills in the art of baking which were either unknown or long-forgotten. The creation of cakes and pastries, delicacies and 'show-stoppers' by skilled professionals and enthusiastic amateurs, has made many shout, 'I could do that!'

My grandmother, however, needed no such TV series. The knowledge passed down from generation to generation of bakers made books on baking and instructional TV programmes redundant. It was *assumed t*hat recipes, tips, basics and special ideas would be passed on to create another generation of skilled bakers. I never once saw my grandmother consult a recipe, cookery book, magazine article, loose-leaf notebook or dog-eared list. Instead, it was a pinch of this and a cupful of that, a handful of one thing and a couple of spoonfuls of another, the white dish for this pie and the large tin for that cake – and her baking was always fantastic. It had all been committed to memory. She'd listened to her mother, practised the baker's art, and could remember it all.

There is much listening to be done if the art of good living is to be well practised. A lot of the wisdom and knowledge of those around us isn't written down. And if good things are committed to memory, and regularly practised so that the skills are kept up to date, then we will have what we need to pass on to the next generation. No book or TV programme will be necessary.

Don't be afraid to give yourself to memory;
for memory has much, yet, to give to you.

October 15 – Sisters

'In the cookies of life, sisters are the chocolate chips.'
Anonymous

If I were being 'politically correct' when I was exploring 'brotherly love' earlier, I should have added 'sisterhood'. But Robert Burns didn't when he wrote: 'Man to man the world o'er shall brothers be for a' that.' I won't either. Instead, I'll share a story ...

St Mary's Episcopal Cathedral is Scotland's largest cathedral, a masterpiece of Victorian architecture. With its three spires dominating Edinburgh's western skyline, it is a landmark throughout the city. *Three* spires? Yes, and for a good reason. Two sisters, Barbara and Mary Walker, left the whole of their property to the Episcopal Church in Scotland, enabling the building of a cathedral dedicated to St Mary the Virgin. The design of Sir George Gilbert Scott was chosen following an architectural competition. The foundation stone was laid in 1874 by the Duke of Buccleuch and Queensberry, and the building was consecrated in 1879. The cost was £110,000, but rising wages curtailed the completion of the chapter house and western spires. The former was added in 1890 and the two additional western spires were added in 1914 – in memory of the founders. So, there is a typical cathedral spire at the east end, and the twin spires in memory of Barbara and Mary stand proudly over the west door. What would the sisters think now of their legacy? Maybe they wouldn't have sought the accolade of two magnificent spires. But, nonetheless, the devotion and generosity of the two sisters is there for all to see.

Not for us, perhaps, two cathedral spires. But might we not stand proud, with our brothers and sisters, in our devotion and generosity, so that people see a landmark which will make them value their memory of us?

What might stand in memory of us when we are gone?

October 16 – Choices, again

'The power of choosing good and evil
is within the reach of all.'
Origen of Alexandria, Origen De Principiis

I love coffee-shops! National chains, small independent places, adjuncts to department stores, I love the café culture – apart, that is, from the increasingly bewildering array of choices coffee-shops seem obliged to deliver. It's not enough that I have to decide 'Would you like a blueberry muffin with that?' or 'Any Danish pastries for you today, sir?' It's that I have to choose what kind of coffee I want in the first place. Long gone are the days when the choice was 'black' or 'white'. *Now* you have to choose between espresso or latté, mocha or cappuccino, tall or short, skinny or fat, frothy or plain, ginger or cinnamon … and that's *before* your companion asks for a tea, and you have to go through another range of choices – Assam or Earl Gray, fruit or herbal, British Rail or Builders'. 'Black coffee with cold milk on the side' is enough for me. And 'No, thank you, I don't want a blueberry muffin with that.'

We have choices in other parts of our living. We're not simply victims of random chance. It's too easy to stay content with whatever comes along. But consideration of options is important. The beginning of the process is to have solid principles to inform our choices. What's best for those I love? What difference will this make? What's the most loving thing to do?

There are some who have little or no choice in anything. It's a case of 'Black coffee with cold milk' or nothing at all. But when we *do* have to make choices, let's do our best to make the right ones and base them on the right principles. And, no, I still don't want a blueberry muffin with that!

The strongest principle of growth lies in human choice.
George Eliot, *Daniel Deronda*

October 17 – Influence again

'To influence a person is to give him one's own soul.'
Oscar Wilde, The Picture of Dorian Gray

I first climbed the 4046 feet of Ben Nevis I was fourteen years old, and did so with the remarkable Bert Bissell. My Boys' Brigade company in Fort William had a visit every year from young people in Dudley in the Midlands, led by this notable mountain climber and peace campaigner. Bert Bissell had founded the Young Men's Bible Class at Vicar Street Methodist Church in Dudley in 1925. Working as a probation officer, he'd led a pilgrimage party from the Bible class to the summit of Ben Nevis on VJ Day, 1945, to construct a 'Peace Cairn'. The expedition was repeated annually thereafter with my BB company now involved, a tradition which continued for some 50 years.

Bert Bissell lived till he was 96. He was the holder of the World Methodist Peace Prize. No one is quite sure how many times he climbed Ben Nevis. Doubtless somebody will figure it out. You can count that kind of thing. But no one will know how many young lives Bert Bissell influenced through the years. You can't count that. Yet we know that *many* lives have been changed, and these lives have changed those of others in turn, because of the faith and commitment to peace of this influential man.

I can count how many times *I've* climbed Ben Nevis. The answer is two! That kind of thing is easy to figure. But how many lives have I influenced through the years? That's the kind of thing no one will ever be able to count. But, if *anyone's* been changed by a fraction of the faith, passion and commitment to peace I've learned from people like Bert Bissell, then that's enough of a Peace Cairn for me.

What stones have you placed in your memorial cairn
for others to see in the years to come?

October 18 – Awareness, again

'In awareness there is no becoming, there is no end to be gained.
There is silent observation without choice and condemnation,
from which there comes understanding.'

J Krishnamurti

'Elegy Written in a Country Churchyard' by the 18th-century poet
Thomas Gray is but one of his impressive poems. I inherited a
book of Gray's poetry from my mother-in-law. I found a marker
in another one of the poems, *Ode on the Death of a Favourite Cat
Drowned in a Tub of Goldfishes*. A comical poem? Not at all! For
here is tragedy, sadness and poignancy wrapped up in the language
of Greek myth and ancient fable.

> *Presumptuous maid! With looks intent*
> *Again she stretched, again she bent,*
> *Nor knew the gulf between.*
> *(Malignant Fate sat by and smiled)*
> *The slippery verge her feet beguiled,*
> *She tumbled headlong in.*
>
> *Eight times emerging from the flood*
> *She mewed to every watery god,*
> *Some speedy aid to send.*
> *No dolphin came, no Nerrid stirred:*
> *Nor cruel Tom nor Susan heard,*
> *A favourite has no friend.*

Why did my mother-in-law choose to mark this particular poem?
It was so that any 'cruel Tom' reading it might be more aware of
tragedy, and take it more seriously in the future.

Awareness always brings new understanding.

October 19 – Rebuke

'In all reprehensions, observe to express rather thy love
than thy anger; and strive rather to convince than exasperate:
but if the matter do require any special indignation,
let it appear to be the zeal of a displeased friend,
rather than the passion of a provoked enemy.'

Thomas Fuller (1608-1661)

In the Church of England a 'tippet' is a long black scarf worn by the minister. It evolved in the 14th century from the long sleeves of the priestly garb, and typically had one end hanging down to the knees. Later 'tippet' became the name for any scarf-like wrap. In some traditions the tippet is referred to as the 'preaching scarf' of my Presbyterian upbringing.

I wish I'd known this when I worked with a man called Ron Tippet. I might have had fun calling him Ron Black Scarf! Ron was a good Christian man with a sincere and humble faith. In a Christian Aid Sunday sermon I said, 'Successive UK governments are equally culpable in their appalling level of overseas aid.' I meant it to hit home. But Ron Tippet was unhappy. He phoned me on the Monday. 'I haven't slept,' he said. 'We need to talk.'

When we met, Ron told me of his time overseas as a civil servant with oversight of UK aid, and his struggles with corruption. He was angry that I'd put the blame on the government and, by association, on him. I learned a lot from Ron – about listening to a wise man who had more experience than I had, as well as the value of an honest, gentle rebuke.

Here was no 'provoked enemy'. Here, instead, was the 'zeal of a displeased friend' and always expressed in love.

*To be rebuked by goodness
is to know goodness as your teacher.*

October 20 – Light

'O death, where *is* thy sting?
O grave, where *is* thy victory?'
Bible: 1 Corinthians 15:55

In Latin, 'tenebrae' means shadows or darkness. In the Episcopal and Roman Catholic traditions, Tenebrae is a religious service for the last three days of Holy Week, from the morning of Maundy Thursday through Good Friday and Holy Saturday, prior to Easter morning. It's designed as a service of mourning, observed in the evening in the darkness of the church, commemorating the suffering and death of Christ and symbolising the darkness over the earth, part of the gospel story of the Crucifixion. In Tenebrae a candelabrum of fifteen candles is used. Accompanied by a series of readings – often from the Lamentations of the Old Testament – and the chanting of Psalms, the candles are progressively extinguished until only one faint, flickering light is left burning.

I have never been to a Tenebrae service. It must be powerfully evocative of the darkness of mourning. And yet one light remains, one fragile, stuttering light. Maybe to plunge the church into total darkness would be too much for people. But that one remaining light symbolises hope ... hope that darkness will *not* have its way and that the grave will not have the ultimate victory. A light *will* continue to shine ...

Tenebrae – the necessary enactment of the gathering darkness, because we've all been there; but a focus also on the never-ending light, which we all need to give us hope for the future.

Light is the first of painters.
There is no object so foul
that intense light
will not make it beautiful.
Ralph Waldo Emerson, *Nature*, Chapter III

October 21 – Knowledge

'When you know a thing, to hold that you know it;
and when you do not know a thing,
to allow that you do not know it –
this is knowledge.'
Confucius, The Confucian Analects

Behind the communion table in Iona Abbey is a cloth, made of embroidered silk, hanging from one side of the chancel to the other and stretching from floor to just above head height. Now, being a mere Presbyterian, it was some surprise to me when a friend pointed out that such a hanging has a name in Episcopal churches and cathedrals. 'It's called a Dossal or Dorsal,' he told me, 'and you get them in most church buildings behind the altar or the Bishop's throne. It's from the French *dos* meaning back. People usually call it the altar screen. But Dossal it is.' And I thought it was just something hung there to cover a rather unattractive stone wall ...

But ... the *next* time we're together admiring a Dossal in some religious building, I'll ask him if he knows where the *Baguette* should be. And I'll explain that a Baguette is a plain or decorated wooden moulding across the top of a Dossal, or suspended above it from a cornice, to enhance the beauty of the Dossal itself. So there! Fifteen-all!

How did I know that? I came across the name in a book I was reading and looked it up! And I'm just *itching* for the opportunity to come out with such a piece of erudition. It's not that my friend and I are always involved in ecclesiastical one-upmanship. It's just that we both like to learn new things. Now, where's my baguette gone?

Being competitive, if it's handled in the right way,
can lead to the expansion of knowledge.

October 22 – Apologies

'Thou wilt lament
Hereafter, when the evil shall be done
And shall admit no cure.'
Homer, The Iliad

In the first baptism I conducted as a minister I got the baby's name wrong! I compounded the felony by getting the gender wrong too, giving the unsuspecting baby boy the similarly sounding name of a girl. I'll not go into the details, but I will say that I sought to alleviate the distress by offering an apology. It didn't work. The mother remained distressed. Her wailing was heard at end of the parish. The family never darkened the door of the church again, at least not while I was there.

Apologies are important, even when we 'shall admit no cure'. So let me offer these thoughts, if for no other reason than to help me get over the memory of that awful occasion. A friend of mine is fond of saying, 'When you realise you've made a mistake, apologise right away. It's easier to eat humble pie while it's still warm.' How true! Often hurt has festered because an apology hasn't been offered soon enough.

GK Chesterton said, 'A stiff apology is a second insult. The injured party does not want to be compensated because he has been wronged; he wants to be healed because he has been hurt.' Sometimes an apology is so unhelpfully offered that it does more harm than good. A minister going out of a church and trying to offer an inept apology is a good example of that! Remember the hurt and the need for healing. So what words of apology have been left unsaid over your graves of hurt and distress?

'The bitterest tears shed over graves
are for words left unsaid and for deeds left undone.'
Harriet Beecher Stowe, *Little Foxes*

October 23 – Vocation

'We may affirm absolutely that nothing great in the world
has been accomplished without passion.'
Georg Wilhelm Friedrich Hegel,
Lectures on the Philosophy of History

In conversation with people in the social work and community
education fields, one of the social workers told us that, when she
was younger, she used to be a nun, serving as a religious sister
within a closed order. Things changed and she left the order,
trained as a social worker, fell in love and married, and now was
the mother of three young children. 'Oh,' someone said, 'you've
left your vocation?' The woman replied gently, 'No, not *left* my
vocation. I've simply exchanged it for several others, including
being a social worker, a wife and a mother. These vocations will
do me for now.'

In the ministry I was told I had a vocation; when my sister
trained as a nurse people said nursing was a vocation; in our local
Catholic diocese the news was that fewer young men were finding
a vocation; when my daughter trained as a nursery nurse she took
'vocational' courses. 'Nothing great ... has been accomplished
without a passion' is quite right.

But there is a danger that this remains a narrow view of the
concept of vocation. Is a committed social worker not following
a vocation by giving it his or her all? Don't wives, husbands and
partners heed an inner prompting to be the best they can be? Is a
parent not committed to the important vocation of parenthood?
None of *them* are 'without passion'. And, thankfully, none of them
is short of great contributions to our world – and that I'm pleased
to 'affirm absolutely'.

Our true vocation is to do the best we can do,
to be the best we can be with whatever we are,
and to be passionately committed to our cause.

October 24 – More music

'If music be the food of love, play on.'
William Shakespeare, Twelfth Night

I don't know who said this, but it bears repeating:

Any world that contains the creative talents of Meat Loaf and Mozart can't be all bad. Any imaginative mind that can create the oboe and the Moog synthesiser gives hope to humanity. Any God who can offer us the voices of Maria Callas and Frank Sinatra has done a good job.

Whoever said it knows the value of music to a worthwhile existence. Of course musical tastes will vary, but what is never up for debate is what music does and what it offers. When you are moved to tears by a piece of music, are you not finding an expression of something deep within you which is beyond words? When you are excited by rhythm so that your feet tap and your hands clap, is there not dancing in your soul? When your heart races when a beautiful song is sung, are you not raised above the mundane to a higher sphere?

This is what prompted the poet Byron to write:

There's music in the sighing of a reed;
There's music in the gushing of a rill;
There's music in all things, if men had ears:
Their earth is but an echo of the spheres.
From 'Don Juan' by George Gordon, Lord Byron

I don't know who offered us the words below. But, given the nature of this reflection, it might well have been me!

Music is what feelings sound like.

October 25 – A deeper silence

'Under all speech that is good for anything
there lies a silence that is better.'

Thomas Carlyle, Sir Walter Scott

4' 33" ('Four minutes, thirty-three seconds') is a composition in three movements by the American composer John Cage. It was composed in 1952 for any instrument or combination of instruments, and the score instructs the performer(s) not to play the instrument(s) during the entire duration of the piece. The first movement has thirty seconds of silence, the second two minutes and twenty three seconds and the third one minute and forty seconds – though there may be times when the piece is played slower and thus with longer movements. I haven't heard the piece myself, but I'm not sure I'd like it. John Cage was an experimental composer, so this kind of modern music might be beyond me. Mind you, I could always get a copy of the score and learn it myself and amaze my friends by playing it from memory!

The piece is usually perceived as 'four minutes thirty-three seconds of silence'. But that's not the way Cage saw it. Instead, he wanted the audience to hear the sounds of the environment while the composition is performed. He was offering his listeners a piece of music through which they could hear Simon and Garfunkel's 'sound of silence'.

I'm still not sure I would like it. But what I do know is this – John Cage is pointing us towards an important truth. So much of the noise of our daily living blocks out any opportunity to be still and truly listen to the silence. When was the last time we were aware of our breathing, or the beating of our heart, or the sighing of the wind, of the ticking of a clock, or the distant song of a bird?

Listen to the sound of silence;
you might be surprised at the music you hear.

October 26 – Wonder

'Wonder is the beginning of wisdom.'

Socrates, Phaedrus

I was changing my daughter's nappy. Modern man ... The baby was moving from milk to solids, and, as a consequence, various combinations of food were being tried. Some of the puréed food was successful. Some wasn't. But if what went *in* was variable, what came *out* at the other end was equally unpredictable. Sometimes it was absolutely foul! But the nappy-changing had to be done. After all, a modern man can't assume that he has sole ownership of the *fun* bits of child-rearing.

I steeled myself. I tried not to look at the mess. I held my breath so I didn't have to smell it, and, when I couldn't hold my breath any longer, I turned away to take a gulp of good air before I returned to my chore. My daughter was unperturbed, unconcerned about my discomfort.

And then I realised the little girl was doing something I hadn't seen before. With jerky but nonetheless clear movements, she was bringing her hands together in front of her face, then taking them away again, closing them together, then pulling them apart. Then I saw what she was doing. There was a light above the bed and she was blocking out the light and opening her hands so she could see it again, shutting it out and revealing it once more, off, on, off, on. A little child was having a new experience – and right in front of my eyes.

In the midst of changing a horrible nappy I was full of wonder at the way a child learns, just as she was full of wonder as she opened her hands and her eyes to something amazing.

If wonder is the beginning of wisdom,
I wonder what kind of wisdom I'll find
when I wonder and wonder some more.

October 27 – Guidance

'Do not lean on your own understanding.'
Bible: Proverbs 3:5

In the *Musée Cognacq-Jay* in Paris there is a dramatic painting by Rembrandt, the Dutch artist, called *Baalam and the Ass*. It depicts the grandly-attired Baalam raising his staff to beat his four-legged beast of burden, while at the same time being threatened with punishment for his actions by the hosts of heaven, swords and all.

The story of Baalam and his ass is found in the Bible in the book of Numbers. Baalam was a heathen prophet summoned by the Moabite King Balak to curse Israel. The story tells us that, on the way to Balak, Baalam's she-ass refuses to walk because an angel is blocking the road. The ass can see the angel but Balaam can't. So he strikes the she-ass with his staff. The ass crushes Baalam's foot against a wall in her terror. Three times she is beaten by her master. Three times she refuses to move. And after a third thrashing, she has had enough. 'What have I done to you that you have struck me three times?' Baalam is terrified. An ass that can speak? So he replies, 'Because you have mocked me. If I had a sword in my hand, I would kill you now.' 'What?' the ass responds. 'Am I not your faithful beast of burden, upon which you have ridden for as long as you can remember? Did I ever cause you any trouble?' Then Baalam's eyes are opened, and he sees not only the angel, but the error of his ways. He falls on his face. He knows what God is saying.

Balaam repented. Thank goodness for that, because if he hadn't, the angel in Rembrandt's painting was clearly going to have his head off!

Guidance – God's or otherwise – can come to us
in the most unexpected of ways –
even when your four-legged transport tries to sort you out!

October 28 – Imposters

'He who pretends to be either a painter or engraver
without being a master of drawing, is an imposter.'
William Blake, The Rossetti Manuscript

Here's another of Aesop's fables which has always fascinated me.

A shipwrecked Chimpanzee had been clinging for a long time to a piece of wreckage when a Dolphin came up and offered to carry him ashore. The exhausted Chimpanzee was so grateful for this kind offer that he immediately accepted. As they moved along, the Chimp began to tell the Dolphin many marvellous tales, places he'd been, people he'd met, things he'd done. But every one of them was a series of lies, each one more fanciful than the last. However, the Dolphin listened without comment. Carrying his passenger to safety was more important.

Eventually, however, the Dolphin had to say something. 'Well, well,' he proclaimed with admiration, 'you are indeed an educated chap. In contrast, my friend, my schooling has been sadly neglected. I only went to sea when I was but a week old.'

Just then they entered a large bay. The Dolphin slowed down, looked around the bay and said to his companion, 'I suppose you know Herring Roads?' The Chimp, thinking this was a man's name and not wanting to appear stupid, replied, 'Do I know Rhodes? Well, I should think so! He's an old college chum of mine, and related to our family by ...'

This was too much for the Dolphin, who suddenly made a great leap, and then, diving quickly, left the imposter in the air for an instant before he fell into the sea and disappeared from sight.

An odd tale, perhaps, but a salutary one. Aesop was right. In the end liars deceive no one but themselves.

Beware of imposters,
for they might be too good to be true.

October 29 – Cruel

'Let no man deceive you with vain words.'
Bible: Ephesians 5:6

I suggested earlier that church communication outlets were a rich source of amusing bloopers! I promised myself I'd stop at two days' worth of items. I failed!

*The outreach committee has enlisted 25 visitors
to make calls on people who are not afflicted with any church.*

*The third verse of Blessed Assurance will be sung
without musical accomplishment.*

*For those of you who have children and don't know it,
we have a crèche downstairs.*

*The Rev. Parkinson spoke briefly,
much to the delight of the audience.*

*Twenty-two members were present at the church meeting
held in the hall on Tuesday evening. Mrs Barrington and Mrs
Creswell sang a duet, 'The Lord Knows Why'.*

*Last Wednesday evening
a 'Songs of Praise' was hell at the Methodist church.*

Words can be funny, even though a person doesn't intend them to be. But it's not funny *at all* when words are *deliberately* spoken to be hurtful – not to amuse, but to be cutting and cruel.

*Laugh with me if I make a 'blooper'.
But chastise me if my words are ever nasty.*

October 30 – Enchantment

'In all things of nature
there is something of the marvellous.'
Aristotle, Parts of Animals

Jodie loved her Enchanted Island. On the best of days, she'd cross the Great Divide to the island of her dreams. She'd discovered the Enchanted Island by accident. But now that she knew its location, she went there as often as she could – on her own, of course. It wasn't that she didn't like sharing. There were plenty of other things to share and people to share them with. But not on an island that was special because she had it to herself.

There was so much to see and do on the Enchanted Island. There was the undergrowth to explore and wild animals to avoid. Keeping a careful eye out for any intruders on her private space was important. And she always had plenty to do – huts to build, plans to make, rituals to enact. It was all marvellous.

In bad weather it was too rough to cross the Great Divide. But on good days she would spend as much time as possible on the Enchanted Island. Today was such a day and Jodie was lost in the island's pleasures. Until, that is, she heard The Voice, quietly at first, and then more loudly and unavoidable in its urgency.

'Jodie! Jodie! Are you there? Come inside now. It's time for tea. Quickly, please. And I hope you're not trampling around in your father's herbaceous border again. How many times have I told you about that? If you stand on his bedding plants, you'll be in real trouble. Come on, girl! It's tea time.' So Jodie set off, back across the Great Divide, in obedience to The Voice's call. But she knew there would be other times when she could return and be drawn easily and quickly into her enchanted delights.

The journey to the land of enchantment begins
with the ticket of a vivid imagination.

October 31 – Work

'All work, even cotton-spinning, is noble; work is alone noble.'
Thomas Carlyle, Past and Present

In his book of mystical tales, *The Wanderer,* Khalil Gibran offers another story, entitled 'Builders of Bridges'.

> *In Antioch where the river Assi goes to meet the sea, a bridge was built to bring one half of the city nearer to the other half. It was built of large stones carried down from among the hills, on the backs of the mules of Antioch. When the bridge was finished, upon a pillar thereof was engraved in Greek and in Aramaic, 'This bridge was builded by King Antiochus II.' And all the people walked across the good bridge over the goodly river Assi. And upon an evening, a youth, deemed by some a little mad, descended to the pillar where the words were engraven, and he covered over the graving with charcoal, and above it wrote, 'The stones of this bridge were brought down from the hills by the mules. In passing to and fro over it you are riding upon the backs of the mules of Antioch, builders of this bridge.' And when the people read what the youth had written, some of them laughed and some marvelled. And some said, 'Ah yes, we know who has done this. Is he not a little mad?' But one mule said, laughing, to another mule, 'Do you not remember that we did carry those stones? And yet until now it has been said that the bridge was builded by King Antiochus.'*

'Credit where credit is due' is a contemporary way of summing up this tale. 'Remember the workers' would be another.

'*A worker who does not need to be ashamed.*'
Bible: II Timothy 2:15

November 1 – Saints

'Let us never forget that if we wish to die like the Saints
we must live like them.
Let us force ourselves to imitate their virtues,
in particular humility and charity.'
Theodore Guerin (Saint Mother Theodore),
Letter to Sisters at Saint Mary's

Working with bereaved people I have often been asked the agonising question, 'Where are they now?' Where has the dead person gone? Is there a heaven? Is the soul eternal? Will there be a meeting up again? These are not just religious questions. The atheist or humanist has the same anxieties. They arise from the fundamental need to remain connected with those who have died, a yearning not to be cut off. It's a grief theory ably explored by Klass, Silverman and Nickman in a book called *Continuing Bonds*. We don't want our bonds with those who have died to be severed.

One response to this deep need in bereaved people comes from the Chicago-based Ecumenical Institute. In life we are influenced by many people – parents, family, friends, role-models, saints and heroes from the past and even fictional characters from the pens of skilled writers. Every decision we make is informed by our relationship with them. It's as if we sit down with them around a large table, listening to one, debating with another, chipping into conversations, overhearing words of wisdom, all to help us move on with life. When someone dies, such is their lasting influence on us that they still remain around our table. We go on communing with them, listening to them and having a lasting relationship with them. They are, and remain, our own saints around our own table. Such continuing bonds can never be broken.

Not even death can force people of importance
to give up their place at our table of saints.

November 2 – The Midas touch

'Greedy eaters dig their graves with their teeth.'
French proverb

'Money makes the world go round,' we are told. Well, maybe …
A Greek legend tells us of Midas, a very wealthy king. Collecting
gold was his whole life. One day as he sat counting his wealth he
saw an old man asleep under a tree. It was Silenus from the court
of Dionysus, god of wine. Midas was cunning and treated Silenus
like a king for ten days before taking him back to Dionysus.
Dionysus was so grateful for the care lavished on his old servant,
he told King Midas he would grant any wish he chose. Midas
asked that anything he touched would be turned to gold.

Dionysus granted his wish but warned him about his greed.
Midas took no heed. He touched a tree and it turned to gold. He
touched the walls of his palace, then his horse, his servant, his
food and finally his children … Everything turned to gold. Midas
couldn't eat, sleep, drink or touch anything because it all turned
to gold.

In the end he went back to find Dionysus and told him that he
wanted to get rid of his golden touch. Dionysus laughed when he
saw the change in the king, but took pity on him and told him to
bathe in the river Pactolus. But King Midas was afraid to get into
the river in case it turned to gold and killed him. So he got a jug
and washed himself down. Little by little his 'golden touch'
washed away. King Midas was relieved. He took jug after jug of
water back to his palace to wash his children, his servants, his
horse and the whole palace. He didn't stop till he had restored
everything to its normal state.

The world stopped for Midas because of his love of money.
Only when he relinquished his greed
did it start to go round again.

November 3 – Wisdom

'Full wise is he that doth himself know.'
Geoffrey Chaucer, The Canterbury Tales

The McEwan Hall is the graduating hall for Edinburgh University. In 1897, William McEwan, a wealthy brewer and politician in the city, commissioned a grand building to be created, at a cost of £115,000. It's an amazing place, circular to the front but D-shaped overall. Inside it's filled with terrific murals. One of the best of these, located high above the centre of the hall, is a scene called 'The Temple of Fame', depicting philosophers and students conversing together. And the whole building is topped by a huge dome, reminiscent of London's Albert Hall, but on a smaller scale.

The McEwan Hall is a fine building. But the finery of it didn't do *me* much good. When I was a student at Edinburgh University the McEwan Hall was often used as an examination hall. And I have to confess that its organ pipes, carvings, murals, 'Temple of Fame' and depictions of philosophers were often more of a distraction than an inspiration for a student who was less prepared for his exams than he should have been.

On the inside of the McEwan Hall's dome is a biblical inscription from Proverbs 4:7:

> *Wisdom is the principal thing, therefore get wisdom,*
> *and with all thy getting, get understanding.*
> *Exalt her and she shall bring thee to honour.*

Maybe if I'd worked on my wisdom *before* I went into my exams I wouldn't have needed inspiration from *anything* the McEwan Hall could offer, and there might have been as much honour in my exam results as there was in a beautiful exam hall.

I need to 'get wisdom' before it slips away.

November 4 – Family

'The family is the natural and fundamental group unit of society
and is entitled to protection by society and the State.'

Article 16(3) of the Universal Declaration of Human Rights

A friend told me the story told of a young woman, who wrote: 'My
sister and I live in the same part of the town but we don't see each
other that often. There's never enough time. My mother lives a
long way away, and when she writes she always asks: "When was
the last time you saw your sister?" I once wrote back: "Three
months ago, I think …" Our mother obviously decided enough
was enough. Shortly afterwards I got a strange letter from her.
"Another of her regular epistles," I thought. But the letter wasn't
finished. All I had were pages one and three. When I looked at it
more carefully, I saw that the letter's greeting was to me *and* my
sister. I was puzzled. Was my mother losing the plot?

I phoned my sister to tell her about my letter and my worries
about mother's state of mind. My sister laughed – not the reaction
I expected. "You'll never guess what *I* got in the post today," she
said. "A letter from mother, addressed to both of us, and it only
has two pages – numbers two and four." The penny dropped!
Mother wasn't going senile after all. She knew exactly what she
was doing. To have all of mother's news, we had to get together to
share the pages to make the letter complete. Since then we each
get half a letter every month and enjoy spending an evening putting the letter together and catching up on news from mother –
and from each other. Finding time doesn't seem to be a problem
any more. Mother is delighted. "When did you last see your
sister?" she asked me recently. "A couple of days ago," I reported.
And I could *feel* my mother smiling down the phone.'

And drops on gate-bars hang in a row,
And rooks in families homeward go,
And so do I.

Thomas Hardy, Weathers

November 5 – Walls again

'We build too many walls and not enough bridges.'
Isaac Newton, Philosophiæ Naturalis Principia Mathematica

The books of Ezra and Nehemiah in the Old Testament cover the period from the fall of Babylon in 539 BC to the second half of the 5th century BC. They recount the return of the children of Israel from exile, the new beginnings for a settled people in Jerusalem and the restoration of worship and a purified Jewish community. Central to this new era is the restoration of the Temple and the rebuilding of the walls of the city. Stage by stage the reconstruction continues. People are raised up to undertake the vital tasks, and successes are marked by great assemblies of the people for rejoicing, celebration and recommitment.

At one point, Nehemiah takes a few men out to inspect the walls. The place is in ruins with rubble everywhere and it's hard for Nehemiah to find a way through the devastation. So, there and then, he makes a promise to his people:

You see the trouble we are in? Jerusalem lies in ruins and its gates have been burned with fire. Come, let us rebuild the walls ... and we will no longer be in disgrace.

With one voice the people reply, 'Let us start rebuilding.' And the work of restoration is under way.

If the fall of the Berlin Wall in 1989 is a symbol of the necessity to break down the walls that divide us and limit our freedom, so the rebuilding of the city walls by Ezra and Nehemiah is a symbol of restoration, of a new beginning of security and peace for a settled people.

Let's continue our rebuilding of what is good and right,
so that our walls stand for all that is safe, peaceful and secure.

November 6 – Me

'To love oneself is the beginning of a life-long romance.'
Oscar Wilde,
Phrases and Philosophies for the Use of the Young

I adore the *Peanuts* cartoons of the late Charles Shultz, especially when he places his characters in the drama of a baseball game. On one occasion the amiable but often bewildered Charlie Brown is standing on the pitcher's mound at the beginning of a game. He notices that the centre-fielder is facing the wrong way. It's crabby and difficult Lucy van Pelt. So Charlie Brown strolls over to her and, in as nice a way as possible, suggests that facing *away* from the action might not be terribly helpful. 'Excuse me,' he says, 'but the game is this way,' pointing towards to the infield.

'I *know* that,' Lucy replies. 'I know, I *know*. But I can't face *that* way. Because when I do the sun shines in my eyes, and I have *very* sensitive and beautiful eyes.'

So Charlie Brown tries a little sarcasm, 'Maybe you'd have us move the whole field around in front of you, eh?'

Still facing *her* way Lucy responds, 'That's a good idea, Charlie Brown. You do just that, 'cause I'm staying right *here!*'

The look on Charlie Brown's face says it all, 'It's me, me, me again. The whole world has to revolve around you, Lucy. You always want things your own way, don't you?' But of course, Charlie Brown would never *dare* to suggest such a thing to Lucy van Pelt. He knows what he is likely to get in return.

My grandmother had a Scots expression for people like Lucy: 'Everyone's oot o' step but oor Jock.' Or put another way, 'She marches to the beat of her own drum.' Just think of the upheaval needed to change round an entire baseball park just because the sun is shining in the centre-fielder's eyes!

Is it 'Me! Me! Me!' all the time?

November 7 – Lasting effects

*'To be capable of steady friendship or lasting love
are the two greatest proofs,
not only of goodness of heart but of strength of mind.'*
Attributed to William Hazlitt

The Mousetrap is a murder-mystery play by Agatha Christie. It opened in the West End of London in 1952 and has been running continuously ever since. With over 24,500 performances it is the longest initial run of any play. It began life in 1947 as a short radio play called *Three Blind Mice*, in honour of Queen Mary, the consort of King George V. It is based on a short story, but Christie asked that the story not be published as long as the play ran in the West End. Because there was already another play entitled *Three Blind Mice* Christie's play had to be renamed. The new name came from Shakespeare's *Hamlet*. It's Hamlet's answer to the King's enquiry about the name of the play whose prologue and first scene the court has just observed. The play is actually *The Murder of Gonzago*, but to the King's question, 'What do you call the play?' Hamlet responds, 'The Mousetrap', because he intends that it 'catch the conscience of the king'.

When she wrote the play, Christie gave the rights to her grandson as a birthday present. And from *The Mousetrap* came a theatrical education charity, 'Mousetrap Theatre Projects', to help young people experience London's theatre. She did not expect her play to run for so long. 'Fourteen months I am going to give it,' someone told her, to which she replied, 'It won't run *that* long. Eight months perhaps. Yes, I think eight months.' She had no idea that a piece of her writing would have such a long-lasting success.

*What, then, of our actions, be they good or bad? Beware! Beware!
Eight months might just be the start of things
that last much longer than we expect!*

November 8 – More light

'Faith is illuminative, not operative.'
Cardinal Newman, Difficulties of Anglicans, Lecture 9

The most celebrated lighthouse of antiquity was built by Ptolemy Soter on the island of Pharos, opposite Alexandria. We're told it could be seen at a distance of forty-two miles. It is, fittingly, one of the seven wonders of the ancient world.

There are also famous lighthouses in our modern times: Eddystone, fourteen miles southwest of Plymouth; the Cordouan lighthouse, at the entrance of the Gironde in France; the Bell Rock, opposite the Firth of Tay in Scotland. And there are many other wonders of modern engineering which light our shores. The light that shines from these lighthouses, be they ancient or modern, warns sailors of danger or guides them safely home.

In a famous cave in New Zealand there is a different kind of light. Sixty miles from Auckland is 'the cave of the glow worms'. It is reached in a boat pulled by a wire for silence. As visitors glide down the stream, they suddenly become aware of a soft light gleaming in the distance. It's like entering a magical fairy world. For, from the top of the cave, thousands of threads hang down from these glowing insects. The light is so bright that it's possible to read a book in the cave. But if there is the slightest noise the bright light dies out, just as if a switch had been turned off.

Whether the light is high above and can be seen for miles, or hangs down gently and offers a soft glow, how sad it would be, and how dangerous, if we were to make the light go out.

Why is it that the brightness of a lighthouse
is measured in 'candle-power'?
It's surely because a candle on its own is very small,
but combine it with lots of others and you get a very bright light.

November 9 – Tested

'Do not tell secrets to those whose faith and silence
you have not already tested.'
Queen Elizabeth I

Sometime, it seems, we are tested more than we should be – or
tested more than other people are. I wonder if you've ever felt that
way. If so, then maybe these are your words.

And if you're being tested right now, are you up for the challenge?

Tested beyond my endurance; tested to do what is right;
Tested right up to the limit; tested to take up the fight;

Tested to challenge what's evil; tested my debts to repay;
Tested, when testing's beyond me; tested, at once to obey;

Tested to face a new challenge; tested to answer the call;
Tested to go where I'm bidden; tested to give up my all;

Tested like no one before me; tested, decisions to make;
Tested with burdens too heavy; tested – my spirit to break?

Tested, and tested, and tested, and tested, and tested, and then ...
Goodness me, would you believe it? I'm tested and tested again ...

Tested, it seems like, for ever. Tested! Do I sound obsessed?
And will I be up for the challenge, ready to cope with the test?

From Welcoming Each Wonder *by Tom Gordon*
Wild Goose Publications, 2010

November 10 – More memories

'God gave us memories
that we might have roses in December.'
JM Barrie, Courage

I went to visit the house in which my grandparents had spent their later years. It was a home full of memories for me – holidays, Christmas, laughter, explorations, celebration, tragedy and much more. How such a modest house could contain so much and how so many people could be crammed into two rooms and a kitchen is beyond me. But, nonetheless, that home was a big part of my childhood development and gave me a store of great memories. Which is just as well, for when I visited the house – it had gone!

Gone was the street of tenements – to be replaced by a modern estate of bungalows, semis and townhouses; gone was the back green of clotheslines and the makeshift football pitch – to be replaced by tidy gardens; gone was the shop on the corner, an Aladdin's cave for a small boy – to be replaced by the pristine layout and soulless efficiency of a Tesco Metro. And my grandparent's flat? Even though there are a couple of houses on the spot where their tenement stood, nothing can replace the uniqueness of that home for me. Bricks and mortar cannot replace the vibrancy of my memories. No physical redevelopment will ever reinvent the influence that makes me what I am. Transformations of the locality can't alter what can never be changed.

Today I'm visiting again the house in which my grandparents spent their later years. But I've not risen from my desk – because it's all still there, where it needs to be, in a memory-bank that I'm always able to visit.

This memory brightens o'er the past, as when the sun concealed
Behind some cloud that near us hangs, shines on a distant field.'
Henry Wadsworth Longfellow, *A Gleam of Sunshine*

November 11 – Remembrance

'I do perceive that the old proverb be not alwaies trew,
for I do finde that the absence of my Nathaniel
doth breede in me the more
continuall remembrance of him.'

Anne, Lady Bacon, To Jane Lady Cornwallis

I was walking in my local park when my eye caught a flash of bright red in the bushes. I went to investigate and found a poppy wreath from the war memorial. It had been blown across the park by the recent storms. I looked around and found half a dozen more wreaths tangled in the undergrowth. A week earlier I'd watched as these poppy wreaths played a central role in the Remembrance Sunday service, as Council and Church, Legion and schools, adults and children laid their tokens of remembrance round the war memorial. The bugler had played the Last Post. Heads had been bowed. A community had remembered. But now, when everyone had finished with their remembrance, the poppy wreaths had been blown away and were stuck in the bushes.

Was this a symbol of what happens to our remembrance? It's for a day, or an hour, or two minutes of silence. But then, all too quickly, it's blown away while life goes on. Remembrance can quickly be forgotten. Remembering is all too brief.

So I gathered up the poppy wreaths from the bushes and laid them round the war memorial again. I don't know how long they stayed there. There was more stormy weather in the next few days. But for a moment at least, for one person, remembrance wasn't just about the events of a Remembrance Sunday, but was another reflective pause on a walk through a local park and onwards in the journey of life.

*Remembrance is the duty we owe to the dead
and the gift we give to the living.*

November 12 – Mourning again

'He that lacks time to mourn, lacks time to mend.
Eternity mourns that. 'Tis an ill cure
For life's worst ills to have no time to feel them.'
Sir Henry Taylor, Philip Van Artevelde

In 1756 Jean Elliot wrote words to an old Scots tune, *The Flowers of the Forest*. As words of mourning they are a powerful expression of the pain of loss. The evocative tune is held in such reverence that it is one of the few that pipers will only perform at funerals or memorial services, and only practise in private or to instruct other pipers.

The Flowers of the Forest is a lament for King James IV, many of his nobles and over ten thousand men who fell at the Battle of Flodden in 1513. Written in Scots, it describes the women's grief at the loss of their young men. Played at the Somme, on the beaches of Normandy, over the hills of the Falklands and on countless Remembrance Sundays, it still calls us all to a rightful and dignified mourning.

I've heard the lilting, at our yowe-milking,
Lassies a-lilting before dawn o' day;
But now they are moaning on ilka green loaning;
'The Floo'rs o' the Forest are a' wede awa'.'

In hairst, at the shearing, nae youths now are jeering,
The bandstarts are lyart, and runkled and grey;
At fair or at preaching, nae wooing, nae fleeching;
The Floo'rs o' the Forest are a' wede awa'.'

yowe = ewes; *lilting* = singing; *ilka* = every; *wede* = withered;
hairst = harvest; *bandstarts* = binders; *lyart* = grizzled;
runkled = crumpled; *fleeching* = coaxing

November 13 – Travelling

'For my part, I travel not to go anywhere, but to go.
I travel for travel's sake.'

Robert Louis Stevenson,
Travels With a Donkey in the Cevenne

I got a text message from my daughter who was on her way north with the family to visit her mother-in-law. It read:

> *It had to happen. No sooner had we turned out of our street and were heading for the bypass, when number one son pipes up from the back of the car, 'Mummy, are we nearly there yet?'*

It's classic, isn't it? A child is so excited about getting to the destination that, short of the adult perspectives of time and distance, impatience spills over into 'Are we there yet?' Every family will have their endless supply of in-the-car distractions, from songs to games, from things to see to stories to make up. And it's all because children are wearied by the long, long journey ...

But, if we are honest, it's not just children who exhibit such impatience and not just on car journeys either. For we all, from time to time, would rather be at the destination and avoid the journey: the enterprise that needs months of planning when it would be easier just to leap right to the end; the course that has to be finished when the certificate and qualifications seem an eternity away; the job search, with the grind of application forms, rejections and interviews, when it would be so much easier if ...

Journeys are a chore – from here to wherever. It would be easier if we could just get there.

'To travel hopefully is a better thing than to arrive.'
Robert Louis Stevenson

November 14 – Politics

'Politics should be the part-time profession of every citizen.'
Henry Brooks Adams, The Education of Henry Adams

We're told that the topics of religion and politics should be avoided in polite company, on the grounds that people hold such strong views on both that discussions can become overheated. As a result, a convivial evening among friends can quickly be ruined. But I'm not so sure.

In his later years, George MacLeod, the founder of the Iona Community, was fond of saying, 'There are only three things that matter: pacifism, politics and personal-pep!' Leaving aside 'personal-pep' for now (his name for the Holy Spirit ...) and having touched on pacifism earlier, George MacLeod believed that a commitment to and involvement with the political process was paramount.

The word 'politics' comes from the Greek and means 'relating to citizens'. It is a system through which the people make collective decisions for the good of all. Some say, 'I'm not involved in politics,' or 'I'll leave the politics to the politicians.' As a result, voter lethargy is a major problem in the UK, and the level of turnout for local and national elections is a blight on modern democracy. By virtue of our citizenship we are already involved in politics. George MacLeod was right. We ought to take it more seriously than we do. Those whom we elect have to be held to account, not just at the ballot box, but by more people being involved in the political process.

Should strong political views be avoided at parties? Well maybe, if it spoils the party for other people. But should the strong voice of political opinion remain silent in our political systems? George MacLeod didn't think so, and neither do I.

'The best politics is right action.'
Mahatma Gandhi

November 15 – Handshakes

'Greet one another with a holy kiss.'
Bible: Romans 16:16

What is a handshake? We know it's a short ritual in which two people grasp each other by the hand, in most cases accompanied by a brief up and down movement. But it's much more than that, isn't it?

Archaeological ruins and ancient texts show that handshaking was practised in ancient Greece in the 5th century BC. It may have been introduced into England by Sir Walter Raleigh in the late 16th century and it's thought to have originated as a gesture of peace by demonstrating that the hand holds no weapon. It's sometimes considered to be in poor taste to show dominance with too strong a handshake. On the other hand (pardon the pun) too feeble a handshake could be viewed as a sign of weakness. Members of the Masonic Brotherhood have a secret handshake. Among some African-American cultures, handshakes can be the beginning of lengthy and well-practised rituals. The current record for the longest handshake is 33 hours and 3 minutes. In 1977 the Mayor of Atlantic City, New Jersey, shook hands with more than 11,000 people in one day.

So, what can be simply defined as a 'short ritual' of greeting has much more to it, it would seem. After all, whether it's ritual or historical, a gesture of peace or brotherhood, weak or strong, one of many or the longest ever, it has the fact of human contact at the root of it. It may not be the 'holy kiss' of the Bible verse above, but touch, greeting and warmth all matter so much.

Don't take a handshake for granted today.
And don't be afraid to offer one.
It might just be what someone else needs –
and might be holier than you think.

November 16 – Tingles

'I shall take the heart ... for brains do not make one happy,
and happiness is the best thing in the world.'
L. Frank Baum, lines for the Tin Woodman
in The Wonderful Wizard of Oz

You'll have heard, 'There were tingles up and down my spine' or 'I felt the hair on the back of my neck stand up' or 'I had goose bumps all over', when something special happens and your body reacts in a 'tingling' kind of way. It happens for me when I read something that touches me deeply. Here's a piece that made me tingle. It's called *The Art of Marriage*, from an anonymous source.

Happiness in marriage is not something that just happens. A good marriage must be created. In marriage the little things are the big things. It's never being too old to hold hands. It's remembering to say 'I love you' at least once a day. It's never going to sleep angry. It's never taking the other for granted; the courtship should not end with the honeymoon, it should continue through the years. It's having a mutual sense of values and common objectives. It is standing together facing the world. It's forming a circle of love that gathers the whole family. It's doing things for each other, not in the attitude of duty or sacrifice but in the spirit of joy. It's speaking words of appreciation and demonstrating gratitude in thoughtful ways. It's not looking for perfection in each other. It's cultivating flexibility, patience, understanding and a sense of humour. It's having the capacity to forgive and forget. It's giving each other an atmosphere in which each can grow old. It's a common search for the good and the beautiful. It's establishing a relationship in which independence is equal, dependence is mutual and obligation is reciprocal. It's not only marrying the right partner; it's being the right partner.

November 17 – Home again

'Home is the place where, when you have to go there,
they have to take you in.'
Robert Frost, The Death of the Hired Man

When I was studying in Washington DC in 1989, I had the privilege of meeting a remarkable man and playing a small part in caring for him as he died. John Levering had been the driving force behind the Servant Leadership School, part of the remarkable expression of Christian community, worship and service that is the Church of the Saviour. I lived with John and his wife, Sara, while John was dying of cancer. John had to be hospitalised from time to time. But each spell in hospital only served to strengthen his desire to be at home.

Being a carer was hard for Sara. To give her a break, I took the caring role for a long weekend. Such was John's graciousness that he made the caring easy. He gave me instructions about cooking, and was patient when I didn't get it right. He allowed me to sit with him and learn from his wisdom, faith and courage. He shared insights from his work as an artist and teacher. He and Sara gave me one of his paintings before he died.

Most of all, John opened up a new understanding of home. Being at home wasn't just about the security of a building, being surrounded by familiarity or having the opportunity to do things in your own time and in your own way. Home was about being at peace, finding an inner space where all was well, and life was complete, and death held no fear. John Levering died at home ... but this was no physical place. It was the place where he found peace and faith, a place where he lived until he died.

Home is where the heart is.
Home is where the love is.
Home is where I ever need to be.

November 18 – Hills

'The gods of the valley are not the gods of the hills,
and you shall understand it.'

Ethan Allen, quoted in Curiosities of Human Nature
by Samuel Griswold Goodrich

The King James version of Psalm 121 comes to us in this form:

I will lift up mine eyes unto the hills; from whence cometh my help. My help cometh from the Lord which made heaven and earth. He will not suffer thy foot to be moved; He that keepeth thee will not slumber. Behold, he that keepeth Israel shall neither slumber nor sleep. The Lord is thy keeper; the Lord is thy shade upon thy right hand. The sun shall not smite thee by day nor the moon by night. The Lord shall preserve thee from all evil; he shall preserve thy soul. The Lord shall preserve thy going out and thy coming in from this time forth and even for evermore.

A Psalm to praise the hills we love? Look to the hills and we will find our God? But consider the Metrical version:

*I to the hills will lift mine eyes.
From whence doth come mine aid?
My safety cometh from the Lord
Who heav'n and earth hath made.*

This 'Psalm of Ascent', which the Israelites sang as they went to worship in Jerusalem's Temple, has a question mark at the end of the second line. When I look to the hills, does my help come from there? No! My God is beyond *even that.*

'I joy'd when to the house of God go up, they said to me.'
Bible: Psalm 122:1

November 19 – Ascents

'Do not despise the bottom rungs in the ascent to greatness.'
Publilius Syrus

The first and last verses of the Metrical version of Psalm 121 which is most commonly sung in churches come to us in this form:

I to the hills will lift mine eyes;
From whence doth come mine aid?
My safety cometh from the Lord,
Who heaven and earth hath made.

The Lord shall keep thy soul; he shall
Preserve thee from all ill.
Henceforth thy going out and in
God keep for ever will.

This is one of fifteen 'Psalms of Ascent' used by pilgrims going 'up' to Jerusalem, the holy city, which was elevated from the valley below. They were sung at the great pilgrimage feasts: the Feast of the Unleavened Bread (commemorating the Exodus) in the spring; the Feast of the Harvest Weeks (Pentecost, the expression of gratitude for the provision of grain) in the early summer; and the Feast of the Booths or Ingathering (Tabernacles – thanksgiving for the final harvest) in the autumn.

We all need 'times of ascent' and to be raised above the ordinary – to celebrate and to share rejoicing with others. When we journey through the valleys, how important it is to lift our eyes from the ordinary to something that is 'extra' ordinary.

Even when we're on our ascent,
we might find a meaning
that makes the whole pilgrimage worthwhile.

November 20 – A way out

'My first plan of escape having failed
I now determined upon another.'
Buffalo Bill (William F Cody), True Tales of the Plains

I've never been guilty of taking my work home. I've *worked* at home sometimes. But I've always been able to leave behind the pressing emotional cases or complex problems of my work. There's a legend from Greek mythology which has something to teach us in this regard.

King Minos was an angry man. The Athenians had killed his son. So, by way of retribution, he ordered that every four years nine youths should be sent to Crete to feed the Minotaur. The Minotaur, half man and half bull, lived in the labyrinth under the palace. And the Minotaur was not to be messed with!

King Aegeus of Athens reckoned that the only way to bring an end to this unhappy state of affairs was for the Minotaur to be killed. His son, Theseus, would be the man for the job. But Ariadne, daughter of King Minos, had fallen in love with Theseus and didn't want to lose him in the labyrinth. So she gave him a big ball of string and a sword. As he entered the maze to find the Minotaur, Theseus let the string out. The Minotaur was killed in a ferocious battle and Theseus found his way back out of the labyrinth by following his string trail.

In any work which involves caring for complex, distressed, broken or vulnerable people you need skills, sensitivity, self-confidence and courage to 'go deep', to enter the labyrinth that surrounds their Minotaur. If you have to do that, make sure you let out your ball of string so that you can find the way back to your own life and loves.

Keep your eye on the door;
you might need to escape sooner than you think.

November 21 – Unprepared

'We have too many high sounding words,
and too few actions that correspond with them.'

Abigail Adams, Letter to John Adams

When my friend was invited to preach at Crathie Kirk when the Queen was in residence at Balmoral, he readied himself for his time as the Queen's houseguest. He prepared his sermon. He even bought himself a new suit. And he followed the instructions issued to him and arrived at the entrance to Balmoral at the designated time. He'd been told he would be greeted at the door, his car would be parked for him, he would be shown to his room and he would be expected to meet with the Queen and her household at the agreed time and say grace before dinner.

But when he arrived there was no one to greet him. The gravelled entrance was empty. No one was standing in the doorway. He was taking his case out of the car when round the corner of Balmoral came a bustling woman wearing a tweed jacket and a Paisley-patterned headscarf and with three corgis on leads in front of her. She was just about to scuttle past when she stopped, and, realising this was the houseguest and that there was no one there to meet him, stepped into the doorway of Balmoral and shouted, 'Anthony …' With that, a footman appeared, picked up my friend's case and ushered him inside. But not before the visiting clergyman realised that the corgi-walking woman was none other than the Queen herself, who was gracious enough to apologise to her guest, and tell him she was looking forward to meeting him properly before dinner. It's not reported what happened to the recalcitrant Anthony, but I suspect he never made the same mistake again.

All the preparations in the world don't prepare us for everything.
Life has a habit of taking us unawares.

November 22 – Rescued

'I would help others out of a fellow-feeling.'
Robert Burton, The Anatomy of Melancholy (1621),
'Democritus to the Reader'

I was eight years old when I forgot my words at the Catholic church annual concert. For my age, I was a bit of a star turn, a Harry Lauder lookalike, with my endearing renditions of *I love a lassie* and *Roamin' in the gloamin'*. I was booked to top the bill at the concert. But why the church had all the entertainers sitting at the back of the stage for the whole show, calling them forward one by one, with each performer returning to their seat and remaining in full view of the audience for the rest of the show, I will never know. But what I *do* know is that I'd never before had to sit that long in full view of a large crowd of people waiting my turn.

I was on last, by which time I was a nervous wreck. I made my way to the front of the stage, bowed, leaned on my crooked stick, smiled, opened my mouth – and not a sound came out. I couldn't remember a single word. The audience began shuffling and fidgeting. That only made things worse. I had blown it.

Then the priest came in from the wings and put his arm round my shoulders. 'Never mind, laddie,' he said. And addressing his parishioners, 'It'll be nerves for a wee boy. And don't I forget the words of the Mass sometimes?' There was knowing laughter, then applause, while the priest led me into the wings to the waiting arms of my mother. I remember little else of that disastrous evening. But what sticks with me was the priest's big arm round my shoulders, and his words that he sometimes forgot things too. I'd been rescued by a patient and understanding man, when my confidence could have been destroyed for ever.

Are you a rescuer,
and, if you are, who needs to be rescued today?

November 23 – Leadership

'A boss says, "Go!" A good leader says, "Let's go!"'
Anonymous

Rudyard Kipling wrote *The Jungle Book* stories, a series of fables using animals to offer moral lessons, in 1894 and 1895 when he was living in Vermont in the USA. But his early childhood years in India, along with a period of time working there as an adult, had given him a rich set of resources from which to draw. In 1914 Lord Baden-Powell announced a junior section for Scouting, to be called 'Wolf Cubbing'. A young boy not old enough to be a wolf or a true Scout could be a baby wolf or Wolf Cub. Baden-Powell asked his friend Kipling for the use of his Jungle Book stories as a motivational framework for Cub-Scouting. Though modern Scouting has removed nearly all the links to *The Jungle Book,* the names of characters are still used. Akela is still a leader, and many Cub Scout packs use an oath called the 'Law of the Pack'.

The Cub Scout follows Akela.
The Cub Scout helps the pack go.
The pack helps the Cub Scout grow.
The Cub Scout gives goodwill.

Whatever the source, the motivation or the context, both Kipling and Baden-Powell knew that young people need to understand important lessons: the community of 'the pack'; that goodwill can be learned and shared; and the role-model of good leadership. When you're still a cub, these are the lessons you need. And if you're an 'Akela' in any form, what a responsibility in leadership you have!

Napoleon once said, 'A leader is a dealer in hope.'
I hope all leaders understand the responsibility of that.

November 24 – Church

' "What is a church?" Let Truth and reason speak,
They would reply, "The faithful, pure and meek,
From Christian folds, the one selected race,
Of all professions, and in every place." '

George Crabbe, The Borough

When I was a minister in my first parish, the tradition, unusually for the Church of Scotland, was the frequent celebration of Holy Communion. The style was distinctive too, for people would come to sit round an extended table at the front of the church. There were thirty places round the table, and people had to come in turn.

One Sunday, I saw Robert and Rhoda approaching the table. Robert was a young man who was trying to cope with the break-up of his marriage, and he cared for his daughter every second weekend. Rhoda was ten years old and Robert was devoted to her. She was severely restricted by Down's Syndrome and was apprehensive about leaving her dad, so, when they came to church, she didn't go out with the Sunday school children, but stayed with Robert. And now he was bringing her to the Communion table.

They took their places. The bread was shared. It came to a woman on the far side of Rhoda. She could have passed it across her to her dad. But instead it was placed in Rhoda's hands and, with help, Rhoda took her piece and passed the bread to Robert. The cup of wine came the other way, and when Robert had taken his sip he gave it to his daughter, who with great dignity took a sip and passed the chalice carefully to the woman on the other side.

That Communion was a parable about what the Church should be. The Sacrament was administered in a welcome at the table, by a sensitive woman, a devoted father, and Rhoda. New ways were being found by the people of God to touch the lives of all.

For Communion to work we have to be truly in community.

November 25 – Gotcha!

'This is our wisdom, to be learners to the end.'
John Calvin, Commentaries on the Prophet Zechariah

Tariq was a Muslim, a patient in the hospice where I was chaplain, and he made no indication that he wished any contact with me. I was surprised, therefore, when one of the nurses said, 'Tariq's asking to see you.' *This is it!* I thought. *This is spiritual, inclusive, multifaith care at its best. Yippee!!* So, calmer on the outside than I was inside, I slipped into Tariq's room and found him sitting up in bed, sipping a glass of iced water, with his newspaper on his knee.

'Ah, Padre!' he said. 'The very man. I need to talk to you about something very important.' My heart raced. *Oh, the rightness of the moment!* 'What can I do for you?' I enquired. There was a deep and meaningful pause … 'I'm stuck, Padre. And I don't know what to do next. You'll be the only one who can help.' *Does it ever get any better than this?* I leaned forward, focused on the frail old Muslim man and asked, 'What are you stuck with, Tariq? How can I help?' Then came the immortal words… 'I'm doing the crossword in the evening paper, Padre, and I'm stuck with 3 across. It's a book of your Bible, four letters, and it begins with an E.'

I knew I could respond immediately. 'That'll be Ezra,' I replied. 'Wonderful!' Tariq exclaimed, and scribbled animatedly in his crossword. And then he turned to me, and issued his second immortal statement. 'Thank you, Padre. That's all. You can go now.' And if Tariq had added 'Gotcha!' I wouldn't have been at all surprised.

We can have a rather high opinion of ourselves at times.
Maybe a gentle teasing from a wise source
might sort us out good and proper!
'Gotcha!' can have much to teach us.

November 26 – Landmarks

'I have been a stranger in a strange land.'
Bible: Exodus 11:22

At either end of the main road through the Morningside area of Edinburgh, there is a landmark at each of the busy crossroads – 'Holy Corner' and 'Morningside Station'. But look for a sign that says 'Morningside Station' or 'Holy Corner' and you'll look in vain. You'll undoubtedly be a 'stranger in a strange land' because you're not 'in the know ...'

'Holy Corner' is easy enough to understand. It's a busy intersection surrounded by four churches, with a fifth just a few metres away. Not all of them are places of worship nowadays, one being an extensive community facility, while another is an annexe to a local university. But all of them are distinctive, church-like buildings. Five churches cheek-by-jowl – and 'Holy Corner' gets its name. 'Morningside Station', on the other hand, is harder to figure. Oh yes, a railway track for freight trains runs under the junction. But a station? No sign of that. For the passenger station, which was once integral to the rail network around the city, is long since gone. 'Morningside Station' is no longer obvious. You have to have local knowledge to understand.

We all have landmarks that matter to us. Some are from a long time ago. Some are recent and hugely influential right now. Some are known to everyone. Some are private, important only to us – because we are 'in the know'. But they are all landmarks which remain significant on our journey. And we don't need any visible sign to indicate what they are or why they matter – just like Morningside Station.

A witness to my commitment to go on, or take a new direction;
a landmark from days gone by or from yesterday;
another signpost on an adventurous journey.

November 27 – A chorus of peace

'The glorious lamp of heaven, the radiant sun, is Nature's eye.'
John Dryden, The Story of Acis, Polyphemus and Galatea

May There Always Be Sunshine is a Russian children's song by Arkady Ostrovsky and Lev Oshanin. The children's poet Korney Chukovsky later wrote that the inspiration for the song had been the four lines of the chorus written in 1928 by a four-year-old boy, Kostya Barannikov. The song earned Tamara Miansarova first prize in 1963 at the Sopot International Song Festival and immediately became popular throughout the USSR, especially among children. It was seen as expressing the people's desire for peace and is one of only a few Soviet-era songs to have remained popular in Russia after the demise of the USSR. Translated into English by Tom Botting, the chorus was popularised by Pete Seeger.

> *May there always be sunshine.*
> *May there always be blue skies,*
> *May there always be Mama,*
> *May there always be me.*

I sang this chorus – in faltering Russian, then reasonable English – in a primary school, taught it to the children and loved the depth of meaning as we sang it together. The following week a little boy presented me with a picture he'd painted inspired by the song. For thirty years I've had his picture on my office wall. With its blue sky filled with a golden sun, and a colourful parent and child in a green field, it still speaks to me of the pleasure of a beautiful world, the nurture of family, the innocence of children and the gift of life. With the people of Russia and an Edinburgh school we can still sing songs that embrace our hopes for peace.

Whatever the song, let the chorus be of peace.

November 28 – Allergies

'Everyone must see daily instances of people
who complain from a mere habit of complaining.'
Richard Graves, Olla Podrida

I recently spent a few days in hospital for minor surgery. I tried to stay as cheerful as possible, and seriously and dutifully answered all the questions put to me – despite being asked the same questions by several different people at different times.

I was 'prepped' for theatre and trundled through the hospital by a taciturn porter. I don't know whether it was *that*, or my apprehension, or the medication I'd been given before I left the ward, but when I was ready to go into theatre and was asked yet another bunch of questions, I just couldn't take it seriously. An anaesthetist asked, 'Well, sir, do have any allergies we should know about?' 'Yes,' I replied, 'lots.' This was clearly not the expected answer and was greeted with a surprised, 'Oh!', a flicking of charts on a clipboard, a whispered conversation behind my head and someone else looking at me seriously and enquiring, 'And what *are* you allergic to?' 'Oh,' I responded, 'let's see. I'm allergic to – people who rustle sweet papers in theatres; cyclists who jump red lights; drivers who don't indicate properly on motorways; the white noise that leaks out of people's earphones on buses; folk who talk loudly on mobile phones; the *Daily Mail*; the misuse of the apostrophe ... Need any more?' I never heard the reply. The anaesthetic was administered before I caused any more problems.

The operation was a success. But I've started working on all these allergies I have in case they make me quite unwell again.

Fill in the gaps:
I'm allergic to ....
I'm trying to deal with ....

November 29 – Heaven

'Heaven will be inherited by every man
who has heaven in his soul.'
Henry Ward Beecher, Life Thoughts

Two monks were discussing the life to come. One insisted it would
be *taliter* – like this life; the other that it would be *aliter* – unlike
it. Finally they agreed that whichever died first should communicate with the one left. In the course of time one died and, true to
his pledge, visited his brother in a dream with this message: *Nec
taliter, nec aliter, sed totaliter aliter.* 'Not as you thought nor as I
thought, but altogether totally different.' I hope I've got the Latin
right ... but I know what the question is about. For I've heard it
often: 'What is heaven like?'

I once asked a Rabbi, 'Is there a heaven?' 'I do not know,' he
answered. 'But if there is, what kind of place will it be, Rabbi?' I
enquired. 'I do not know,' was his reply. 'But perhaps you are
asking the wrong questions. You ask me if I *know*. And I do not.
But if you were to ask me what I *believe,* that would be a different
matter. Begin from where you are,' he continued, 'not from where
you think you should be. Work outwards from what you understand, and don't worry about what is beyond your grasp.'

So, like the monks, I do not know what the life to come will
be like. So I begin from where I am and work outwards from there.
When the people who mattered to me were alive, we shared love
together. Now they are gone, we still share love together. When I
die, will we not continue to share love? Where that is, I still do
not know. What it will be like, I have no idea. But if love matters,
it will not die, and where it continues, that will be eternity for me.

Knowing about heaven is beyond my grasp.
Understanding the importance of love is where I am.
So that is where I begin – and end.

November 30 – Kilts

'Tradition refuses to submit to the small and arrogant oligarchy
of those who merely happen to be walking about.'
GK Chesterton, The Ethics of Elfland: Orthodoxy

Most weddings in Scotland now include guests who wear kilts. As
well as the groom, best man and other principals, many of the
guests are bedecked in tartan. Very few weddings are based on the
'morning dress' more common a few decades ago. Now weddings
are a riot colour, each man wearing the tartan of his clan and
proud to do so. Clearly, kilts are 'in vogue'.

It wasn't always so. There was a time in Scotland when the
wearing of tartan of any sort was banned, and flouters of the law
were subject to fines and even imprisonment. After the ill-fated
Jacobite Rebellion of Charles Edward Stuart in 1745, Scottish
national dress was outlawed. As 'the butcher Cumberland' did his
worst to smash the Highland clans into submission, so the government of the day sought to destroy their culture and traditions.
If they had no heritage, they had no loyalty to their past. If they
had no past, they were no present threat.

The horrors of ethnic cleansing in modern times – in the
Balkans and Rwanda, for example – are current evidences of the
same approach. There are painful lessons to be learned from such
tragedies. We live in a multicultural world where the rich heritage
of ancient civilisations can enhance the lives of those who have
never been exposed to such things. The past matters. There is
much in people's heritage from which we can learn – and that
includes the cultural background of our own country.

So let's keep the kilts on show, and, at the same time, celebrate
all the other examples of cultural diversity.

On St Andrew's day, we give thanks for a nation
which has always welcomed diversity.

December 1 – Frosts

'In the bleak mid-winter frosty winds made moan.'
Christina Rossetti, Poetic Works, *1904*

Rhubarb is usually considered to be a vegetable. However, in 1947 a New York court decided that, since it was used in the USA as a fruit, it was to be counted as such for the purposes of regulations and duties. I don't want to start a 'fruit or veg' debate in these pages. But it gives me the opportunity to tell you that I love rhubarb, and that rhubarb crumble is one of the puddings that make the frosts of the winter more bearable.

During a recent mild spell of winter weather I heard a rhubarb-grower complaining that there wasn't *enough* frost! This wasn't so people like me would use more of her rhubarb as a comfort against the rigors of the winter. It was because *without* a good frost the rhubarb doesn't grow properly. The frost needs to get into the roots of the rhubarb – before it's taken inside for 'forcing' – to break down the roots and release their goodness. 'There's an awful lot of energy stored in them roots,' she explained, 'and if it's not released, the goodness doesn't get out.'

We complain about the frosts of the winter. We complain about the darkness of loss too, and the bitter frosts of pain and sorrow that accompany it. They too have to be endured. But if we look on frosts as necessary to get into the roots of our rhubarb and release the energy and growth stored there, then maybe the darkness and pain of loss are equally necessary to release the unseen resources that we all have within us. If they're not released, they can't provide what we need.

If our bitter frosts can open up our dormant resources,
then, when the spring comes,
hopefulness, strength and a capacity to move forward
will surely follow.

December 2 – Regret

'Deep as first love, and wild with all regret.'
Alfred Tennyson, The Princess

Puffins are my favourite birds. They breed in large colonies on coastal cliffs or offshore islands, nesting in crevices among rocks or in burrows in the soil. The Tufted Puffin and Horned Puffin are found in the North Pacific Ocean and the Atlantic Puffin in the North Atlantic Ocean. It's the Atlantic Puffin I know and love.

These puffins are stocky, short-winged and short-tailed birds, with black upper parts and white or brownish-grey underparts. The head has a black cap, the face is mainly white, the feet are orange-red and the bill is large and colourful during the breeding season. These fascinating and comic seabirds are, in my opinion, absolutely gorgeous. That's why I still carry a deep regret that I had an opportunity to see them close up – and missed it!

While I was sharing a week with a church group on Iona, we were offered the chance to visit the island of Staffa, with the prospect of seeing and photographing puffins close up. I'm not a good sailor so I chose not to go on the trip – even though I would miss seeing my favourite bird. When the party returned, they only confirmed my disappointment. Several had got within feet of the puffin colony. Their photographs were spectacular. Their enjoyment was complete.

Am I still disappointed? Yes, I am. Can I live with my regret? I just have to, as we all have to with the many regrets we gather from life's journeys. Do I still love puffins? I certainly do. Will I get to be close to them one day? I hope so – provided there's not an hour's choppy sea journey on a small boat between them and me.

'It's better to act and to regret than to regret not to have acted.'
Mellin de Saint-Gelais, *Quatrains*, LXXVIII

December 3 – Golden

'A world-without-end bargain.'
William Shakespeare, Love's Labour's Lost

I was invited by a couple to assist them in renewing their vows at
their golden wedding. It was a privilege to be close to the enduring
love that had sustained a marriage for fifty years.

> When we were newly one, we took the time
> To nurture love in joyful, carefree days,
> To live one life and share each other's ways.
> When we were good, each moment was sublime.
>
> When we were young at heart, we made the choice
> To venture forth and drink the best of wine,
> And find that place where heaven and earth combine.
> When we were one, we made the world rejoice.
>
> When we could trust our love, we joined the dance
> That leads to family life with children's cries,
> And coped with sweet hellos and sad goodbyes.
> When we were right, we offered life the chance.
>
> When we were in our prime, we valued more
> Of what was deep and lasting in our years,
> And found a different love in joy and tears ...
> When we grew old, we had our treasure store.
>
> When we were older yet, in each embrace
> We found we'd saved the best of wine till last,
> A love so rich it could not be surpassed.
> When we are one, we're ever blessed by grace.

From *A Blessing to Follow*, Tom Gordon, Wild Goose Publications, 2009

December 4 – Arguments

'Real knowledge is to know the extent of one's ignorance.'
Confucius, The Confucian Analects

In his book *Don Quixote*, Miguel Cervantes tells us of the hero's obsession with books on chivalry. But sometimes Don Quixote's reading got him tied in knots.

> *He often found passages like 'the reason of the unreason with which my reason is afflicted so weakens my reason that with reason I murmur at your beauty;' or again, 'the high heavens, that of your divinity divinely fortify you with the stars, render you deserving of the desert your greatness deserves.' Over conceits of this sort the poor gentleman lost his wits, and used to lie awake striving to understand them and worm the meaning out of them.*

No wonder he lost his wits! It's one thing, though, getting into a tangle with what you're reading, but it's quite another when what you've learned creates conflict with other people. Cervantes continues:

> *Many an argument did he have with the curate of his village ... as to which had been the better knight, Palmerin of England or Amadis of Gaul. Master Nicholas, the village barber, however, used to say that neither of them came up to the Knight of Phoebus, and that if there was any that could compare with him it was Don Galaor, the brother of Amadis ...*

Don Quixote knew that learning was important – even the complicated things. But when learning makes you believe you are always right, beware of the conflict that might ensue.

Knowledge is haunted by the ghost of certainty.

December 5 – Intimidation

'There is a stubbornness about me that never can bear
to be frightened at the will of others. My courage always rises
at every attempt to intimidate me.'
Jane Austen, Pride and Prejudice

In the wake of the bombings at the Boston Marathon in April 2013, the 37,000 runners in the London Marathon a week later observed a minute's silence at the start of the race. Elite athletes and fun-runners stood in solidarity with the marathon participants in Boston, the families of those who had lost their lives and all the worldwide victims of terrorism. As thousands applauded at the end of the silence, BBC commentator Steve Cram said, 'The terrorists picked the wrong group to try to intimidate. Marathon runners will not be intimidated.'

What is it about marathon runners that would cause a commentator to make such a bold assertion? It's to do with a commitment to a task that may, at times, seem overwhelming. As I said earlier, I ran two marathons when I was younger. I know about the commitment of marathon runners – to months of long hours of training; to raising money for a chosen charity; to the challenge of running 26.2 miles; to keeping going when your body is crying out for rest; to making it to the finish. That commitment has diverse sources. People may run in memory of someone who has died; because they have a passion for a charity; for self-improvement; because they want to achieve a dream; or they might just want to prove that they can do it.

Steve Cram is right. Marathon runners are not to be intimidated. But nor should anyone be who has a commitment to justice and peace in the face of terrorism and hatred. The task may, at times, seem overwhelming. But we have to affirm that, marathon runners that we are, we too will not be intimidated.

Intimidation is the last resort of the bullying coward.

December 6 – Connections again

'Humankind has not woven the web of life.
We are but one thread within it.
Whatever we do to the web, we do to ourselves.
All things are bound together.
All things connect.'
Chief Seattle

People thought Jesus' disciples were completely mad when they talked about sharing fish and bread on a lakeside with someone who was dead. 'You're stuck in your fantasy,' they said. 'You're holding on to him. You're not prepared to accept that he's gone.' But they told their doubters to stop talking nonsense. They'd always shared fish and bread with their friend and life wouldn't be the same if they didn't share it with him now. In the sharing he was there. That was important, because they still needed to be connected with him. They wouldn't have it any other way.

Difficult to conceptualise? Well, maybe so. But then ... I worked with a woman who'd been widowed for eighteen months. She had a psychiatrist who was giving her a hard time because she still had her husband's toothbrush beside hers in the rack in the bathroom. 'You're stuck in your grief,' he'd said. 'You're holding on to him. You're not prepared to accept that he's gone.' But she told him to stop talking nonsense, and that perhaps he should see a good psychiatrist – or at least someone who understood the processes of grief and what it's like to mourn for your husband. She'd always had a red and a blue toothbrush together in the bathroom and it wouldn't be the same if one of them wasn't there. The red toothbrush reminded her of her husband. That was important, because she still needed to be connected to him. She wouldn't have it any other way.

Connections with the dead matter to the living.

December 7 – Nature

'Mountains are earth's undecaying monuments.'
Nathaniel Hawthorne, The Notch of the White Mountains

Ailsa Craig is a small island in the Firth of Clyde formed from the volcanic plug of an extinct volcano. It famously provides the blue granite for the manufacture of curling stones, and served as a haven for Roman Catholics during the Scottish Reformation in the 16th century and as a prison in the 18th and 19th centuries. Now the uninhabited island is a bird sanctuary, a home for huge numbers of gannets and puffins.

The name is an anglicising of the Gaelic *Aillse Creag*, meaning 'fairy rock'. An alternative name is *Creag Ealasaid*, 'Elizabeth's rock'. The first element, *Aillse*, may represent *Allt Shasann*, 'cliff of the English'. For travellers, it's sometimes known as 'Paddy's Milestone', being approximately halfway on the sea journey between Belfast and Glasgow, a traditional route of emigration for Irish labourers coming to Scotland. The island is known by other names too: *A' Chreag* – the rock; *Creag Alasdair* – Alasdair's rock; *Ealasaid a' Chuain* – Elizabeth of the ocean.

But none of them is right, because this island has been claimed and named by my wife and her brother. It's a family tradition that Ailsa Craig is actually called 'John's Dumpling'. I don't know why, but my wife will not have it any other way.

It's amazing that a wonder of nature which has existed for eons of time can be rediscovered by successive generations and remind a sister of a dumpling brother, and bring to mind happy family times. Creation is recreated in the pleasure it gives.

Nature belongs to each of us
and not to one individual or group.
Wonders cannot be claimed or defined.

December 8 – Hospitality

'Given to hospitality.'
Bible: Romans 12:13

I like having visitors. I haven't always, for visitors – especially unexpected – can be an intrusion into a busy day and an interruption of careful plans. But I enjoy visitors now, because of what they mean, what they bring and what they leave behind.

What do they mean? It's about keeping in contact with people who matter. Whether it's an arranged visit with folk you haven't seen for a while or an unplanned 'drop in' visit, human contact matters. The singer Eric Bogle wrote a song called 'Reason for it all' after being deeply moved by a newspaper account of the death of Clare Campbell in a Sydney suburb. She'd probably lain dead at home for months. The only letters behind the door were junk mail and circulars. Bogle tells us he was grateful for the regularity of his own human contact, and how distressed he was that someone, in the crowded busyness of a city, could lie dead for so long because she had no human contact.

What do these visitors bring? Not just the obligatory bottle of wine or box of chocolates, but, like travellers from afar, they bring news and thoughts, developments and ideas, stories of what is happening to them. In short, they bring themselves – the new, changed, interesting, unique selves that they are.

And what do they leave behind? Not just forgotten gloves and current information. They leave people who are changed. We are fundamentally altered by every human contact, richer for the worth of any visit. All the more reason why we too might be 'given to hospitality' as St Paul encouraged the Christians in the early Church to be.

Who might I visit today? What will I bring them?
And what difference will it make?

December 9 – Still coping

'Do not fear the winds of adversity.
A kite rises against the wind rather than with it.'
Anonymous

When I was a parish minister I had a student working with me who was totally blind. He had lost his sight when he was a child, but now, as an adult, wanted no special treatment because of his disability. He became one of the team, taking his responsibility for the work allocated to him and absorbing the wisdom of more experienced practitioners. On one occasion, at our weekly staff planning meeting, we were allocating house calls. We talked through each set of visits and clarified the expectations for particular people. And off we all went to fulfil our responsibilities.

Later that day I was standing at the street door of a refurbished tenement stair, trying to work out which of the eight buzzers I should press to gain access to the home I was to visit. Then I realised to my horror that we had given a blind student a set of house calls for similar tenement blocks. How on *earth* was he going to know which buzzer to press?

When we met later in the week to review how our visits had gone, he reported that he had completed all his calls. I apologised for making things difficult for him by my thoughtlessness in allocating the house calls. He smiled and told me I needn't have worried. 'I'm used to coping with things like that,' he said. 'I just stand by the street door and wait till I hear someone come along. Then I ask the stranger to press the appropriate buzzer. Everyone's pleased to help. Doing it that way comes as naturally to me as seeing the buzzers and finding the right one does to you.'

*If we spend too long looking at a closed door and cursing our fate,
we may not see other doors that could be lying open for us.*

December 10 – Songs

'Sir, we are a nest of singing birds.'
James Boswell, The Life of Samuel Johnson

Robert Louis Stevenson offers this insight in his *Songs of Travel*:

Bright is the ring of words when the right man rings them.
Fair the fall of songs when the singer sings them.

While there is no doubt that the right words offered by the right person at the right time can often be enormously effective, the effect of a song – words and music together – can be even more powerful. It has the ability to soothe and disturb, to create emotion and excite the spirit, to cause tingles in the spine and a deep beating of the heart. There have been many times when a song has moved me to tears … a folk song, or an operatic aria, a choral piece or a solo melody. I'm more than happy in Johnson's 'nest of singing birds'. But what if a song, sung or heard, does nothing to move or uplift?

The Psalmist encourages his people in exile to ask: *'How can we sing the Lord's song in a strange land?'* (Psalm 137:4) How indeed?

I knew a family who had a lovely seven-year-old son who died of leukaemia. His parents had watched by his bedside in their home as his life drained away. In the next room lay their tiny daughter, six months old. When their son died, they were left with what his mother described as 'a thousand whys'. She was a singer, and sought in her mind and heart to find some words she knew or a familiar melody that would offer some solace and peace. But, as she said, 'All I heard was silence, for the whole world had stopped its singing.'

Sing it loud! Sing it proud! Sing it now!

December 11 – Nurture

'My lovely living Boy,
My hope, my hap, my Love, my life, my joy.'
Guillaume de Salluste Du Bartas, Divine Weekes and Workes

The 'nature' or 'nurture' debate has always interested me. What makes us what we are? Are we predisposed to be a certain kind of person with no control over how we turn out? That's the 'nature' argument. Or are we moulded by the environment in which we live, influenced by our upbringing, family life, community? That's the 'nurture' part. 'Nature' or 'nurture' – which matters most?

During a Science Festival in Edinburgh a while ago I attended a seminar addressed by two people – a crime-fiction author and a lecturer in forensic psychology. Both offered insights into the workings of the criminal mind, how the writer can portray that on the page and how the forensic psychologist works with it in the profiling of offenders.

As part of her presentation, the forensic psychologist made this remarkable assertion: the same make-up that drives the psychopath to become a mass-murderer is also found in leading politicians and the CEOs of major companies. Of course that doesn't mean that politicians and people in business and commerce are scary psychopaths. But it does indicate that what is in a person – the nature part – can be influenced by other factors – the nurture part. And how the two interact determine whether you're a psychopathic killer or a Government Minister.

I'll need to do more thinking on all of that, I suspect. But it leaves me with this important truth – nurture matters! Who knows how the scariest of people could have turned out if only they had been nurtured in the proper way?

Who knows what might be lost if the seeds of talent and skill aren't valued and nurtured at a tender age?

December 12 – Simplicity

''Tis the gift to be simple, 'tis the gift to be free.'
Joseph Brackett, Simple Gifts

From a very early age, my elder grandson took to calling the remote control for the TV the 'doofer'. He didn't come up with the name himself. It was the name his parents used, and he just picked it up – the name, that is, not the doofer. Actually, he became very adept at negotiating his way around the doofer and even had to teach his grandfather how it worked. But then, children pick these things up very quickly – like the doofer *and* the way it operates.

Our doofer is always getting lost. It's never there when you need it, and it's always somewhere you don't want it to be – between the seat-cushion and the arm of the sofa; under a pile of newspapers; in the toilet where you took it by mistake; on the telephone cradle, because it looks the same as the phone. And then when you *do* find it, how do you change the clock on the recorder again? And where's the 'record' button? And how do you get into the menu? And what's the 'parental control'? Arrgghh! Where's my grandson when I need him?

On top of all of *that*, what happens when you have more than one doofer? Which one is for the hi-fi, and why does it look so much like the one for the DVD player? And which one switches the TV on first, or do you do the set-top box and then the TV? And why am I using the phone to try to change the channel anyway?

Doofers are a symbol of how complicated life has become – for grandfathers, if not for dextrous grandsons. Sometimes I long for a simpler life. Maybe I'll just do away with doofers and all the things that they're supposed to operate, and just sit for a while in silence and be still. You don't need a doofer for that, do you?

Keep it simple; keep it true;
keep it honest; that will do.

December 13 – Talent

'Talent develops in quiet places,
character in the full current of human life.'
Johann Wolfgang von Goethe, Torquato Tasso

In primary school I was told by an art teacher, 'You can't draw for toffee!' I didn't actually *want* toffee, just encouragement. In high school I had a fantastic English teacher. I never heard *him* say, 'You can't write for toffee.' All I got was encouragement. If I can now write anything decent, it's David Chalmers I have to thank.

What can I offer? What can I give?
What can I bring you today?
What can I do now? What do you need?
What do you want me to say?

What can I help with? What's to be done?
What are my skills to prepare?
What am I good at? What's any use?
What are my offerings to share?

Bring me your tenderness; offer your touch;
Give me your comfort again;
Hold out your hopefulness; stay when I cry;
Be by my side through my pain.

Hold me and help me; for that's what I need.
Be a companion that's true.
You have the talent; you have the skill.
All that I'm wanting is you.

From Welcoming Each Wonder *by Tom Gordon*
Wild Goose Publications, 2010

December 14 – My way

'Remorse is the poison of life.'
Charlotte Brontë, Jane Eyre

I've never been asked for the famous song of Edith Piaf, *Non, je regrette rien*, to be played at a funeral. I have, however, been faced with the request for another pseudo-biographical song – Frank Sinatra's *My way*. It's the most often requested piece of secular music for funerals, top of the crematorium hit-parade, it would seem. From Sinatra's own version, through renditions by Elvis Presley and others, to brass-band and orchestral versions, *My way* tops the funeral charts.

But why? It appears that when people look at any life, be it chequered or ordinary, there is something in the uniqueness and individuality of that life that needs to be celebrated. Whether a person selects it for their own funeral, or mourners choose it for someone they love, *My way* says what needs to be said. As in Edith Piaf's song, there is something in this choice that is biographical. 'I have no regrets.' 'I did it my way.' There need be no arrogance in that. It need contain no fatalism or pessimism. We are what we are. We did what we did. We achieved what we achieved. This is the truth of it all. This is our honesty. I did it my way ...

Whether for a funeral or in assessing our own life, when we are listening to *No regrets* or *My way*, we might experience a wistfulness about the past. We might look at what's gone by and wonder how it might have been different. We might even try to fix things, or, as in the movie *Sliding Doors*, try to work out how our life could have been if one thing had happened rather than another. But don't tie yourself in knots. It's ultimately a fruitless exercise. We can learn from the past, but it can't be changed.

If 'my way' is your way
what way is that?

December 15 – Waiting

'God made all the creatures,
and gave them our love and our fear,
To give sign we and they are his children,
one family here.'

Robert Browning, Saul, Dramatic Romances and Lyrics

I'm a collector of antiquarian books. I've bought them on the internet, ordered them from catalogues, been in contact with out-of-print book specialists, followed up recommendations from friends and, of course, scoured second-hand bookshops. I can't tell you the thrill of finding a book I've been searching for – to make up a set, replace a damaged copy or begin a new part of my collection.

There's a story Jesus told of a son who came back home. *He* was needed to complete a set, a family that wasn't the same without him. He was out there somewhere, but nobody knew where. There was a collector waiting at home, a father who had a passion for a son who'd gone away. The collector had a gap in his collection, and there was a lost son who fitted the bill.

Among the many angles that have fascinated me in this story, there is this one – the collector did nothing to complete his collection. He scoured no shops, studied no catalogues, perused no lists, contacted no specialists, followed no advice. He just sat at home, and he waited, dreamed, hoped and prayed, because he believed that his sought-after treasure would come to him.

A lazy collector? Not committed enough? No passion for finding things? I don't think so. For if he'd been trailing round the countryside and the young man had come back to find an empty house and no warm welcome home, what then?

Somewhere today,
is there someone who is waiting for you to turn up
to complete their collection and to welcome you home?

December 16 – Baby's world

'Sweet babe, in thy face
Soft desires I can trace,
Secret joys and secret smiles,
Little pretty infant wiles.'
William Blake, A Cradle Song

Here is a poem by Rabindranath Tagore called *Baby's World:*

I wish I could take a quiet corner
in the heart of my baby's very own world.
I know it has stars that talk to him,
and a sky that stoops down to his face
to amuse him with its silly clouds and rainbows.
Those who make believe to be dumb,
and look as if they never could move,
come creeping to his window with their stories
and with trays crowded with bright toys.
I wish I could travel by the road that crosses my baby's mind,
and out beyond all bounds;
where messengers run errands for no cause
between the kingdoms of kings of no history;
where Reason makes kites of her laws and flies them,
and the Truth sets Fact free from its fetters.

How I wish I could live in a world uncluttered with reason, in a permanent state of wonder, where stars speak, clouds are silly and rainbows make me laugh, and where I can learn the embrace of love and understand my uniqueness for the first time.

I wish I could enter the heart of a child,
So that, sometimes, in my adult world,
I see things through that child's eyes.

December 17 – Revelation again

'*'Tis Revelation satisfies all doubts,*
Explains all mysteries except her own,
And so illuminates the path of life,
That fools discover it, and stray no more.'
William Cowper, The Task

I'm not prone to exaggeration, nor am I familiar with dramatic revelations from God. But once ...

I was on a silent retreat in the Wellspring Retreat Centre on the outskirts of Washington DC as part of my study leave with the Church of the Saviour. I'd never been on a silent retreat before. It's hard for me to be silent for half an hour, far less the two and a half days of the retreat. But it seemed right. I needed the space. A silent retreat fitted the bill.

It was day two. I'd taken myself off to sit beside a little lake in the grounds and found myself fascinated by a family of geese in the reeds by the lake. I was completely absorbed by the tenderness, beauty, wonder and naturalness of what I was watching. And, right there, God spoke. 'Keep it simple,' was the message. I didn't hear it at first. I just had a sense of something. And it came again, clearer and insistent. 'Keep it simple.'

I don't know *how* God spoke, whether it was real or imagined, actual or prayerful, by voice or a deepened sense inside me. I don't know how. But I do know *why* ... for simplicity was something I needed to find in an overcomplicated faith and a confused understanding of ministry, calling and purpose. God had something to say. 'Keep it simple' was his message. And it was my job to listen.

Revelation – a gift of insight and importance;
a promise of knowledge and purpose.
Do I have my antenna tuned to the message?

December 18 – Windows

'Nothing is more dangerous to reason
than the flights of the imagination.'
David Hume, A Treatise of Human Nature

Adam always sat by the window. You could see him when you walked by. He didn't mind you looking at him through his window. In fact, he welcomed it. He was just happy seeing you seeing him.

Adam always sat by the window, because it was Adam's way of engaging with the world. He couldn't go out by himself, and so the front room was his home. He liked it well enough. It was warm, comfortable and interesting. He could fall asleep by the fire or poke around for things to do. But it was *much* more fun looking out of the window at the wonderful world out there.

Adam always sat by the window, and because he couldn't get out there as he would have liked, he loved making up stories for himself about the people he saw going by. The postman was a regular, and Adam loved it when he saw him coming up the path and rattling the letterbox with the mail. It was always exciting to investigate what the postman had brought. But where was he off to next? How did he spend the rest of his day? And what about the two girls at the bus stop? Always the same time each morning, the same last-minute cigarette, constant chatter, texting as they spoke. Where were they going? Would they be fun to be with? More stories to ponder, and more pleasure from the world 'out there'.

Adam always sat by the window. But the *reason* he sat by the window was to watch for Elaine coming home. And when she did, he would run to the front door, bark loudly, jump up for a welcome pat, wag his tail like crazy and lick her face. After all, sitting by the window was all about waiting to welcome your whole world when she came back.

Might reason go out the window when we use our imagination?

December 19 – Roots

'People will not look forward to posterity,
who never look backward to their ancestors.'
Edmund Burke, Reflections on the Revolution in France

My wife and I were just sitting down to lunch one Sunday when the doorbell rang. Somewhat irritated by the interruption I answered the door to find myself faced with a family of four, a mother, father and two school-aged children. 'I'm sorry to disturb you,' the man said, 'but I was wondering if we could take a photograph of the outside of your house.' Now more surprised than irritated, and knowing that my mid-terrace house is in no sense spectacular, I agreed, but also enquired as to why he would want such a photograph. 'Oh,' he replied, 'we're on holiday from Australia and we're researching our Scottish and Irish roots. And, as far as we can tell, my grandmother's sister lived in this house in the early part of the 20th century.'

Soon we were in animated conversation about dates and names, family history and connections. I invited them in, and while the house has been modernised somewhat over the years, the basic layout hasn't changed. The stair banisters are original, as are the cornices in several rooms and the mantelpiece in the lounge. They were all duly photographed. We told stories of what we'd found when we renovated the property. We unearthed the title deeds of the house and traced names back to the original owners. They were photographed as well. The Australians said they felt really connected to their family history.

When they were leaving, one of the girls turned to her sister and said, 'Wow! We'll have some essay to write when we get back to school about, "What I did in the holidays", won't we?'

Roots go down deep
so that the branches of the Family Tree can flourish.

December 20 – Success

'Faith, mighty faith, the promise sees, and looks to that alone;
Laughs at impossibilities, and cries "It shall be done".'
Charles Wesley, Hymns and Sacred Poems

At the gate of the Canongate Kirk on Edinburgh's Royal Mile there is a life-sized bronze sculpture of the Scottish poet Robert Fergusson. This 18th-century contemporary of Robert Burns died tragically and prematurely. But had he lived and blossomed as a poet, he could have been numbered with the greats.

Fergusson was a sensitive and vulnerable man. Despite his early promise he suffered from severe depression at a young age. He later became insane after incurring injuries from a fall. Rumour has it he was drunk at the time, drink being his escape from his self-doubt and dark thoughts. He died in what was then the 'City Bedlam' – the institution for the insane – at the age of 24. He is laid to rest by the west wall of the Canongate kirkyard.

It would be easy to confine Fergusson to obscurity, dismiss him as unsuccessful, or mock him as an insane drunkard. But we should not. Fergusson was an important influence on Robert Burns, and Burns never forgot it. He wrote this for Fergusson's headstone:

No sculptured Marble here nor pompous lay,
No storied urn nor animated bust,
This simple Stone directs pale Scotia's way
To pour her Sorrows o'er her Poet's Dust.

Thankfully Burns wasn't so haughty with success that he failed to acknowledge the influence on his early years of the talent of poets such as Robert Fergusson.

Let us never dismiss as failures
those who don't measure up to what the world calls success.

December 21 – Redemption again

'Condemned into everlasting redemption for this.'
William Shakespeare, Much Ado About Nothing

In our brokenness, we all need to know what redemption means.

Fashioned and made with real beauty and form;
Cherished and loved since the day I was born;
Broken and lost, now a victim of shame;
Tarnished and spoiled, I'm thrown out of the game;

Far from a home of true welcome and peace;
Tortured by doubt, with no blessèd release;
Outside the walls of calm shelter and rest;
Missing the times when the loved ones are blessed.

Where is my home now, my purpose, my worth?
Where is the meaning I've craved since my birth?
Where is the rescue, the word from above?
Where is the faith, or the hope, or the love?

Come now my child, for I know who you are;
Come now in brokenness; come from afar;
Come with your questions, your sins and your shame;
Come from your wilderness; rejoin the game;

Come with your fears and your worries and grief;
Come with your doubts and your lack of belief;
Come, though you've plotted and selfishly schemed;
Come! You're forgiven. Now, you're redeemed.

From Welcoming Each Wonder *by Tom Gordon*
Wild Goose Publications, 2010

December 22 – Profit

'Profit comes from what's there,
usefulness comes from what's not there.'
Chinese proverb

Jesus told a story of a successful farmer who, with successive bumper harvests, had more grain than he could cope with. So he built bigger and bigger barns. Successful farmer, bigger barns, more profit, more money, bigger farms, more success, bigger barns ... and so the cycle continues in the joys of the boom years. But without having to wait for the 'bust' period when the bottom fell out of the grain market ... he died!

What good are his store of grain and his bigger barns now, eh? The punchline for Jesus is:

*What does it profit a man if he gains the whole world
and loses his own soul?*
Matthew 12:16

There is nothing wrong with profit. There is no evil in success. There is nothing fundamentally bad in the trappings of wealth. But when profit becomes a god that twists people away from concern for others, what then? Bill Gates, the founder of Microsoft, became one of the wealthiest men in the world. He also founded a charity called The Bill and Melinda Gates Foundation, which is dedicated to bringing innovations in health, development and learning to the global community. One of its straplines is 'All lives have equal value.' That says something about a man who *has* built bigger and bigger barns, but who hasn't lost his own soul in the process.

*Profit is not bad of itself.
But the focus on profit above all else, well ...*

December 23 – Carols

' "I have often thought," says Sir Roger, "it happens very well
that Christmas should fall in the Middle of winter." '

Joseph Addison in The Spectator

'Why do we only sing Christmas carols at Christmas?' one of my
friends said. Maybe we should look behind the familiarity more
than we do. Take, for example, the carol *O little town of Bethlehem*.

O little town of Bethlehem, how still we see thee lie;
Above thy deep and dreamless sleep, the silent stars go by.
Yet in thy dark streets shineth the everlasting light;
The hopes and fears of all the years are met in thee tonight.

The words were written in 1868 for his Sunday school by Rev.
Phillips Brooks of Philadelphia. The original melody, 'St Louis',
was composed by Lewis Redner, an American real-estate businessman and amateur organist, and it is still often sung to this
tune. The carol was hardly known in the UK when it appeared in
the English Hymnal in 1906 with the words set to Vaughan
Williams' arrangement of a traditional English tune, 'Forest
Green'. Brooks was inspired to write his hymn on a trip to the
Holy Land. Having ridden on horseback from Jerusalem to Bethlehem, he attended midnight mass. 'I remember standing in the
old church in Bethlehem close to the spot where Jesus was born,'
he wrote, 'when the whole church was ringing hour after hour
with splendid hymns of praise to God, how I could hear voices I
knew well telling each other of the wonderful night of the Saviour's birth.'

O holy Child of Bethlehem, descend to us, we pray;
Cast out our sin and enter in; be born in us today.
We hear the Christmas angels the great glad tidings tell;
O come to us, abide with us, our Lord Emmanuel.

December 24 – Bethlehem

'O little town of Bethlehem, how still we see thee lie;
Above thy deep and dreamless sleep, the silent stars go by.
Yet in thy dark streets shineth the everlasting light;
The hopes and fears of all the years are met in thee tonight.'

Rev. Phillips Brooks

I visited Bethlehem early in 2013 as part of a pilgrimage to the Holy Land. I was not disappointed by the pilgrimage experience, and I am left with many formative images, feelings and memories. Not all of the impressions were positive, however, and one of these happened in Bethlehem. Of course I was well prepared to leave behind any lingering sentimentality of an idyllic rural setting, of peaceful stables and pastoral stillness. For I knew that the city of Bethlehem, as a continuation of urban south Jerusalem, was a busy, modern environment, and that the Church of the Nativity was as far removed from Christmas card images as it is possible to get. But what I was not prepared for was The Wall.

Bethlehem is a Palestinian city in the Central West Bank and it is divided by the West Bank Barrier. Israeli separated from Palestinian, Palestinian from Israeli, with a guarded checkpoint to control the passage from one side to the other. A Palestinian Christian woman told me that sometimes she isn't able to get to church in Jerusalem because she isn't allowed through the wall.

Whatever Bethlehem is today, it is not a 'little town' and does not 'lie still'. Yet it should be our prayer that in its dark and fearful streets a light *will* shine, and that the promise of love and reconciliation will see walls coming down. Our hopes and fears still meet in Bethlehem tonight.

*Let us pray on this Christmas Eve
that our hopes and dreams of peace
triumph over the fears and darkness of hate and prejudice.*

December 25 – More than the X-factor

'We hear the beating of wings over Bethlehem and a light that is not of the sun or of the stars shines in the midnight sky. Let the beauty of the story take away all narrowness, all thought of formal creeds. Let it be remembered as a story that has happened again and again, to men of many different races, that has been expressed through many religions, that has been called by many different names. Time and space and language lay no limitations upon human brotherhood.'
The New York Times, *25 December 1937*

Christians complain about the commercialisation of Christmas. The meaning is lost, they say, as the religious content of Christmas is squeezed out. The symbol of this, they continue, is the use of 'Xmas'. Jesus appears to have become an X, the 'unknown quantity' at Christmas time. 'Put Christ back into Christmas,' is the cry.

But they needn't worry, for *Xmas* isn't a secular version of Christmas at all. The X actually stands for the Greek letter 'Chi'. In the early years of the Christian Church Greek was the language of commerce, trade and education. So Christ – pronounced Christos in Greek – was Χριστος. X became the short form for Christ's name, and for centuries Xmas was regularly used by religious scholars. So the truth is that Xmas and Christmas are the same – except for their letters. Christ has *never* been removed from Christmas, no matter how hard people have tried.

December 25th was fixed as the date for Christians to celebrate the birth of Jesus in order to conveniently merge it with a pagan festival. It could be argued that the celebration came *first* and the rejoicing at the birth of Jesus was the *completion* of it all. Maybe we'll still be left with people complaining that Christ is left out of Christmas. But for me Christ has never gone away. There's 'x' factor in that.

If there's an 'x' at all, let it mark an important spot.

December 26 – Goodwill

'However many holy words you read,
However many you speak,
What good will they do you if you do not act upon them?'
Buddha

Boxing Day, the day following Christmas Day, is traditionally the day when servants and tradesmen would receive a gift, known as a 'Christmas box', from their superiors or employers. Today, Boxing Day is better known as a bank or public holiday.

No one really knows where 'boxing' comes from. In Europe, there has been a tradition since the Middle Ages of giving money and other gifts to those who were needy or in menial or 'service' positions – akin to the 'Christmas bonus' of our modern era. In ancient, pre-Christian Rome, Saturnalia was a celebration during which slave owners would switch roles with their slaves. Indeed, in some branches of the armed forces there is a similar swapping of roles, with officers and enlisted personnel changing places for the day (though it would be hoped that here the slave and slave-owner analogy would break down).

Perhaps the most significant aspect of Boxing Day comes from South Africa, for in 1994 December 26th was renamed the 'Day of Goodwill'. 1994 saw the first fully democratic elections in the Republic of South Africa, a visible end of the era of apartheid. The Day of Goodwill, therefore, was an important symbol that the spirit of Christmas needed to be carried over to the next day, and the day after, and the day after that, and for every succeeding day, so that a country could continue to have goodwill at its core, for the good of all its people.

Goodwill shouldn't be trapped in a box.
Let it out, so that everyone can benefit.

December 27 – Students

'What is the end of study? Let me know.'
William Shakespeare, Love's Labour's Lost

A student got 0% in an exam – and yet all the questions appear to be answered correctly. Or is it just me?

Q: In which battle did Napoleon die?
A: His last one.

Q: Where was the Declaration of Independence signed?
A: At the bottom of the page.

Q: In the USA, the Blue River runs in which state?
A: Liquid.

Q: What looks like half an apple?
A: The other half.

Q: How can you lift an elephant with one hand?
A: It is impossible to find an elephant with one hand.

Q: If you had three apples and four oranges in one hand and four apples and three oranges in the other, what would you have?
A: Very large hands.

Q: If it took eight men ten days to build a wall, how long would it take four men to build it?
A: No time at all. The wall is already built.

Q: How can you drop an egg onto a concrete floor without cracking it?
A: Any way at all. Concrete floors are notoriously hard to crack.

A little learning is a dang'rous thing ...
Alexander Pope, *An Essay on Criticism*

December 28 – Hopes and dreams

'Every child comes with the message
that God is not yet discouraged of man.'
Rabindranath Tagore, in Stray Birds

Kes is a 1969 film directed by Ken Loach. It's based on the novel
A Kestrel for a Knave, written by Barry Hines. It tells the story of
15-year-old Billy Casper, who is bullied, both at home by his half-
brother, Jud, and at school. Billy is on the road to nowhere, and
his greatest fear is ending up working down the pit.

Billy has little going for him until he finds an outlet through
training a kestrel he's taken from a nest on a farm. His interest in
learning falconry prompts him to steal a book on the subject from
a second-hand bookshop, as he is underage and can't get a bor-
rower's card from the public library. As the relationship between
Billy and 'Kes', the kestrel, improves during the training, so do
Billy's outlook and horizons. For the first time, Billy receives
praise, from his English teacher, after delivering an impromptu
talk on his relationship with the bird.

Jud leaves money and instructions for Billy to place a bet on
two horses, but Billy spends the money on chips and on meat for
his bird, having been told that the horses are unlikely to win.
However, the horses do win. Furious at Billy for losing him his
bet but unable to find him, Jud takes revenge by killing his kestrel.

Billy had hope, and that hope had come to him from an unexpected source. Kes was Billy's future. A trained kestrel had given
Billy what he never expected to find – a future with possibilities.
When Billy Casper retrieves the body of his dead friend from the
trash and buries it in the garden, have the hopes and dreams of
this young man been buried too?

When hope is chosen, anything is possible.
Dreams are answers to questions we've never asked.

December 29 – More changes

'Plus ça change, plus c'est la même chose.'
(The more it changes, the more it's the same thing.)
Jean-Baptiste Alphonse Karr, in his journal Les Guêpes (The Wasps)

I live close to a working harbour in a fishing village on the East Lothian coast. Being at sea level and halfway up the Firth of Forth, the weather is relatively mild. However, there are times when the coastline takes a fair battering, especially with a combination of high tides and the spring or autumn gales.

It's fascinating to walk by the harbour and along the shoreline after a storm and to see the changes. Broken lobster-creels and torn fragments of fishing nets are cast up on the beach. Here and there on the rocks lie a discarded tyre, a length of rope or a faded oilskin. Poking through the sand is an old wellington boot or a rusty tin can.

And there are also changes in the layout of the shore. A sand-bank can be moved three or four metres. An area of pebbles may now be completely covered over. A stony section might have disappeared, the stones having been dragged away to expose a bank of grey sand. One part of the beach may be higher, another lower. The storm has done its worst. Changes abound.

But not everything is different – the line of jagged rocks hasn't shifted. The seagulls gather again on the breakwater. The lobster-creel markers still bob on the water. The habitual heron has returned to stand guard over the harbour mouth. The view across to Fife is as spectacular as ever. And another day dawns ...

Of course we become disturbed by the changes we have to face. Perhaps then we might value all the more what stays the same, trust in the things that matter and believe that life, like my shore-line, is more stable and unchangeable than we might think.

Trust in what you know. Know what you should trust in.

December 30 – Lost days

'Listen to the Exhortation of the Dawn!
Look to this Day! For it is Life,
The very Life of Life.'
Salutation of the Dawn *from the Sanskrit*

One of my favourite TV programmes is 'QI', presided over by the inimitable Stephen Fry. So here's a QI question: 'What is quite interesting about the 30th of December 2011 for the citizens of the Samoan Islands?' On Samoa, December 30th 2011 *didn't happen*. For economic purposes – to be closer in time to their main trading partners in Eastern Australia and New Zealand – the Samoans felt it would be better to be three hours ahead of their near neighbours than twenty-one hours behind. So they decided to 'jump westwards' across the International Date Line and skip a day. As a result, at the end of 2011, they went from December 29th to 31st, missing out the 30th altogether. As a celebration of this momentous event, church bells rang, sirens wailed and prayers were said at special services – to mark a day that never happened.

Towards the end of a year, as we take stock of what's gone by, there will be some who wish a day could have been missed out of their own year – or a week, or a month, or even the whole year. Tragedy, loss, sadness, disaster and a host of other bad things are hard in the remembering so that we will wish they had never happened. But the reality is that we can't skip any day. Life brings us the bad with the good. The experience of both moulds us and shapes us. If we *all* lost December 30th, then my aunt would have no birthday to celebrate for one thing. So bells will ring for good days and sirens will wail for bad ones, because they're part of the deal and, in time, fit together for a greater purpose.

Our prayers are for balance,
so that every day might have its place.

December 31 – Amen

'Then all the people said, "Amen!"'
Bible: 1 Chronicles 16:36

When I was young, the two most universally understood words in the English language were 'Coke' and 'Amen'. There might be others that are equally well known nowadays, like 'CNN', 'Microsoft' or 'Google'. But I'll stick with what I know and, because there are other drinks as good as Coke, I'll concentrate, for the last day of the year, on 'Amen'.

'Amen' is a declaration of affirmation. With its roots in the Hebrew Bible and the New Testament, it's generally been used in Christian worship as a concluding word for prayers and hymns. It is sometimes translated as 'verily' or 'truly', but I've also heard it explained as 'so let it be', or 'so be it', a declaration of affirmation for what has gone before. Indeed, it's also utilised freely in popular culture. Which of us hasn't heard, or even offered, 'I'll say "Amen" to that,' when something positive has happened.

In some churches there is an 'amen corner' or 'amen section', a group of the congregation who are likely to call out 'Amen' in response to points they approve of in a preacher's sermon. I like that! An *excellent* affirmation for what's been said.

At the end of a year, I hope and pray you can say 'Amen'. Maybe it's a 'Yes!' to having survived a hard time that you're happy to see the back of, and a welcome 'So be it' to what's to come. Maybe it's a shout of gratitude for good things that have been experienced, or an 'Amen!' as an affirmation for what's gone before. Whatever your circumstances, join with me to offer together that universal cry, 'I'll say, "Amen" to all of that.'

'Amen' to a year gone by.
'Amen' to the promise of what's yet to come.

Index – by subject

Permissions

January 6: The quotation from 'The journey of the Magi' by T S Eliot is accessed from 'The Poetry Archive' and used by permission of Faber UK.

January 28: The quotation from the Office of the UN High Commissioner for Human Rights (OHCHR) originates from OHCHR and is used with the permission of the UN High Commissioner.

January 27: The text relating to Holocaust Memorial Day (HMD) is reproduced freely from the UK's Statement of Commitment to HMD.

April 15: The information on 'Fresh Start' is accessed from their website – http://www.freshstartweb.org.uk – and is quoted with permission.

July 10: The quotation from *The Grove Concise Dictionary of Music* edited by Stanlie (1994), 38w from 'Harmony', is used by permission of Oxford University Press, USA.

Wild Goose Publications is part of the Iona Community:

- An ecumenical movement of men and women from different walks of life and different traditions in the Christian church
- Committed to the gospel of Jesus Christ, and to following where that leads, even into the unknown
- Engaged together, and with people of goodwill across the world, in acting, reflecting and praying for justice, peace and the integrity of creation
- Convinced that the inclusive community we seek must be embodied in the community we practise

Together with our staff, we are responsible for:

- Our islands residential centres of Iona Abbey, the MacLeod Centre on Iona, and Camas Adventure Centre on the Ross of Mull

and in Glasgow:

- The administration of the Community
- Our work with young people
- Our publishing house, Wild Goose Publications
- Our association in the revitalising of worship with the Wild Goose Resource Group

The Iona Community was founded in Glasgow in 1938 by George MacLeod, minister, visionary and prophetic witness for peace, in the context of the poverty and despair of the Depression. Its original task of rebuilding the monastic ruins of Iona Abbey became a sign of hopeful rebuilding of community in Scotland and beyond. Today, we are about 250 Members, mostly in Britain, and 1500 Associate Members, with 1400 Friends worldwide. Together and apart, 'we follow the light we have, and pray for more light'.

For information on the Iona Community contact:
The Iona Community, Fourth Floor, Savoy House, 140 Sauchiehall Street, Glasgow G2 3DH, UK. Phone: 0141 332 6343
e-mail: admin@iona.org.uk; web: www.iona.org.uk

For enquiries about visiting Iona, please contact:
Iona Abbey, Isle of Iona, Argyll PA76 6SN, UK. Phone: 01681 700404
e-mail: ionacomm@iona.org.uk